ROBIN BATGIRL
FRESH BLOOD

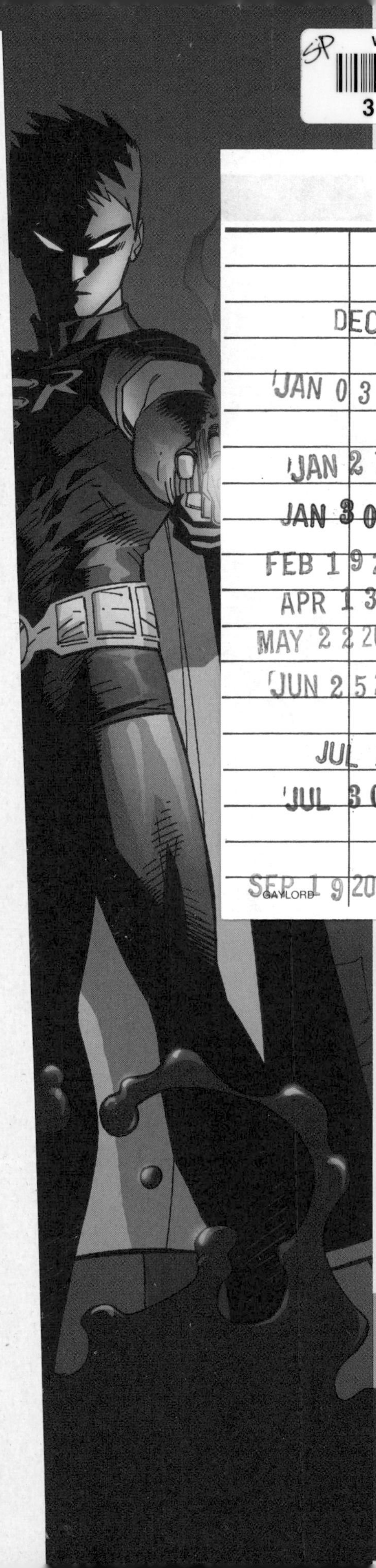

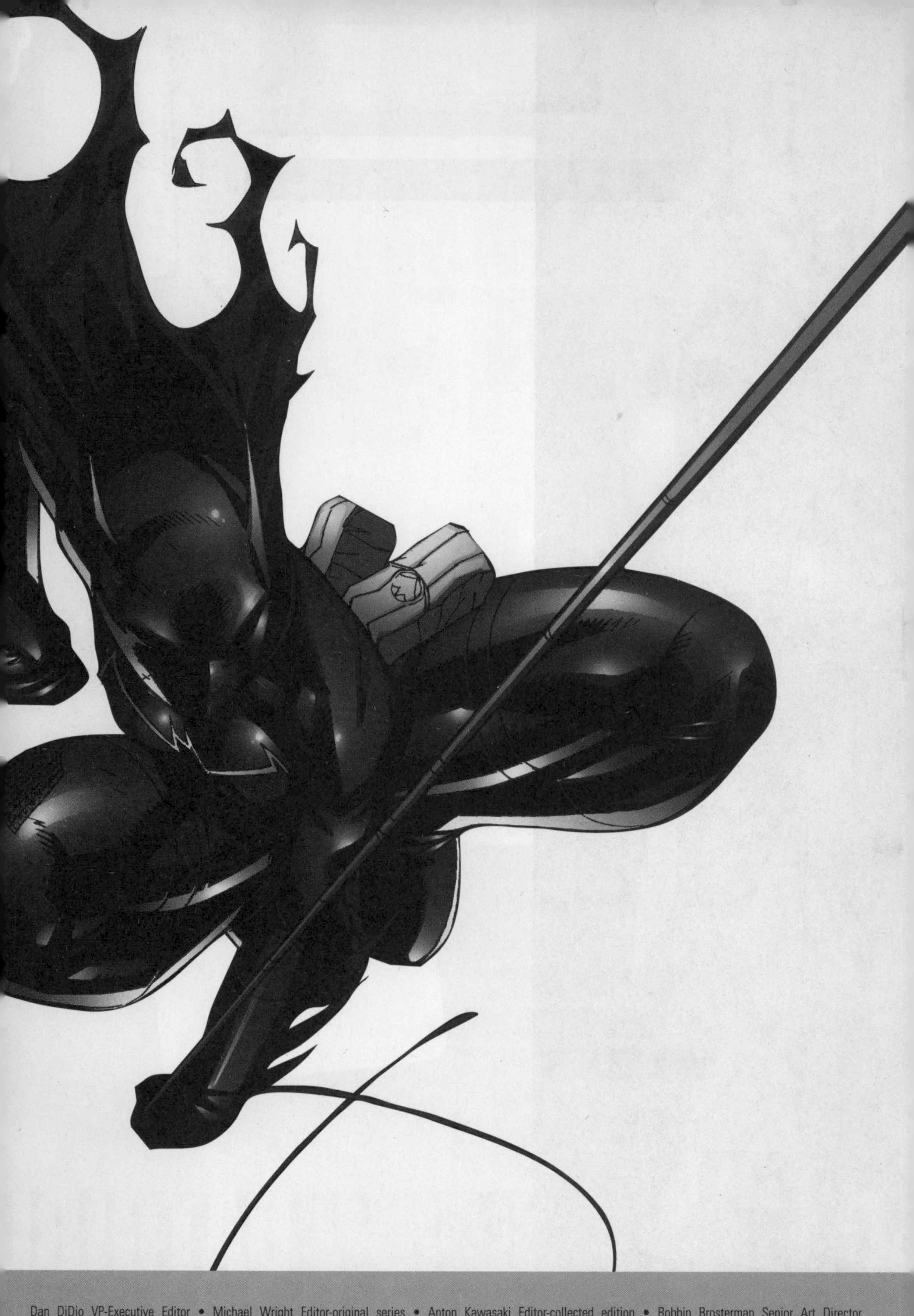

ROBIN BATGIRL
FRESH BLOOD

BILL WILLINGHAM
ANDERSEN GABRYCH
WRITERS

DAMION SCOTT
ALÉ GARZA &
JESSE DELPERDANG
ARTISTS

GUY MAJOR
WILDSTORM FX
COLORISTS

PHIL BALSMAN
ROB LEIGH
LETTERERS

DAMION SCOTT
ALÉ GARZA &
JESSE DELPERDANG
ORIGINAL COVERS

ROBIN/BATGIRL: FRESH BLOOD
Published by DC Comics. Cover and compilation copyright © 2005 DC Comics. All Rights Reserved. Originally published in single magazine form in ROBIN #132, 133 and BATGIRL #58, 59. Copyright © 2005 DC Comics. All Rights Reserved. All characters, their distinctive likenesses and related elements featured in this publication are trademarks of DC Comics. The stories, characters and incidents featured in this publication are entirely fictional. DC Comics does not read or accept unsolicited submissions of ideas, stories or artwork. DC Comics, 1700 Broadway, New York, NY 10019. A Warner Bros. Entertainment Company. Printed in Canada. First Printing.
ISBN: 1-4012-0433-3
Cover art by Damion Scott
Publication design by Jennifer Redding

BATGIRL

Cassandra Cain was trained from birth by her father, assassin David Cain. She never learned to speak, but mastered reading other people, perfecting one fighting form after another. She would have been Cain's masterwork had she not rejected killing and fled his care. In Gotham City she found a true calling following the footsteps of Batman and is now learning how to be a crimefighter. Under Barbara Gordon's watchful eye, she is also learning what it means to be a young woman.

WHAT HAS GONE BEFORE

Over the years, Batman has developed several contingency plans to cover any worst-case scenarios that might arise in his city of Gotham. One such "war game" scenario involved the city's underworld uniting under the Dark Knight's control. It was a plan that was never meant to be initiated.

Stephanie Brown, the Spoiler, unleashed the plan in hopes of proving to her mentor Batman that she was worthy of his trust. Instead, things spiraled out of control despite the best efforts of Batman and his allies to contain the violence. Gotham faced one of the deadliest gang wars in its history, and before it was over, many lives would be lost — including Spoiler's.

For Tim Drake, who had a relationship with Stephanie as Robin, it was a devastating blow. Even worse, Tim's father Jack was also recently killed in a separate incident. Tim continued as Robin but because of his need to escape the ghosts of Gotham City has recently relocated to Blüdhaven. Batman asked Batgirl to move there as well to keep an eye on Tim, but she has her own reasons for being there — mainly to once and for all become truly independent.

The third to wear the costume and name, Tim Drake was at the Haly Circus the night the Graysons were killed, sending young Dick on his path to become Robin. When Tim saw Robin perform the exact same acrobatic trick that Dick Grayson executed with the Flying Graysons, he deduced the Dynamic Duo's identity. Over time he followed their careers and when the second Robin was killed, it was Tim who brought Batman back from the darkness. Since then he has trained hard to be Robin, learning not only from Batman but from his peers, first with Young Justice and currently with a re-formed Teen Titans.

ROBIN

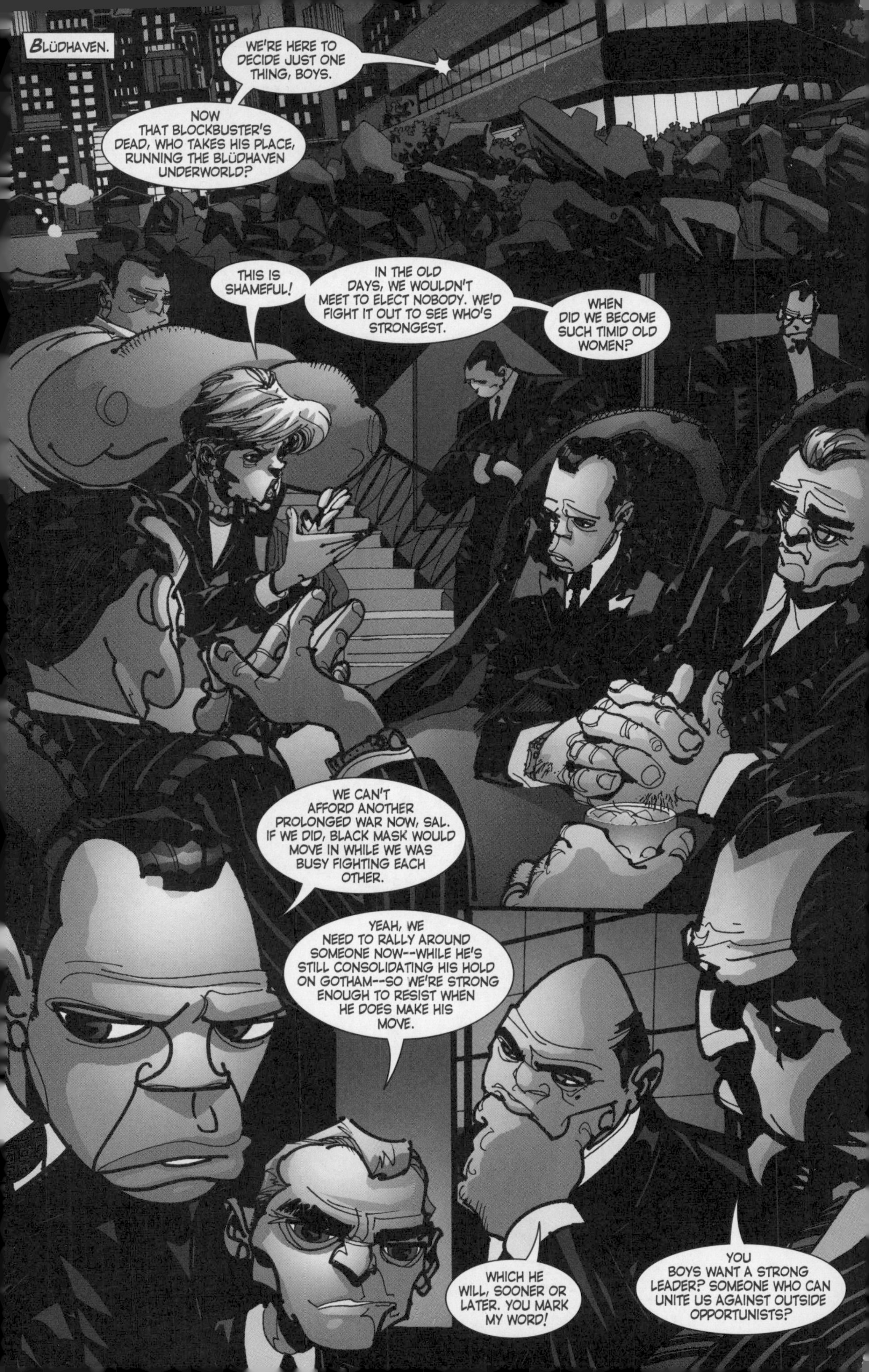
BLÜDHAVEN.
WE'RE HERE TO DECIDE JUST ONE THING, BOYS.
NOW THAT BLOCKBUSTER'S DEAD, WHO TAKES HIS PLACE, RUNNING THE BLÜDHAVEN UNDERWORLD?
THIS IS SHAMEFUL!
IN THE OLD DAYS, WE WOULDN'T MEET TO ELECT NOBODY. WE'D FIGHT IT OUT TO SEE WHO'S STRONGEST.
WHEN DID WE BECOME SUCH TIMID OLD WOMEN?
WE CAN'T AFFORD ANOTHER PROLONGED WAR NOW, SAL. IF WE DID, BLACK MASK WOULD MOVE IN WHILE WE WAS BUSY FIGHTING EACH OTHER.
YEAH, WE NEED TO RALLY AROUND SOMEONE NOW--WHILE HE'S STILL CONSOLIDATING HIS HOLD ON GOTHAM--SO WE'RE STRONG ENOUGH TO RESIST WHEN HE DOES MAKE HIS MOVE.
WHICH HE WILL, SOONER OR LATER. YOU MARK MY WORD!
YOU BOYS WANT A STRONG LEADER? SOMEONE WHO CAN UNITE US AGAINST OUTSIDE OPPORTUNISTS?

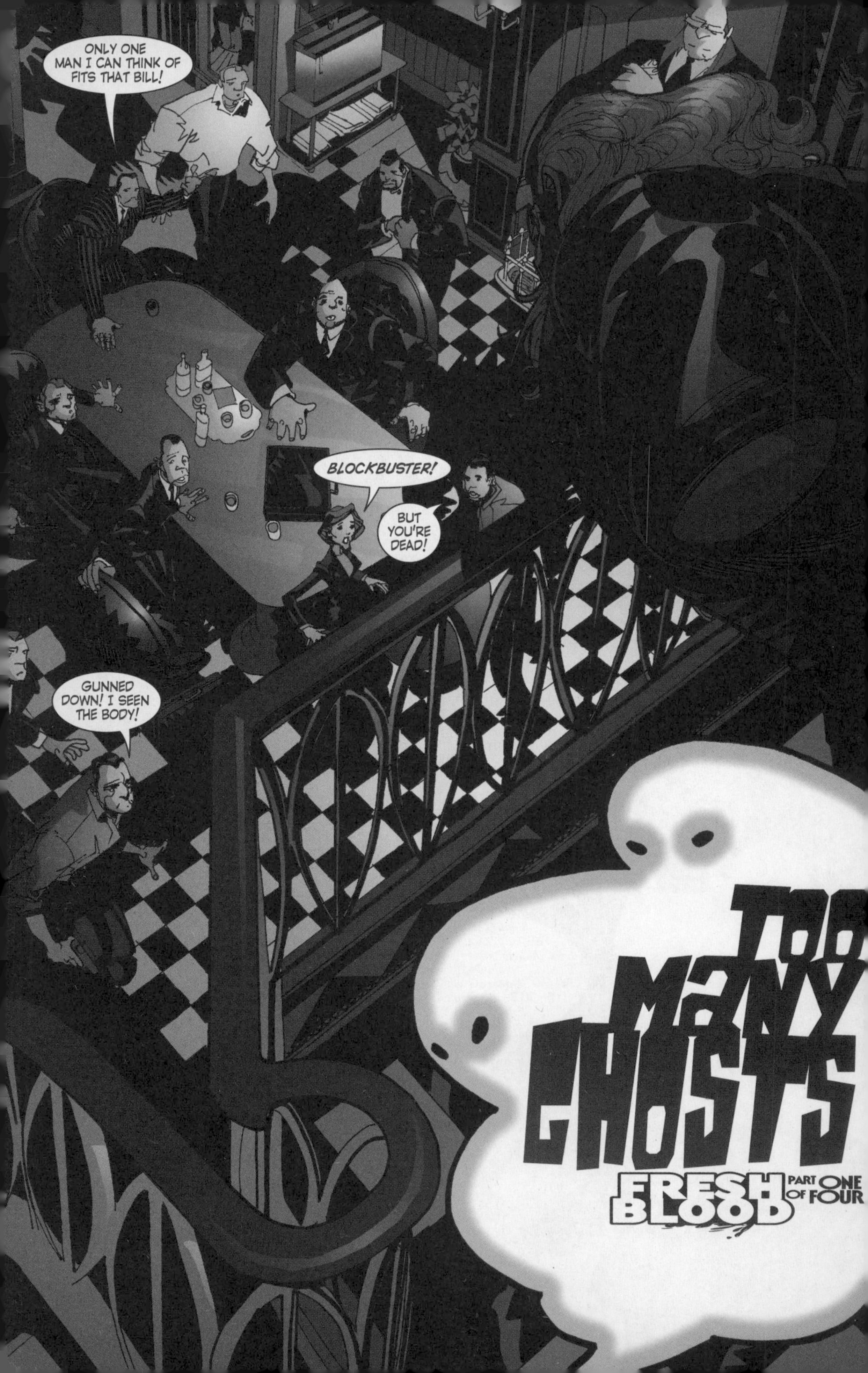
ONLY ONE MAN I CAN THINK OF FITS THAT BILL!
BLOCKBUSTER!
BUT YOU'RE DEAD!
GUNNED DOWN! I SEEN THE BODY!
TOO MANY GHOSTS
FRESH BLOOD
PART ONE OF FOUR

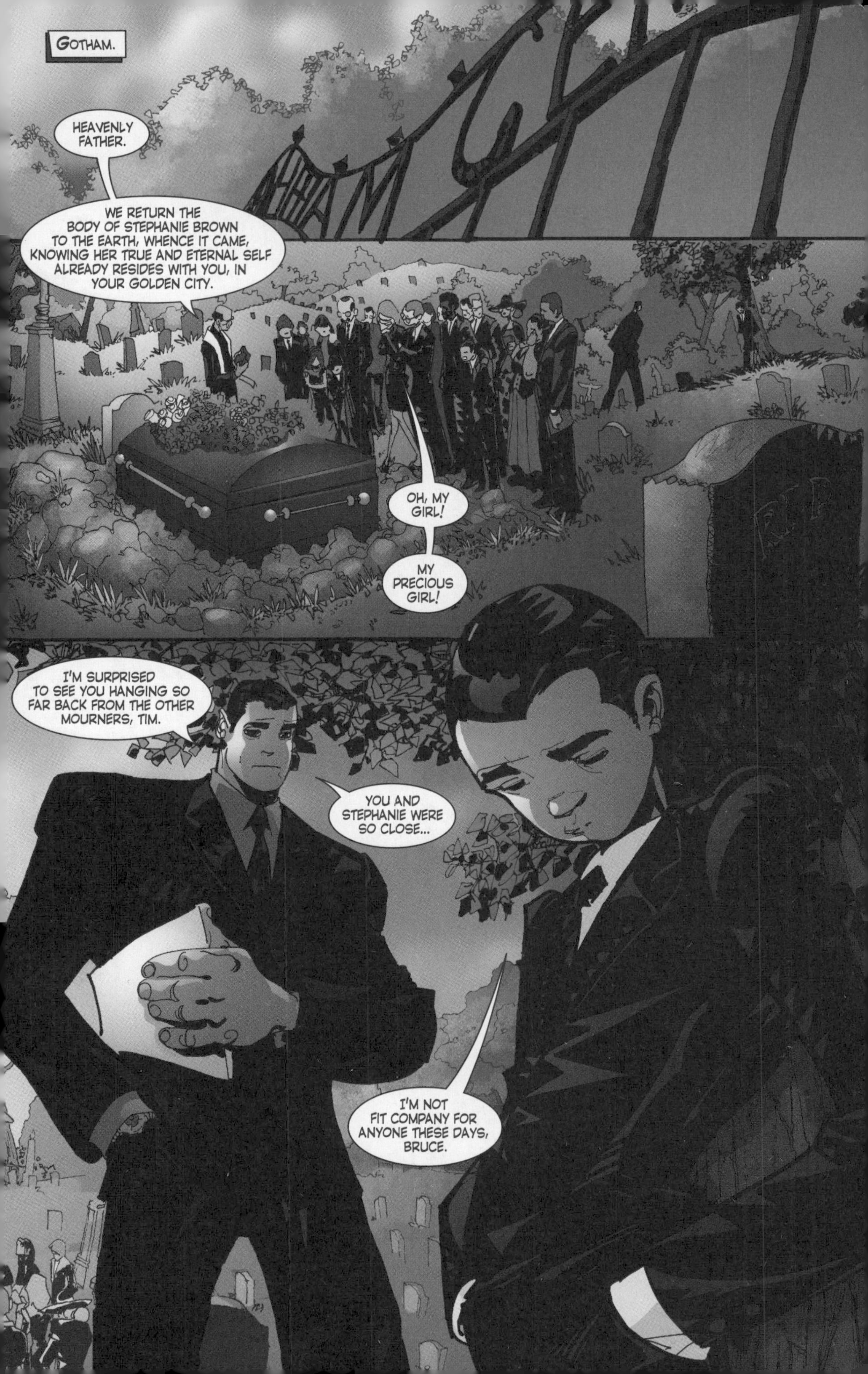
GOTHAM.
HEAVENLY FATHER.
WE RETURN THE BODY OF STEPHANIE BROWN TO THE EARTH, WHENCE IT CAME, KNOWING HER TRUE AND ETERNAL SELF ALREADY RESIDES WITH YOU, IN YOUR GOLDEN CITY.
OH, MY GIRL!
MY PRECIOUS GIRL!
I'M SURPRISED TO SEE YOU HANGING SO FAR BACK FROM THE OTHER MOURNERS, TIM.
YOU AND STEPHANIE WERE SO CLOSE...
I'M NOT FIT COMPANY FOR ANYONE THESE DAYS, BRUCE.

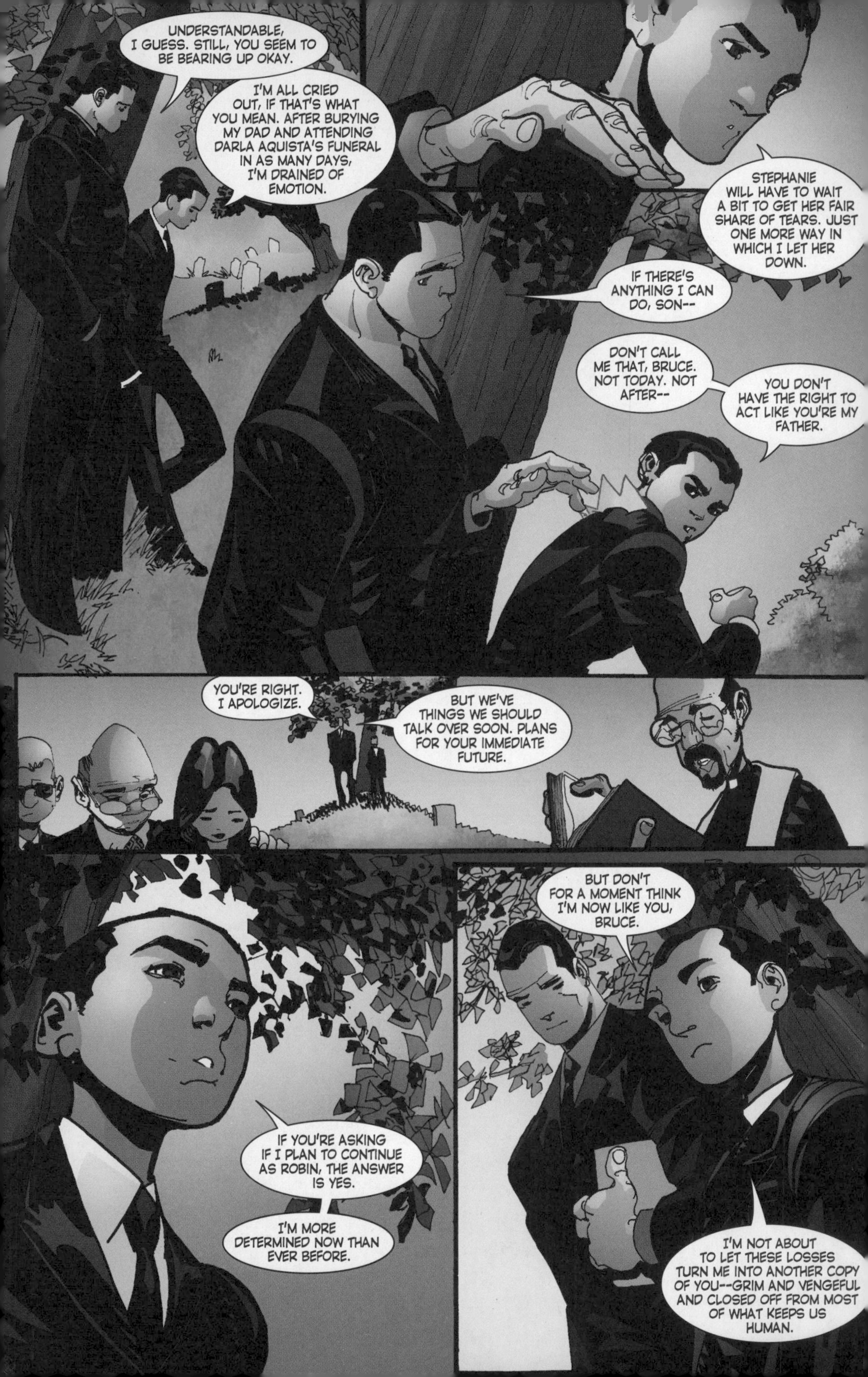
UNDERSTANDABLE, I GUESS. STILL, YOU SEEM TO BE BEARING UP OKAY.
I'M ALL CRIED OUT, IF THAT'S WHAT YOU MEAN. AFTER BURYING MY DAD AND ATTENDING DARLA AQUISTA'S FUNERAL IN AS MANY DAYS, I'M DRAINED OF EMOTION.
STEPHANIE WILL HAVE TO WAIT A BIT TO GET HER FAIR SHARE OF TEARS. JUST ONE MORE WAY IN WHICH I LET HER DOWN.
IF THERE'S ANYTHING I CAN DO, SON--
DON'T CALL ME THAT, BRUCE. NOT TODAY. NOT AFTER--
YOU DON'T HAVE THE RIGHT TO ACT LIKE YOU'RE MY FATHER.
YOU'RE RIGHT. I APOLOGIZE.
BUT WE'VE THINGS WE SHOULD TALK OVER SOON. PLANS FOR YOUR IMMEDIATE FUTURE.
IF YOU'RE ASKING IF I PLAN TO CONTINUE AS ROBIN, THE ANSWER IS YES.
I'M MORE DETERMINED NOW THAN EVER BEFORE.
BUT DON'T FOR A MOMENT THINK I'M NOW LIKE YOU, BRUCE.
I'M NOT ABOUT TO LET THESE LOSSES TURN ME INTO ANOTHER COPY OF YOU--GRIM AND VENGEFUL AND CLOSED OFF FROM MOST OF WHAT KEEPS US HUMAN.

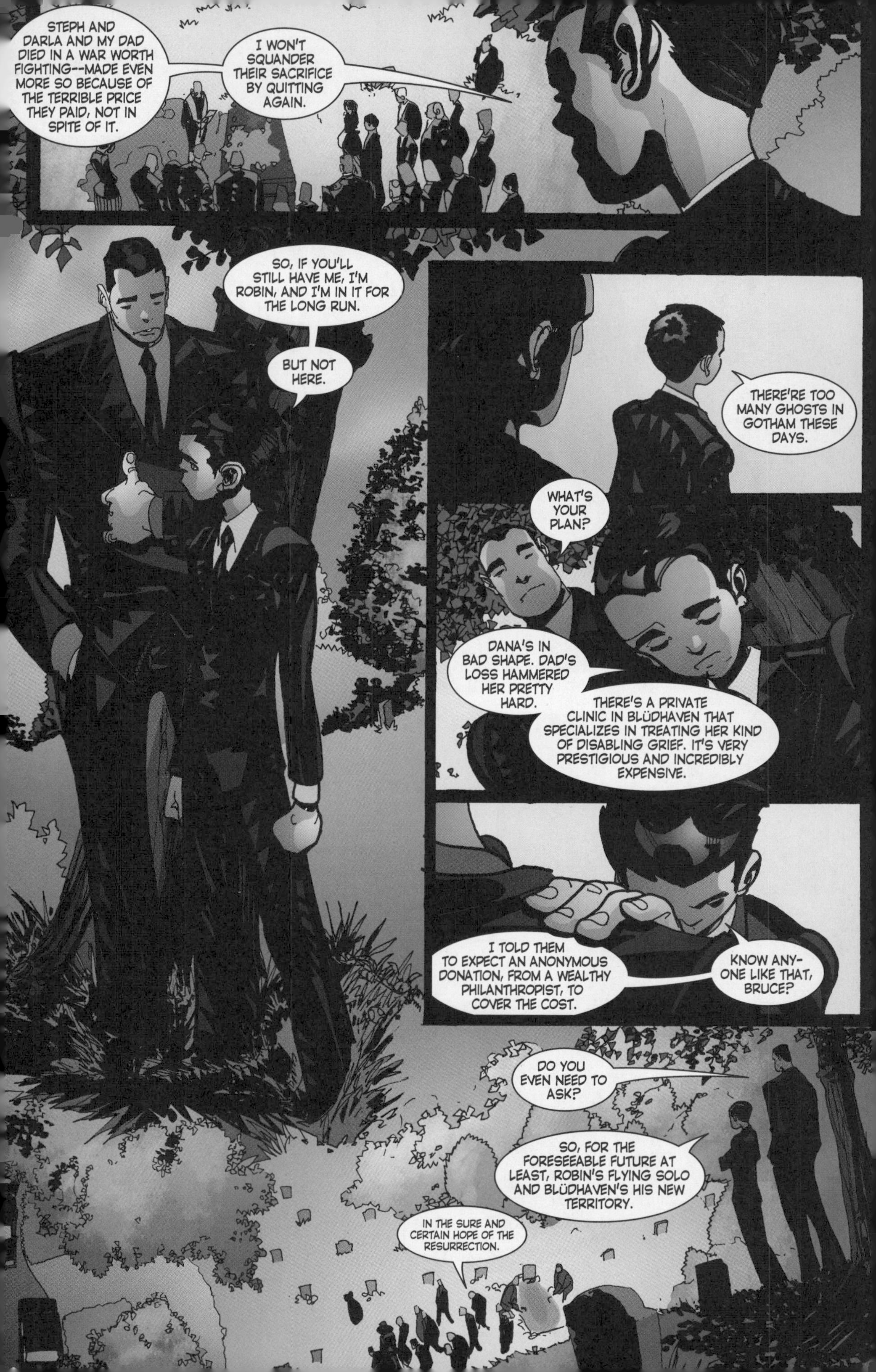
STEPH AND DARLA AND MY DAD DIED IN A WAR WORTH FIGHTING--MADE EVEN MORE SO BECAUSE OF THE TERRIBLE PRICE THEY PAID, NOT IN SPITE OF IT.
I WON'T SQUANDER THEIR SACRIFICE BY QUITTING AGAIN.
SO, IF YOU'LL STILL HAVE ME, I'M ROBIN, AND I'M IN IT FOR THE LONG RUN.
BUT NOT HERE.
THERE'RE TOO MANY GHOSTS IN GOTHAM THESE DAYS.
WHAT'S YOUR PLAN?
DANA'S IN BAD SHAPE. DAD'S LOSS HAMMERED HER PRETTY HARD.
THERE'S A PRIVATE CLINIC IN BLÜDHAVEN THAT SPECIALIZES IN TREATING HER KIND OF DISABLING GRIEF. IT'S VERY PRESTIGIOUS AND INCREDIBLY EXPENSIVE.
I TOLD THEM TO EXPECT AN ANONYMOUS DONATION, FROM A WEALTHY PHILANTHROPIST, TO COVER THE COST.
KNOW ANYONE LIKE THAT, BRUCE?
DO YOU EVEN NEED TO ASK?
SO, FOR THE FORESEEABLE FUTURE AT LEAST, ROBIN'S FLYING SOLO AND BLÜDHAVEN'S HIS NEW TERRITORY.
IN THE SURE AND CERTAIN HOPE OF THE RESURRECTION.

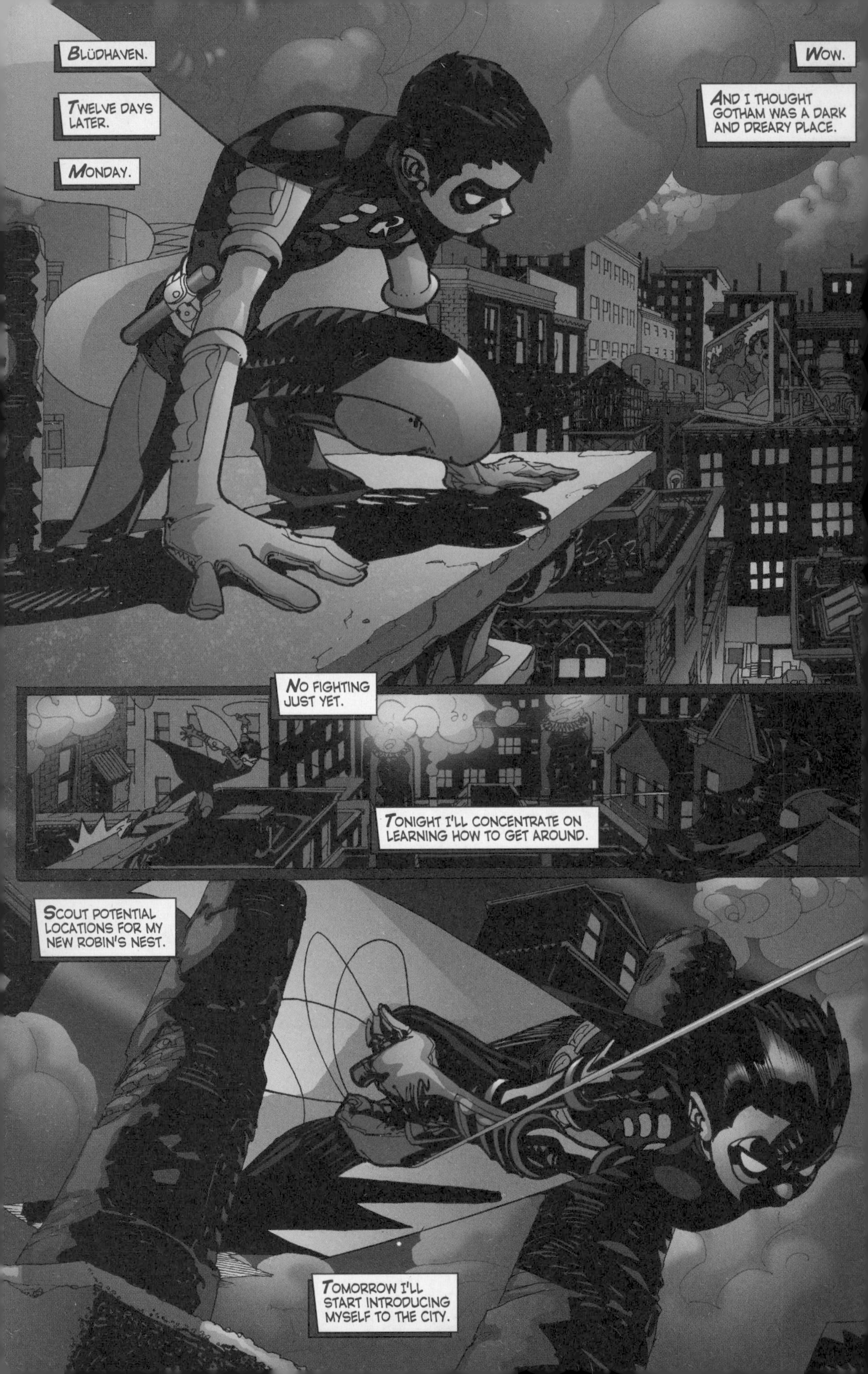
BLÜDHAVEN.
TWELVE DAYS LATER.
MONDAY.
WOW.
AND I THOUGHT GOTHAM WAS A DARK AND DREARY PLACE.
NO FIGHTING JUST YET.
TONIGHT I'LL CONCENTRATE ON LEARNING HOW TO GET AROUND.
SCOUT POTENTIAL LOCATIONS FOR MY NEW ROBIN'S NEST.
TOMORROW I'LL START INTRODUCING MYSELF TO THE CITY.

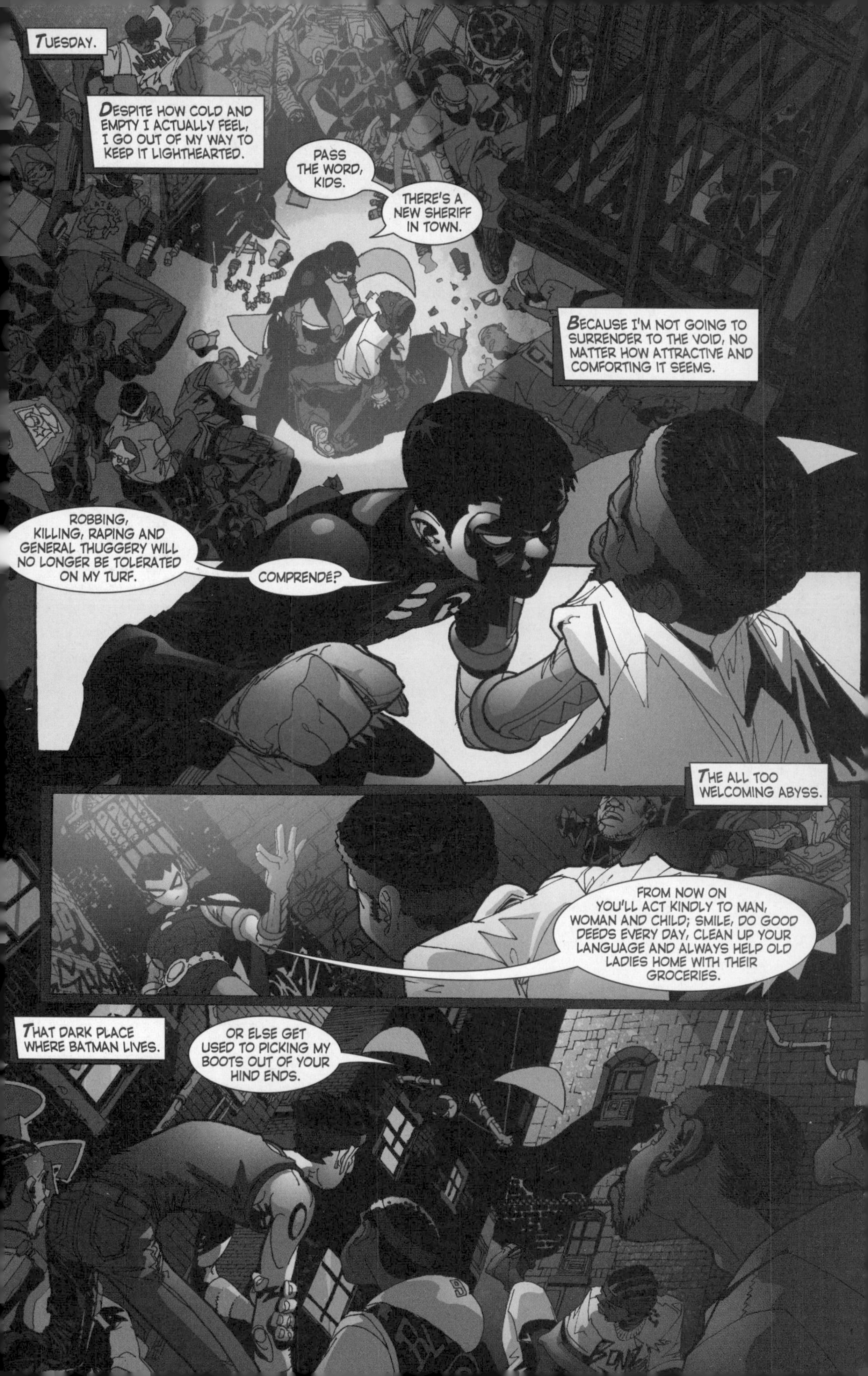
TUESDAY.
DESPITE HOW COLD AND EMPTY I ACTUALLY FEEL, I GO OUT OF MY WAY TO KEEP IT LIGHTHEARTED.
PASS THE WORD, KIDS.
THERE'S A NEW SHERIFF IN TOWN.
BECAUSE I'M NOT GOING TO SURRENDER TO THE VOID, NO MATTER HOW ATTRACTIVE AND COMFORTING IT SEEMS.
ROBBING, KILLING, RAPING AND GENERAL THUGGERY WILL NO LONGER BE TOLERATED ON MY TURF.
COMPRENDE?
THE ALL TOO WELCOMING ABYSS.
FROM NOW ON YOU'LL ACT KINDLY TO MAN, WOMAN AND CHILD; SMILE, DO GOOD DEEDS EVERY DAY, CLEAN UP YOUR LANGUAGE AND ALWAYS HELP OLD LADIES HOME WITH THEIR GROCERIES.
THAT DARK PLACE WHERE BATMAN LIVES.
OR ELSE GET USED TO PICKING MY BOOTS OUT OF YOUR HIND ENDS.

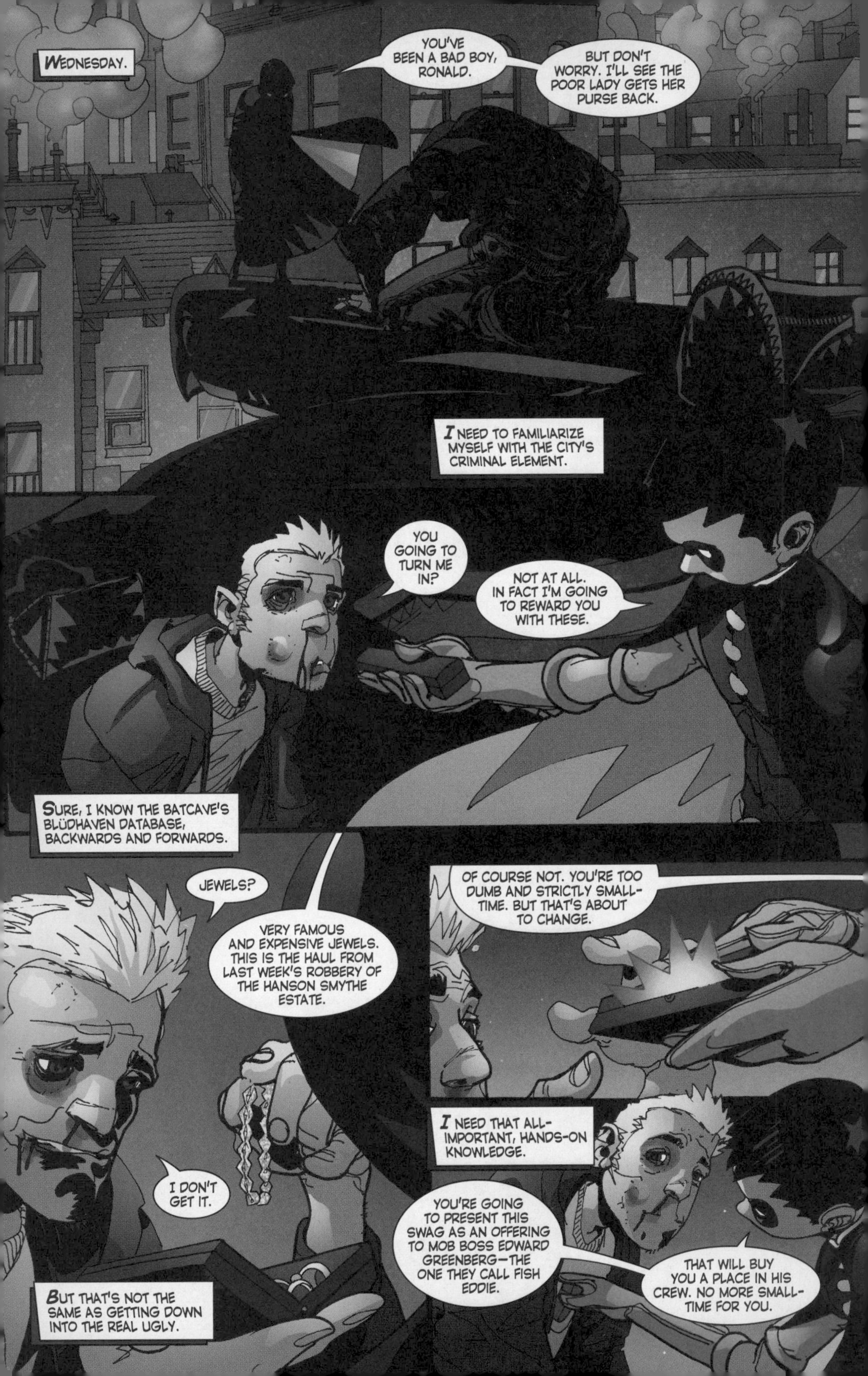
WEDNESDAY.
YOU'VE BEEN A BAD BOY, RONALD.
BUT DON'T WORRY. I'LL SEE THE POOR LADY GETS HER PURSE BACK.
I NEED TO FAMILIARIZE MYSELF WITH THE CITY'S CRIMINAL ELEMENT.
YOU GOING TO TURN ME IN?
NOT AT ALL. IN FACT I'M GOING TO REWARD YOU WITH THESE.
SURE, I KNOW THE BATCAVE'S BLÜDHAVEN DATABASE, BACKWARDS AND FORWARDS.
JEWELS?
VERY FAMOUS AND EXPENSIVE JEWELS. THIS IS THE HAUL FROM LAST WEEK'S ROBBERY OF THE HANSON SMYTHE ESTATE.
I DON'T GET IT.
BUT THAT'S NOT THE SAME AS GETTING DOWN INTO THE REAL UGLY.
OF COURSE NOT. YOU'RE TOO DUMB AND STRICTLY SMALL-TIME. BUT THAT'S ABOUT TO CHANGE.
I NEED THAT ALL-IMPORTANT, HANDS-ON KNOWLEDGE.
YOU'RE GOING TO PRESENT THIS SWAG AS AN OFFERING TO MOB BOSS EDWARD GREENBERG—THE ONE THEY CALL FISH EDDIE.
THAT WILL BUY YOU A PLACE IN HIS CREW. NO MORE SMALL-TIME FOR YOU.

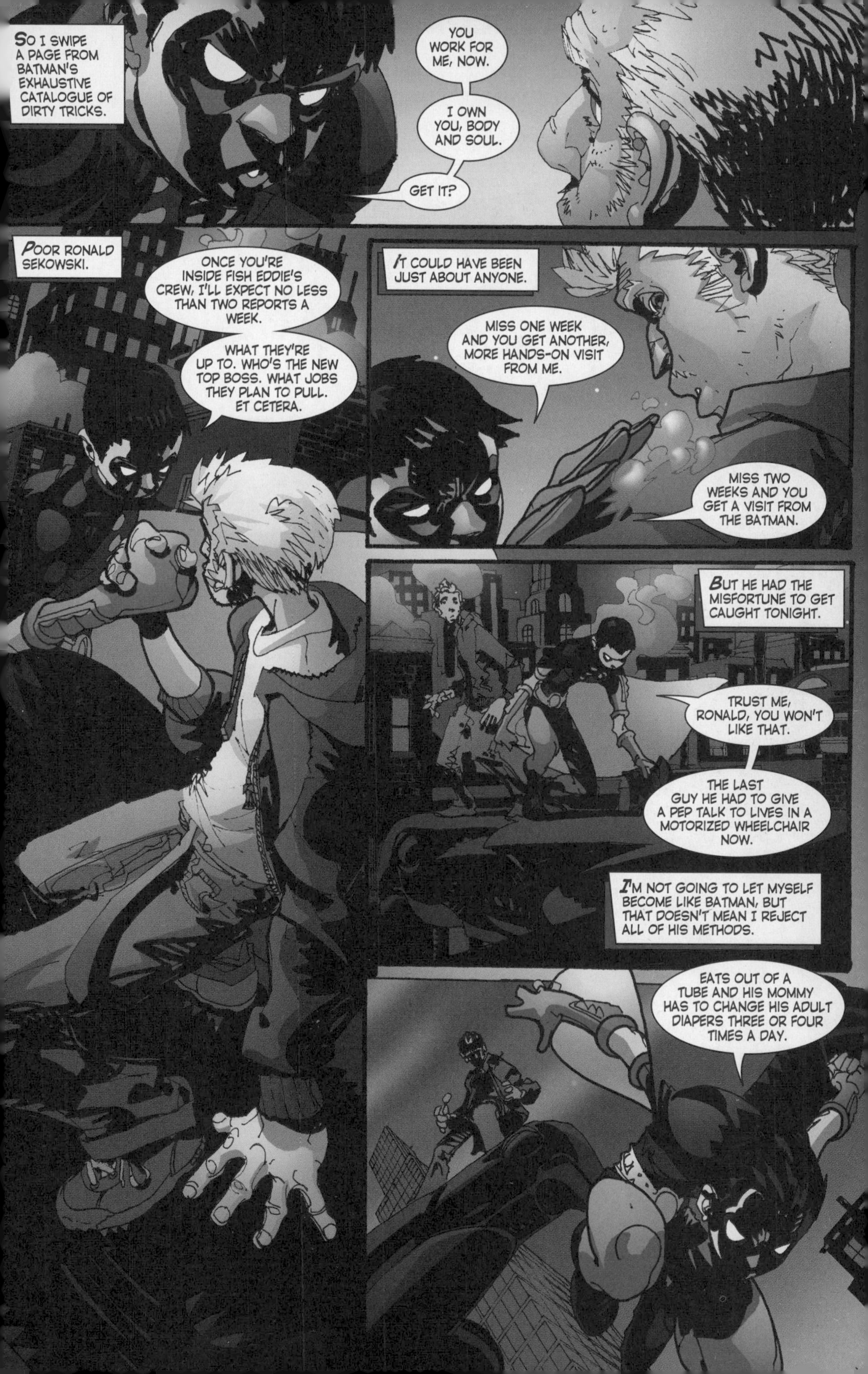
SO I SWIPE A PAGE FROM BATMAN'S EXHAUSTIVE CATALOGUE OF DIRTY TRICKS.
YOU WORK FOR ME, NOW.
I OWN YOU, BODY AND SOUL.
GET IT?
POOR RONALD SEKOWSKI.
ONCE YOU'RE INSIDE FISH EDDIE'S CREW, I'LL EXPECT NO LESS THAN TWO REPORTS A WEEK.
WHAT THEY'RE UP TO. WHO'S THE NEW TOP BOSS. WHAT JOBS THEY PLAN TO PULL. ET CETERA.
IT COULD HAVE BEEN JUST ABOUT ANYONE.
MISS ONE WEEK AND YOU GET ANOTHER, MORE HANDS-ON VISIT FROM ME.
MISS TWO WEEKS AND YOU GET A VISIT FROM THE BATMAN.
BUT HE HAD THE MISFORTUNE TO GET CAUGHT TONIGHT.
TRUST ME, RONALD, YOU WON'T LIKE THAT.
THE LAST GUY HE HAD TO GIVE A PEP TALK TO LIVES IN A MOTORIZED WHEELCHAIR NOW.
I'M NOT GOING TO LET MYSELF BECOME LIKE BATMAN, BUT THAT DOESN'T MEAN I REJECT ALL OF HIS METHODS.
EATS OUT OF A TUBE AND HIS MOMMY HAS TO CHANGE HIS ADULT DIAPERS THREE OR FOUR TIMES A DAY.

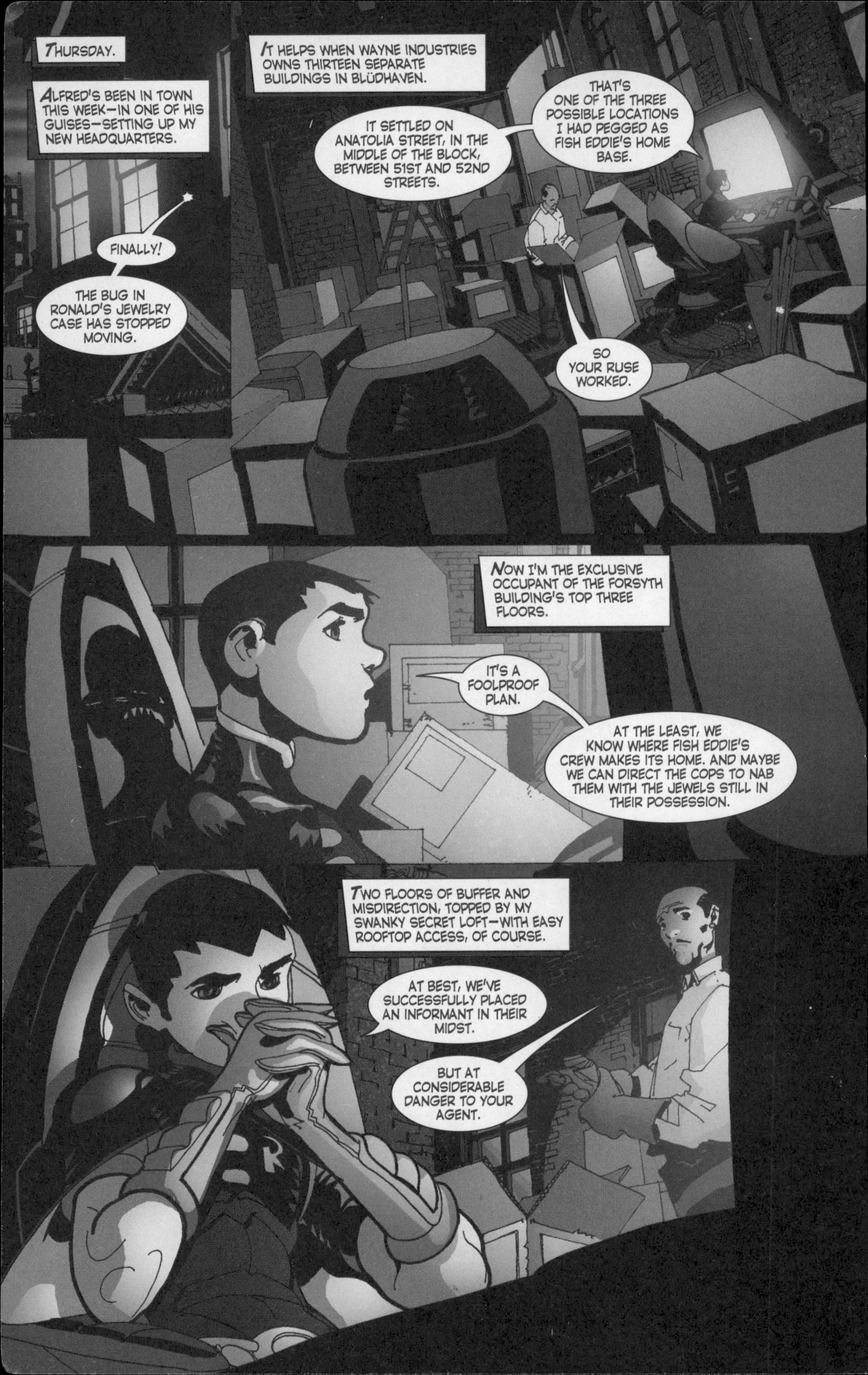
THURSDAY.
ALFRED'S BEEN IN TOWN THIS WEEK—IN ONE OF HIS GUISES—SETTING UP MY NEW HEADQUARTERS.
IT HELPS WHEN WAYNE INDUSTRIES OWNS THIRTEEN SEPARATE BUILDINGS IN BLÜDHAVEN.
FINALLY!
THE BUG IN RONALD'S JEWELRY CASE HAS STOPPED MOVING.
IT SETTLED ON ANATOLIA STREET, IN THE MIDDLE OF THE BLOCK, BETWEEN 51ST AND 52ND STREETS.
THAT'S ONE OF THE THREE POSSIBLE LOCATIONS I HAD PEGGED AS FISH EDDIE'S HOME BASE.
SO YOUR RUSE WORKED.
NOW I'M THE EXCLUSIVE OCCUPANT OF THE FORSYTH BUILDING'S TOP THREE FLOORS.
IT'S A FOOLPROOF PLAN.
AT THE LEAST, WE KNOW WHERE FISH EDDIE'S CREW MAKES ITS HOME. AND MAYBE WE CAN DIRECT THE COPS TO NAB THEM WITH THE JEWELS STILL IN THEIR POSSESSION.
TWO FLOORS OF BUFFER AND MISDIRECTION, TOPPED BY MY SWANKY SECRET LOFT—WITH EASY ROOFTOP ACCESS, OF COURSE.
AT BEST, WE'VE SUCCESSFULLY PLACED AN INFORMANT IN THEIR MIDST.
BUT AT CONSIDERABLE DANGER TO YOUR AGENT.

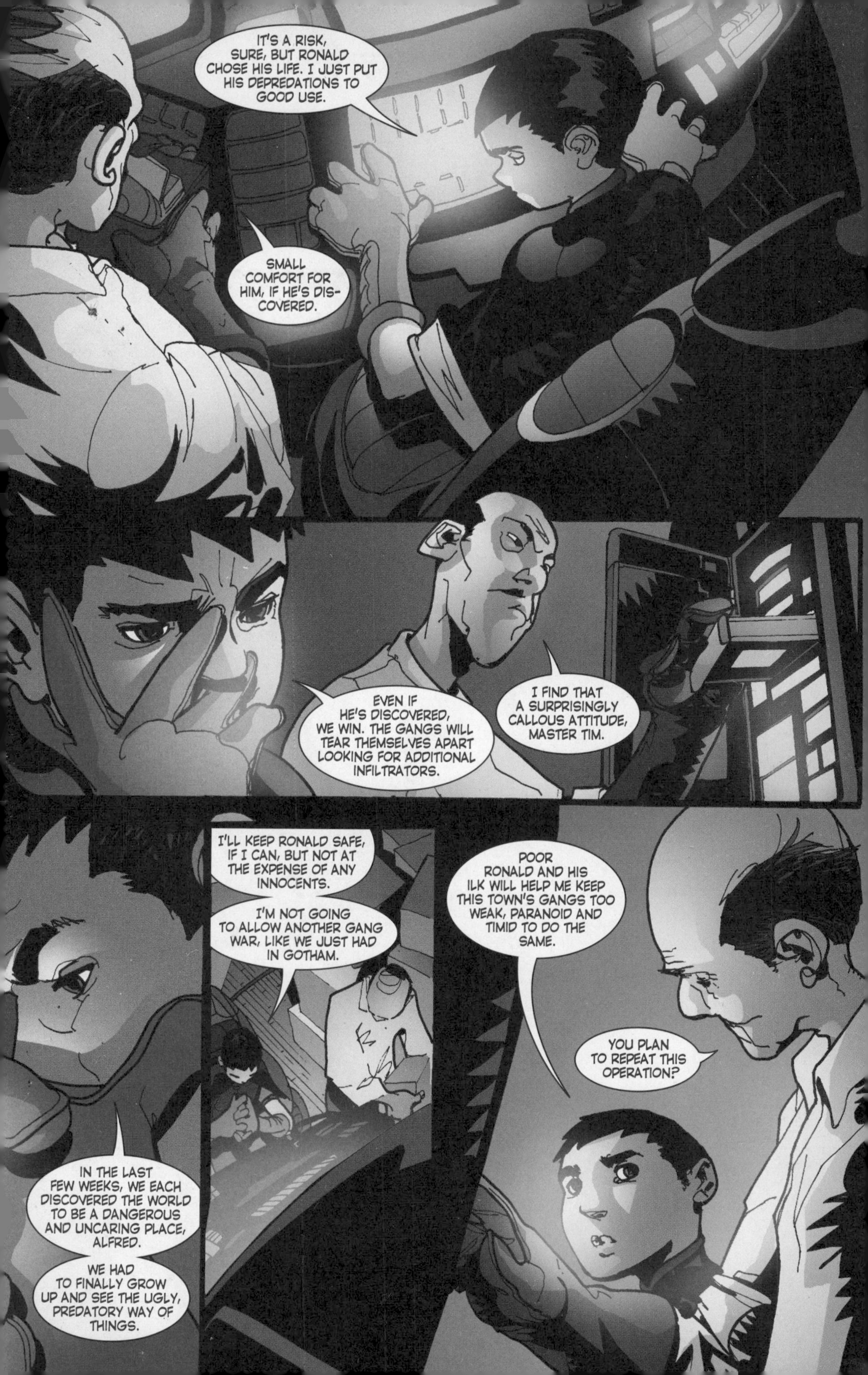
IT'S A RISK, SURE, BUT RONALD CHOSE HIS LIFE. I JUST PUT HIS DEPREDATIONS TO GOOD USE.
SMALL COMFORT FOR HIM, IF HE'S DIS-COVERED.
EVEN IF HE'S DISCOVERED, WE WIN. THE GANGS WILL TEAR THEMSELVES APART LOOKING FOR ADDITIONAL INFILTRATORS.
I FIND THAT A SURPRISINGLY CALLOUS ATTITUDE, MASTER TIM.
IN THE LAST FEW WEEKS, WE EACH DISCOVERED THE WORLD TO BE A DANGEROUS AND UNCARING PLACE, ALFRED.
WE HAD TO FINALLY GROW UP AND SEE THE UGLY, PREDATORY WAY OF THINGS.
I'LL KEEP RONALD SAFE, IF I CAN, BUT NOT AT THE EXPENSE OF ANY INNOCENTS.
I'M NOT GOING TO ALLOW ANOTHER GANG WAR, LIKE WE JUST HAD IN GOTHAM.
POOR RONALD AND HIS ILK WILL HELP ME KEEP THIS TOWN'S GANGS TOO WEAK, PARANOID AND TIMID TO DO THE SAME.
YOU PLAN TO REPEAT THIS OPERATION?

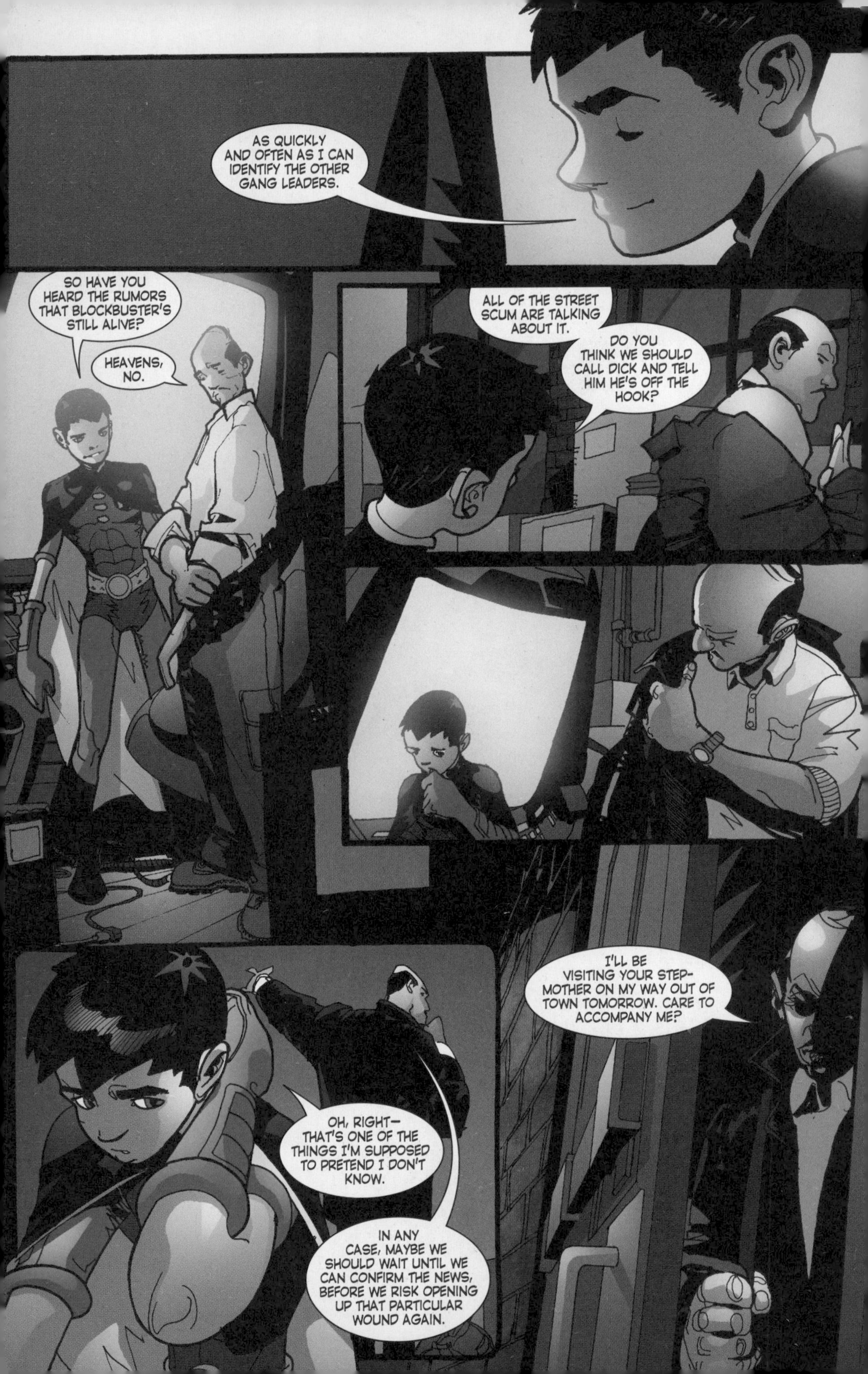
AS QUICKLY AND OFTEN AS I CAN IDENTIFY THE OTHER GANG LEADERS.
SO HAVE YOU HEARD THE RUMORS THAT BLOCKBUSTER'S STILL ALIVE?
HEAVENS, NO.
ALL OF THE STREET SCUM ARE TALKING ABOUT IT.
DO YOU THINK WE SHOULD CALL DICK AND TELL HIM HE'S OFF THE HOOK?
I'LL BE VISITING YOUR STEP-MOTHER ON MY WAY OUT OF TOWN TOMORROW. CARE TO ACCOMPANY ME?
OH, RIGHT— THAT'S ONE OF THE THINGS I'M SUPPOSED TO PRETEND I DON'T KNOW.
IN ANY CASE, MAYBE WE SHOULD WAIT UNTIL WE CAN CONFIRM THE NEWS, BEFORE WE RISK OPENING UP THAT PARTICULAR WOUND AGAIN.

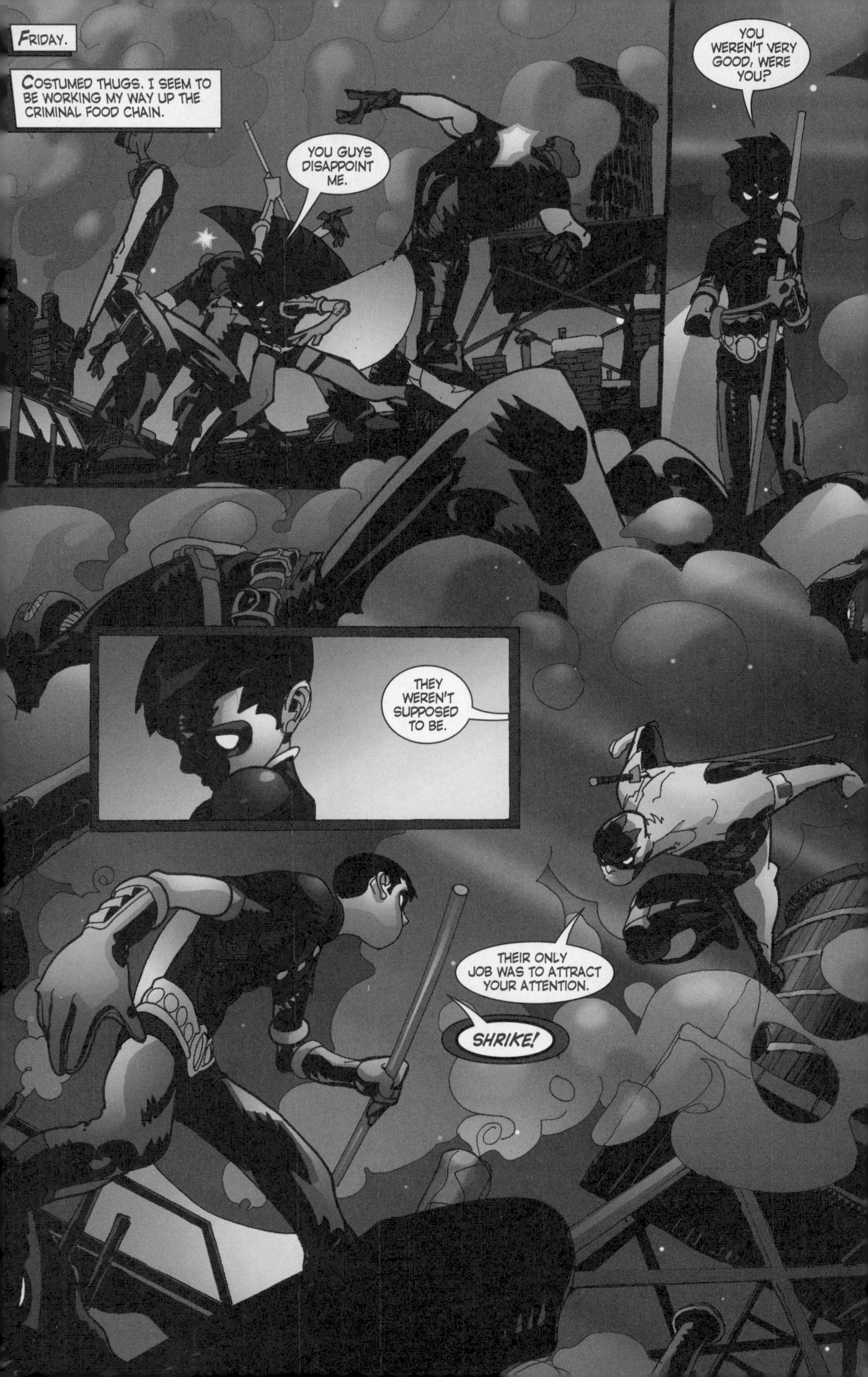
FRIDAY.
COSTUMED THUGS. I SEEM TO BE WORKING MY WAY UP THE CRIMINAL FOOD CHAIN.
YOU GUYS DISAPPOINT ME.
YOU WEREN'T VERY GOOD, WERE YOU?
THEY WEREN'T SUPPOSED TO BE.
THEIR ONLY JOB WAS TO ATTRACT YOUR ATTENTION.
SHRIKE!

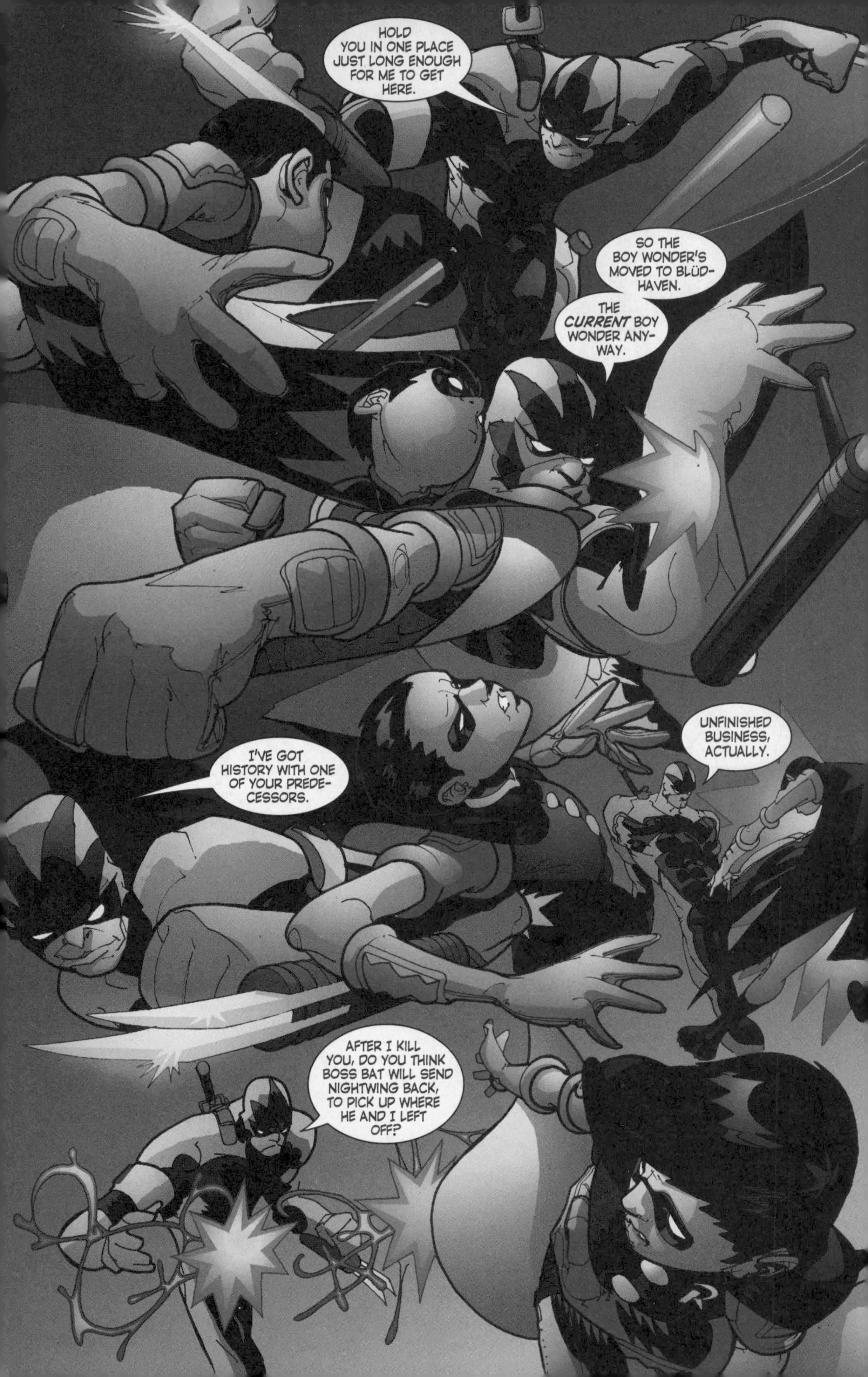
HOLD YOU IN ONE PLACE JUST LONG ENOUGH FOR ME TO GET HERE.
SO THE BOY WONDER'S MOVED TO BLÜDHAVEN.
THE CURRENT BOY WONDER ANYWAY.
I'VE GOT HISTORY WITH ONE OF YOUR PREDECESSORS.
UNFINISHED BUSINESS, ACTUALLY.
AFTER I KILL YOU, DO YOU THINK BOSS BAT WILL SEND NIGHTWING BACK, TO PICK UP WHERE HE AND I LEFT OFF?

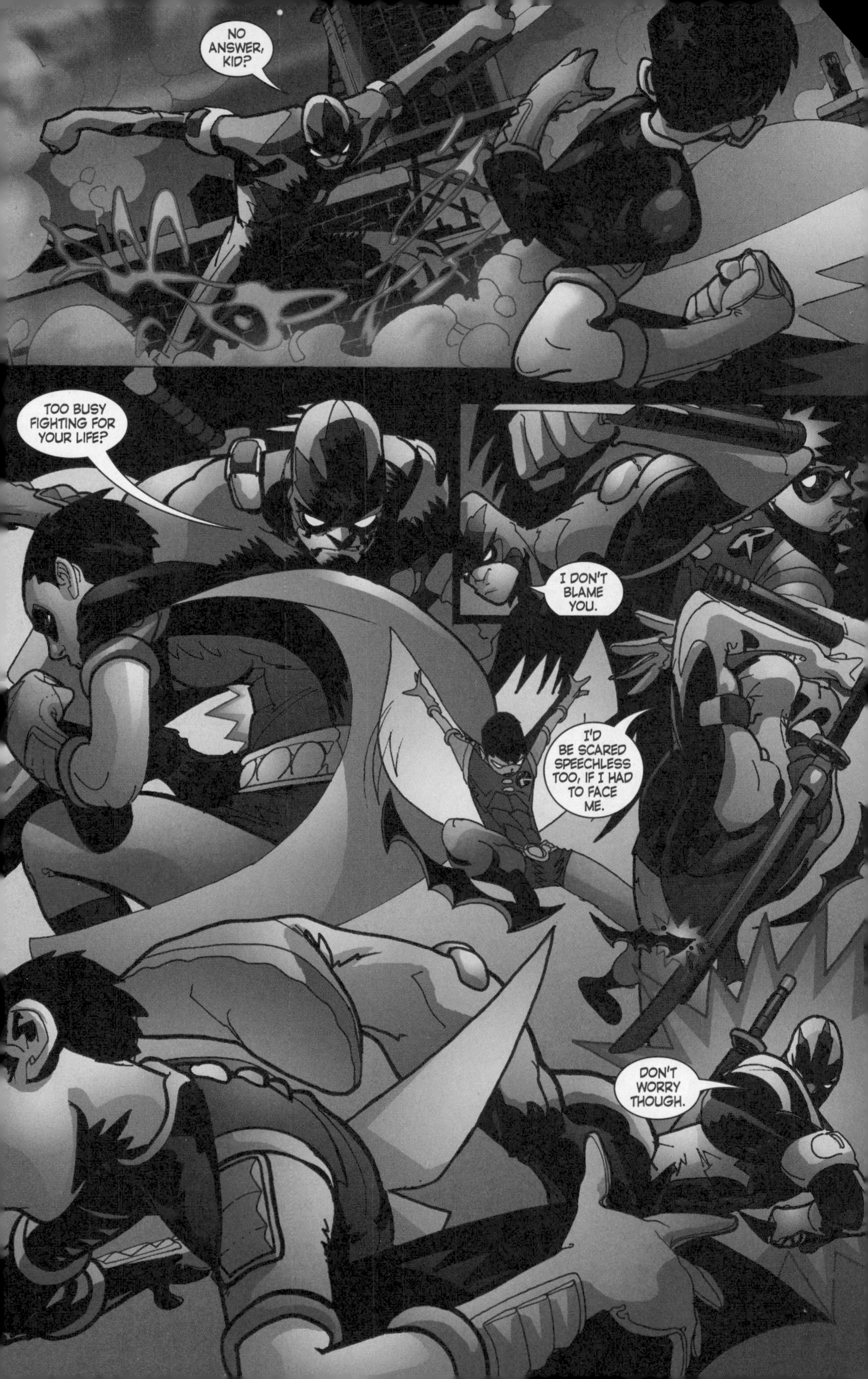
NO ANSWER, KID?
TOO BUSY FIGHTING FOR YOUR LIFE?
I DON'T BLAME YOU.
I'D BE SCARED SPEECHLESS TOO, IF I HAD TO FACE ME.
DON'T WORRY THOUGH.

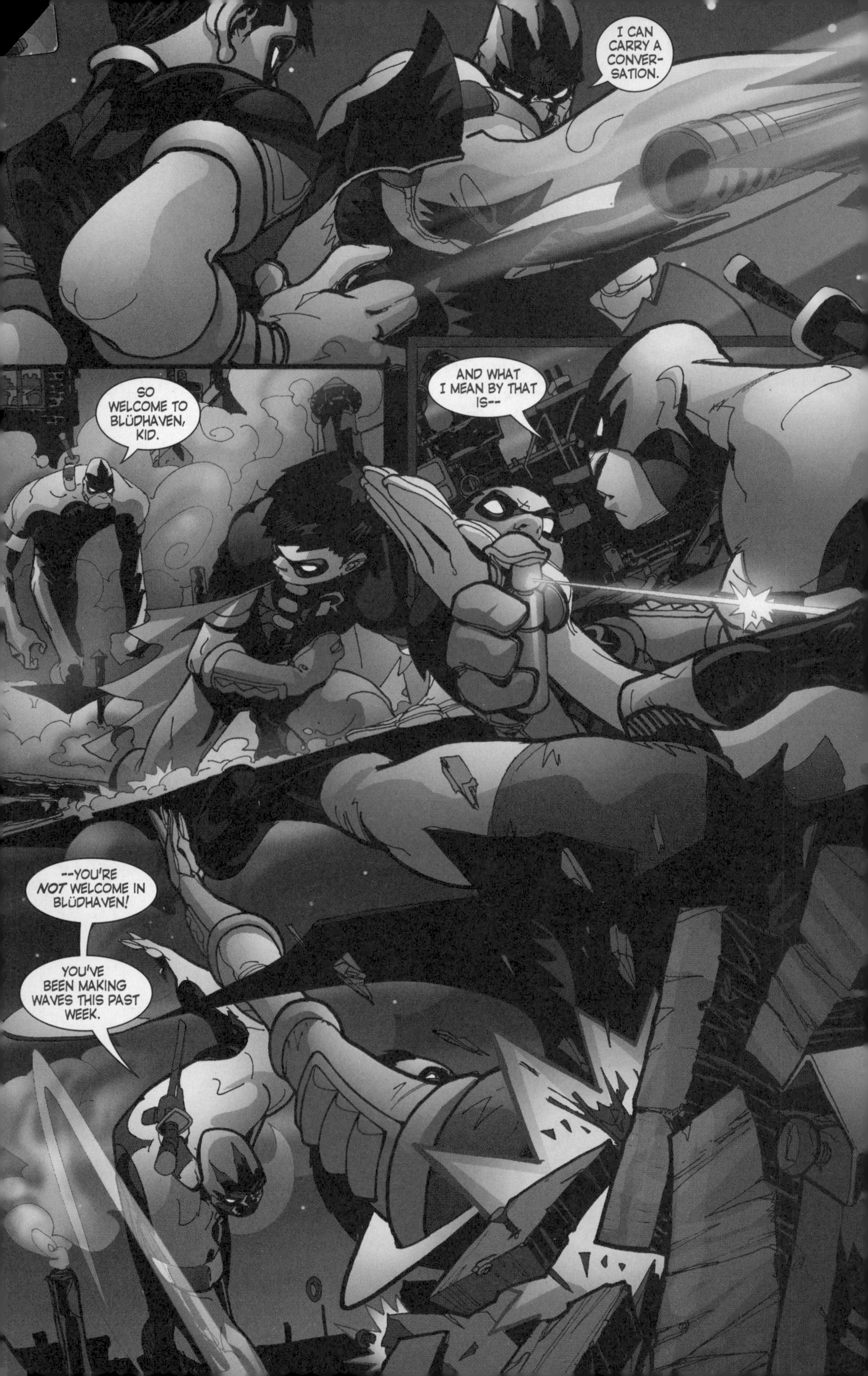

I CAN CARRY A CONVER-SATION.
SO WELCOME TO BLÜDHAVEN, KID.
AND WHAT I MEAN BY THAT IS--
--YOU'RE *NOT* WELCOME IN BLÜDHAVEN!
YOU'VE BEEN MAKING WAVES THIS PAST WEEK.

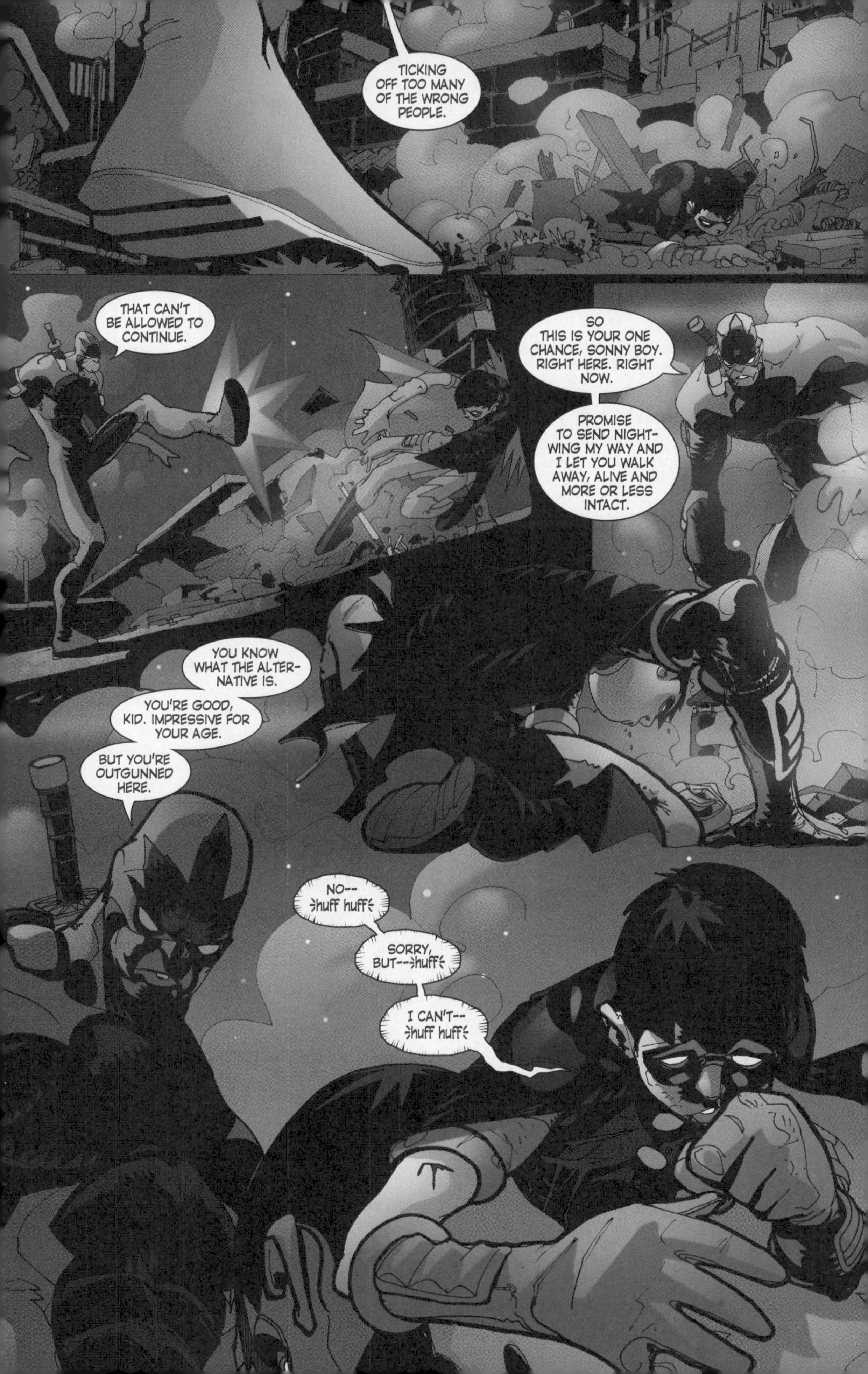
TICKING OFF TOO MANY OF THE WRONG PEOPLE.
THAT CAN'T BE ALLOWED TO CONTINUE.
SO THIS IS YOUR ONE CHANCE, SONNY BOY. RIGHT HERE. RIGHT NOW.
PROMISE TO SEND NIGHT-WING MY WAY AND I LET YOU WALK AWAY, ALIVE AND MORE OR LESS INTACT.
YOU KNOW WHAT THE ALTER-NATIVE IS.
YOU'RE GOOD, KID. IMPRESSIVE FOR YOUR AGE.
BUT YOU'RE OUTGUNNED HERE.
NO-- huff huff
SORRY, BUT-- huff
I CAN'T-- huff huff

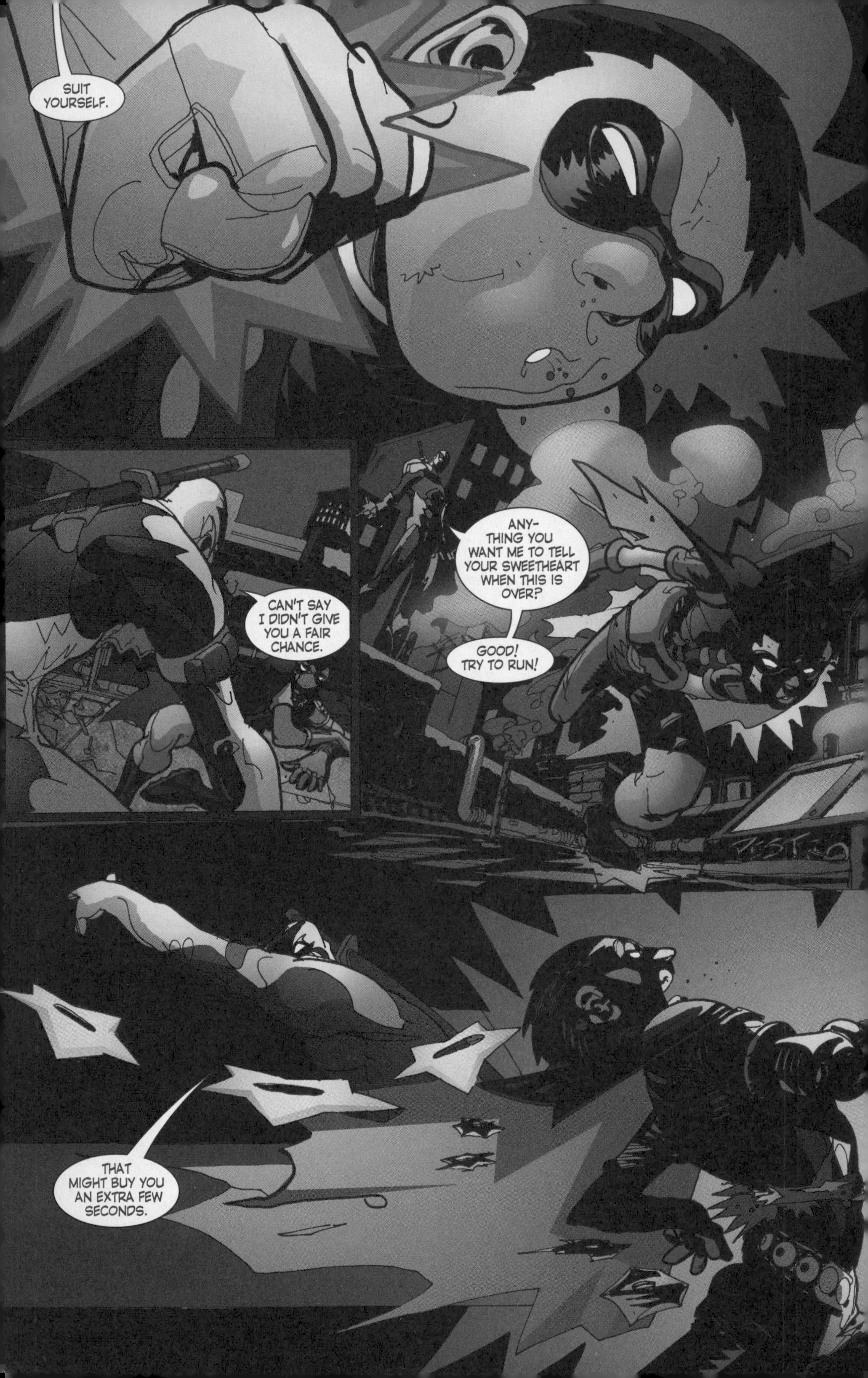
SUIT YOURSELF.
CAN'T SAY I DIDN'T GIVE YOU A FAIR CHANCE.
ANY-THING YOU WANT ME TO TELL YOUR SWEETHEART WHEN THIS IS OVER?
GOOD! TRY TO RUN!
THAT MIGHT BUY YOU AN EXTRA FEW SECONDS.

AT THAT MOMENT...

SO HOW WAS TIM, ALFRED?

DISTURBING.

STILL SAD? THAT'S JUST GOING TO TAKE TIME TO--

OH, HE WAS SAD, CERTAINLY-- BUT ALSO MORE THAN THAT.

HE'S CHANGED CONSIDERABLY OVER THESE PAST HORRIBLE DAYS.

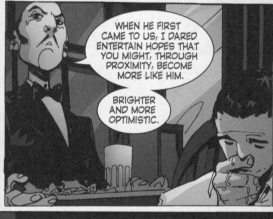

WHEN HE FIRST CAME TO US, I DARED ENTERTAIN HOPES THAT YOU MIGHT, THROUGH PROXIMITY, BECOME MORE LIKE HIM.

BRIGHTER AND MORE OPTIMISTIC.

BUT I'M AFRAID EXACTLY THE OPPOSITE HAS OCCURRED.

I'M AFRAID HE'S BECOME MORE LIKE YOU.

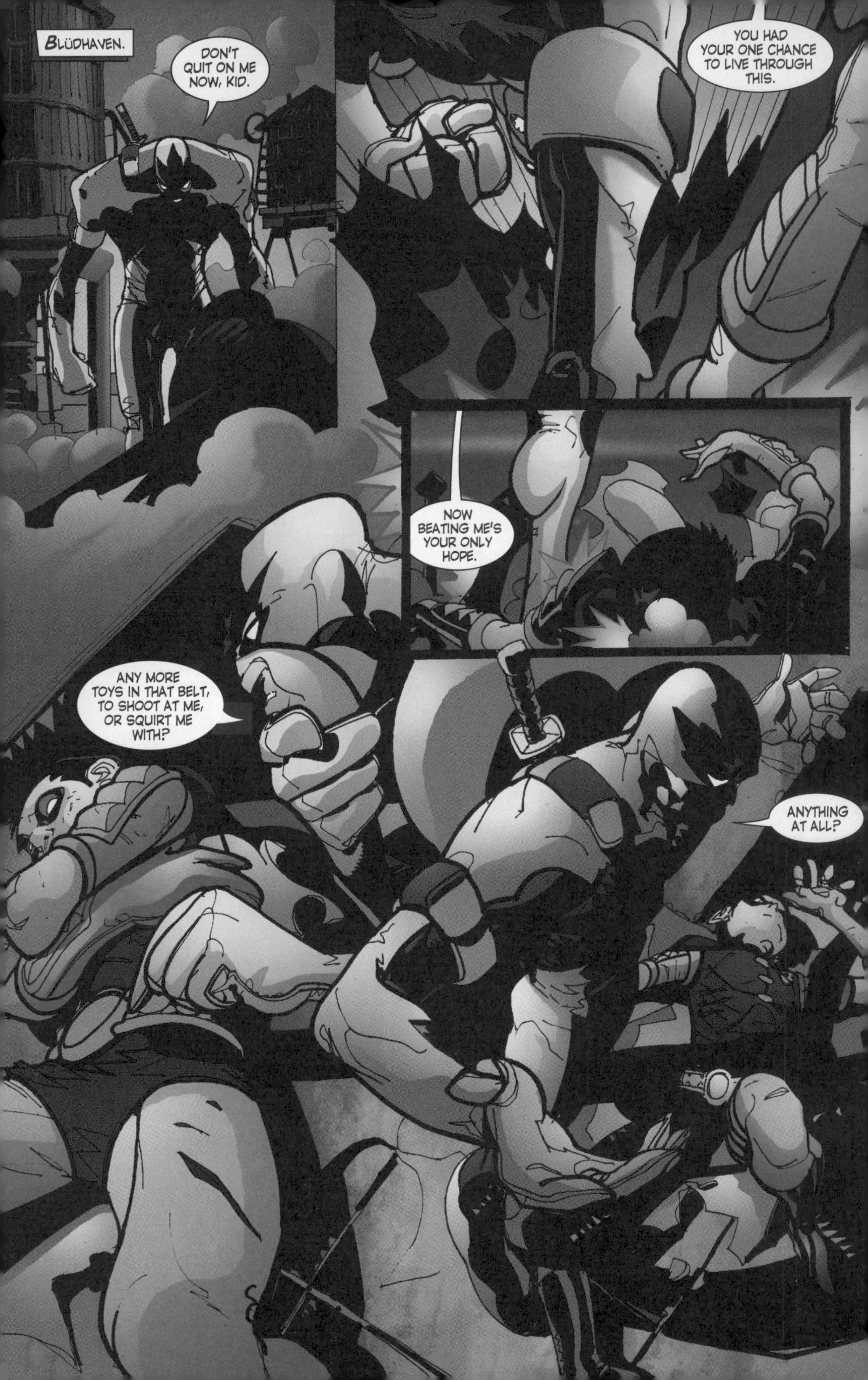
BLÜDHAVEN.
DON'T QUIT ON ME NOW, KID.
YOU HAD YOUR ONE CHANCE TO LIVE THROUGH THIS.
NOW BEATING ME'S YOUR ONLY HOPE.
ANY MORE TOYS IN THAT BELT, TO SHOOT AT ME, OR SQUIRT ME WITH?
ANYTHING AT ALL?

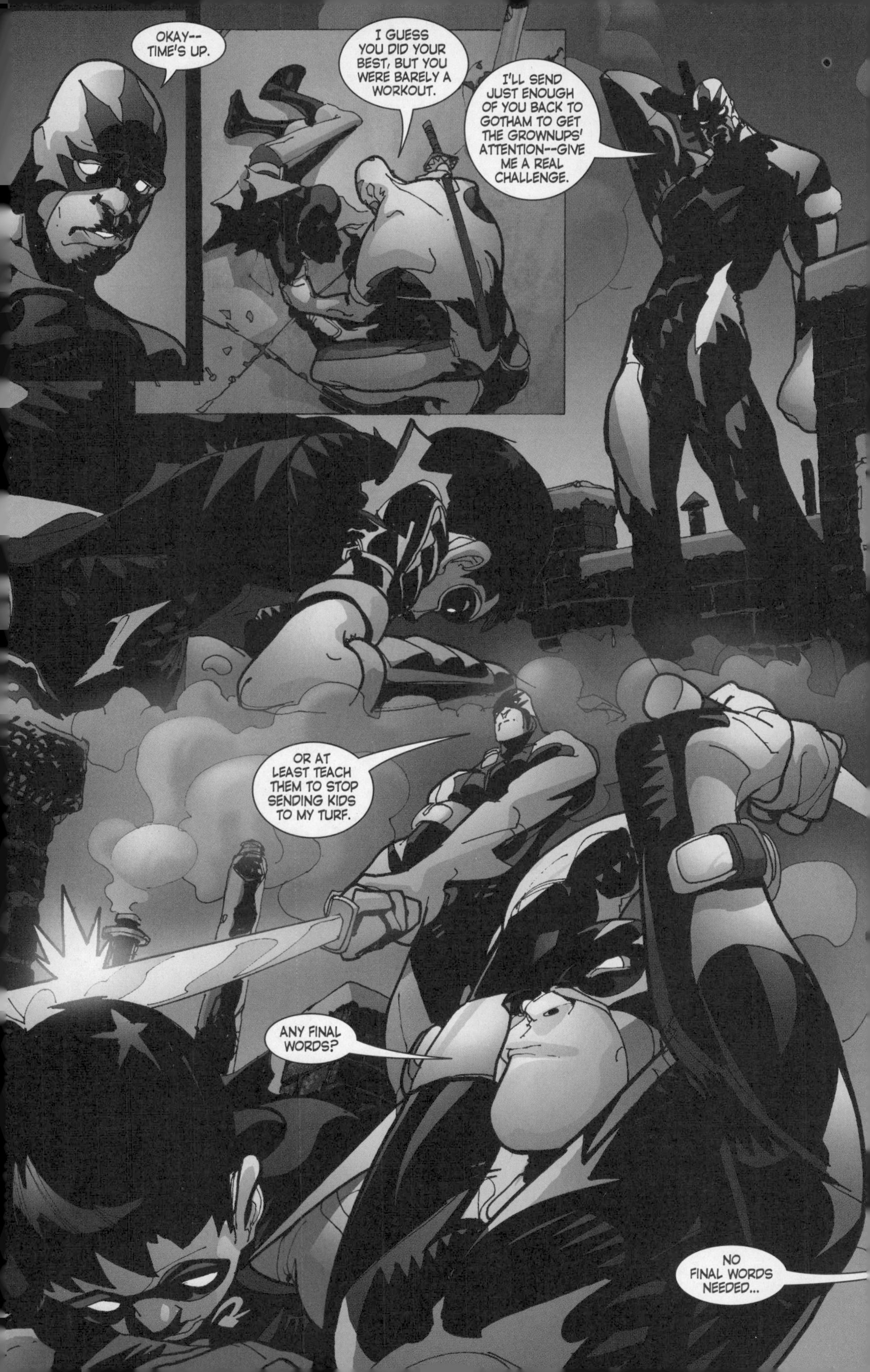
OKAY--
TIME'S UP.
I GUESS
YOU DID YOUR
BEST, BUT YOU
WERE BARELY A
WORKOUT.
I'LL SEND
JUST ENOUGH
OF YOU BACK TO
GOTHAM TO GET
THE GROWNUPS'
ATTENTION--GIVE
ME A REAL
CHALLENGE.
OR AT
LEAST TEACH
THEM TO STOP
SENDING KIDS
TO MY TURF.
ANY FINAL
WORDS?
NO
FINAL WORDS
NEEDED...

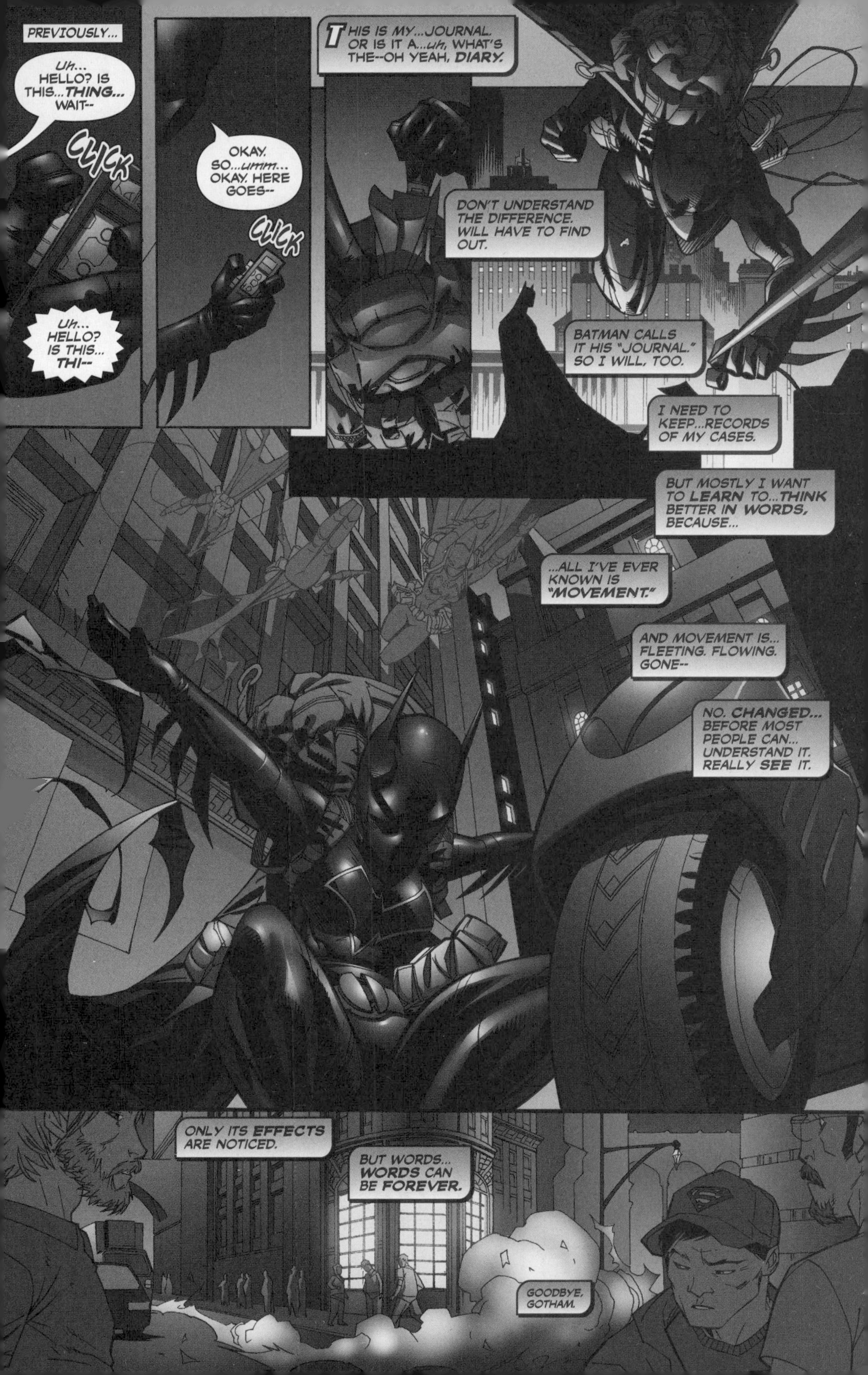
PREVIOUSLY...
Uh... HELLO? IS THIS...THING... WAIT--
CLICK
Uh... HELLO? IS THIS... THI--
OKAY. SO...umm... OKAY. HERE GOES--
CLICK
THIS IS MY...JOURNAL. OR IS IT A...uh, WHAT'S THE--OH YEAH, DIARY.
DON'T UNDERSTAND THE DIFFERENCE. WILL HAVE TO FIND OUT.
BATMAN CALLS IT HIS "JOURNAL." SO I WILL, TOO.
I NEED TO KEEP...RECORDS OF MY CASES.
BUT MOSTLY I WANT TO LEARN TO...THINK BETTER IN WORDS, BECAUSE...
...ALL I'VE EVER KNOWN IS "MOVEMENT."
AND MOVEMENT IS... FLEETING. FLOWING. GONE--
NO. CHANGED... BEFORE MOST PEOPLE CAN... UNDERSTAND IT. REALLY SEE IT.
ONLY ITS EFFECTS ARE NOTICED.
BUT WORDS... WORDS CAN BE FOREVER.
GOODBYE, GOTHAM.

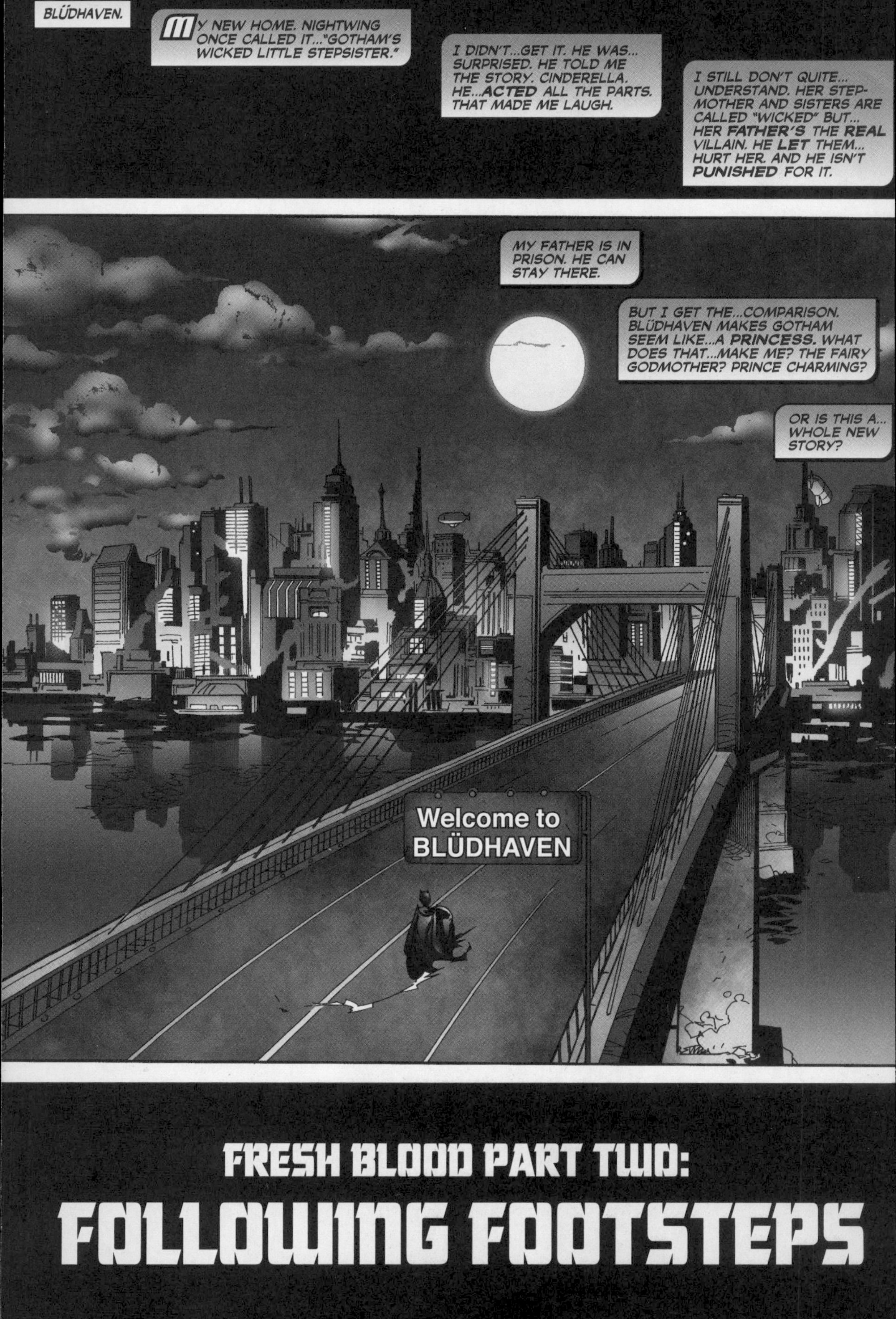
BLÜDHAVEN.
MY NEW HOME. NIGHTWING ONCE CALLED IT..."GOTHAM'S WICKED LITTLE STEPSISTER."
I DIDN'T...GET IT. HE WAS... SURPRISED. HE TOLD ME THE STORY. CINDERELLA. HE...ACTED ALL THE PARTS. THAT MADE ME LAUGH.
I STILL DON'T QUITE... UNDERSTAND. HER STEP-MOTHER AND SISTERS ARE CALLED "WICKED" BUT... HER FATHER'S THE REAL VILLAIN. HE LET THEM... HURT HER. AND HE ISN'T PUNISHED FOR IT.
MY FATHER IS IN PRISON. HE CAN STAY THERE.
BUT I GET THE...COMPARISON. BLÜDHAVEN MAKES GOTHAM SEEM LIKE...A PRINCESS. WHAT DOES THAT...MAKE ME? THE FAIRY GODMOTHER? PRINCE CHARMING?
OR IS THIS A... WHOLE NEW STORY?
Welcome to BLÜDHAVEN
FRESH BLOOD PART TWO:
FOLLOWING FOOTSTEPS

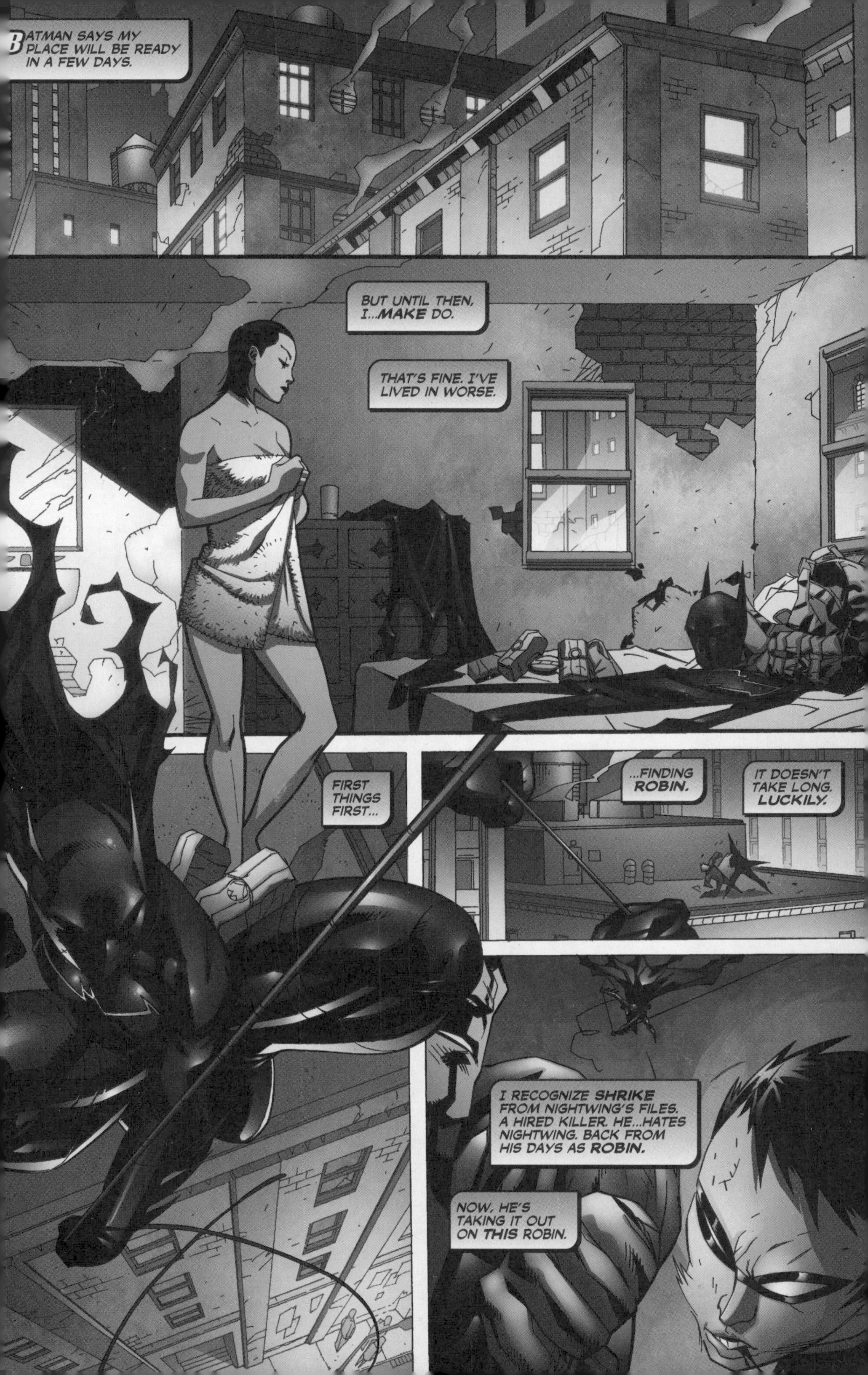
BATMAN SAYS MY PLACE WILL BE READY IN A FEW DAYS.
BUT UNTIL THEN, I...MAKE DO.
THAT'S FINE. I'VE LIVED IN WORSE.
FIRST THINGS FIRST...
...FINDING ROBIN.
IT DOESN'T TAKE LONG. LUCKILY.
I RECOGNIZE SHRIKE FROM NIGHTWING'S FILES. A HIRED KILLER. HE...HATES NIGHTWING. BACK FROM HIS DAYS AS ROBIN.
NOW, HE'S TAKING IT OUT ON THIS ROBIN.

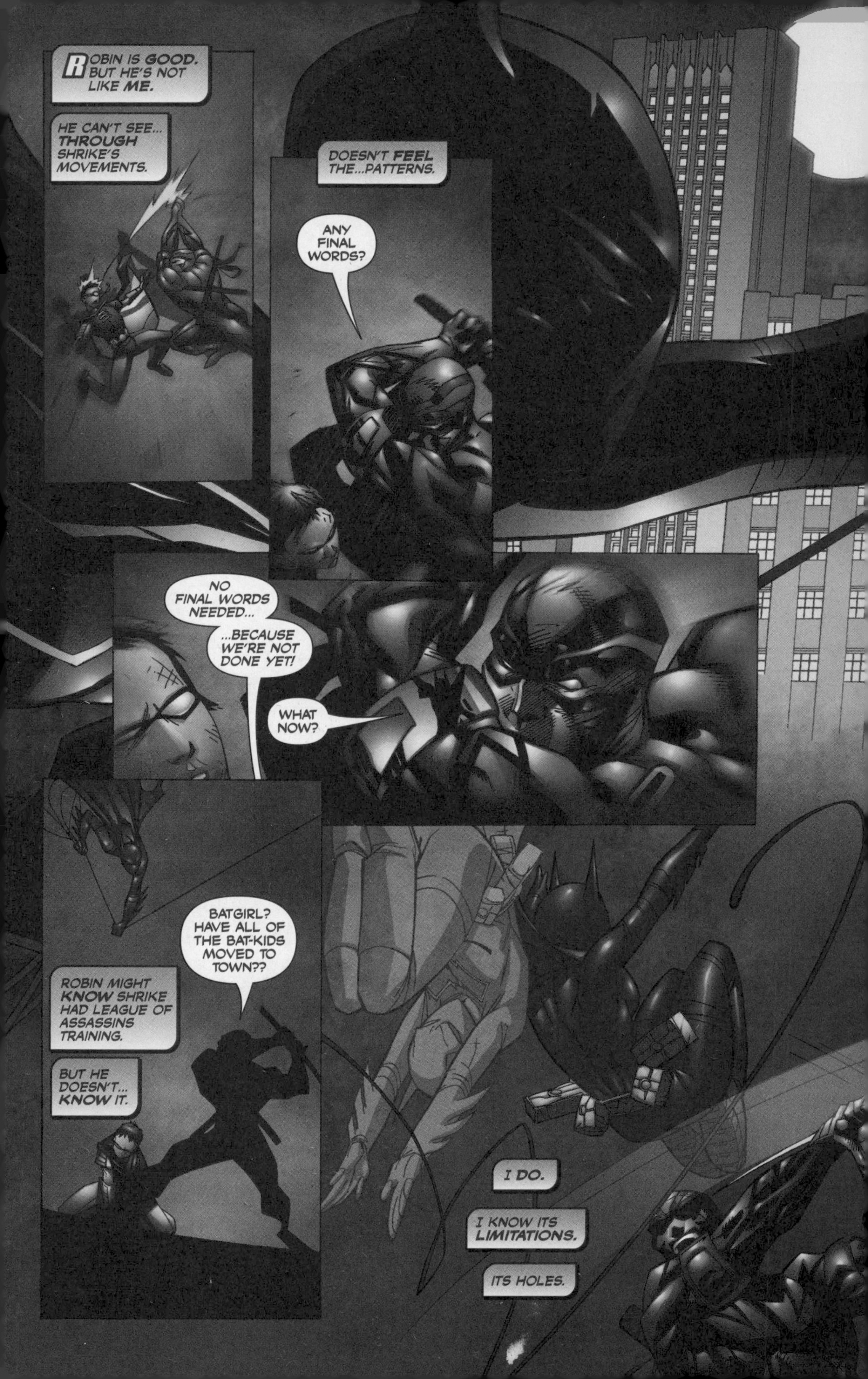
ROBIN IS GOOD. BUT HE'S NOT LIKE ME.
HE CAN'T SEE... THROUGH SHRIKE'S MOVEMENTS.
DOESN'T FEEL THE...PATTERNS.
ANY FINAL WORDS?
NO FINAL WORDS NEEDED...
...BECAUSE WE'RE NOT DONE YET!
WHAT NOW?
BATGIRL? HAVE ALL OF THE BAT-KIDS MOVED TO TOWN??
ROBIN MIGHT KNOW SHRIKE HAD LEAGUE OF ASSASSINS TRAINING.
BUT HE DOESN'T... KNOW IT.
I DO.
I KNOW ITS LIMITATIONS.
ITS HOLES.

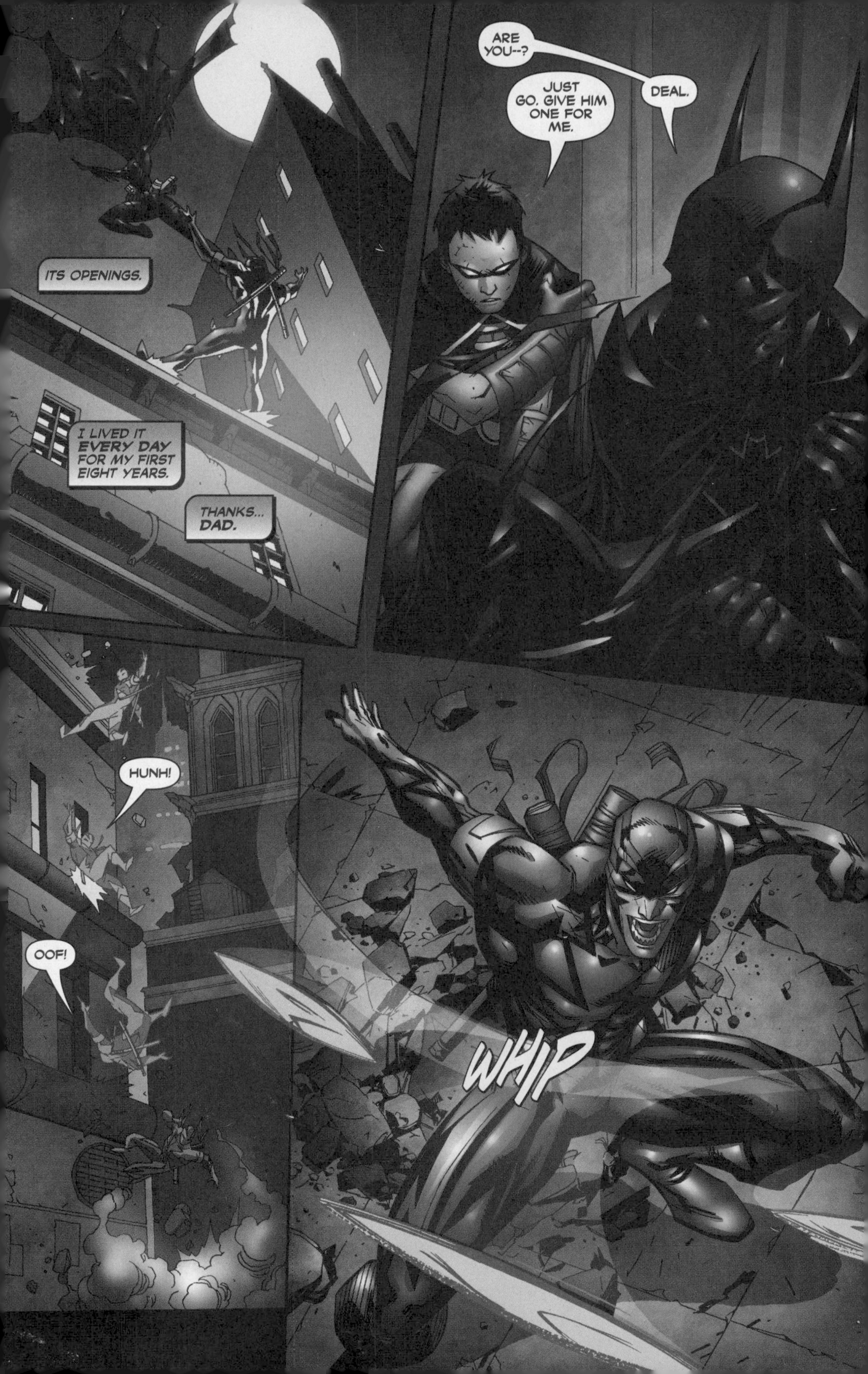

ITS OPENINGS.
I LIVED IT EVERY DAY FOR MY FIRST EIGHT YEARS.
THANKS... DAD.
ARE YOU--?
JUST GO. GIVE HIM ONE FOR ME.
DEAL.
HUNH!
OOF!
WHIP

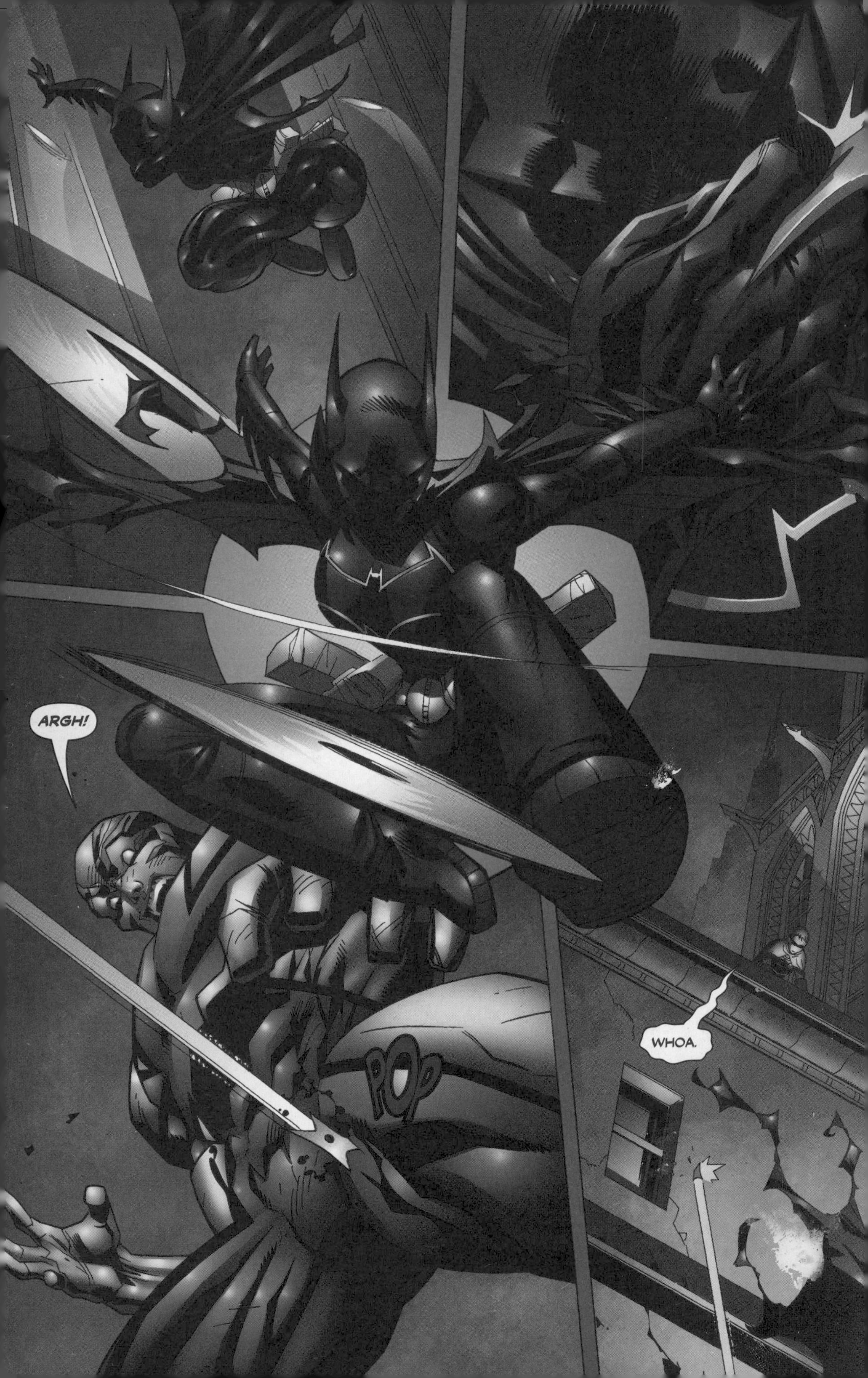
ARGH!
POP
WHOA.

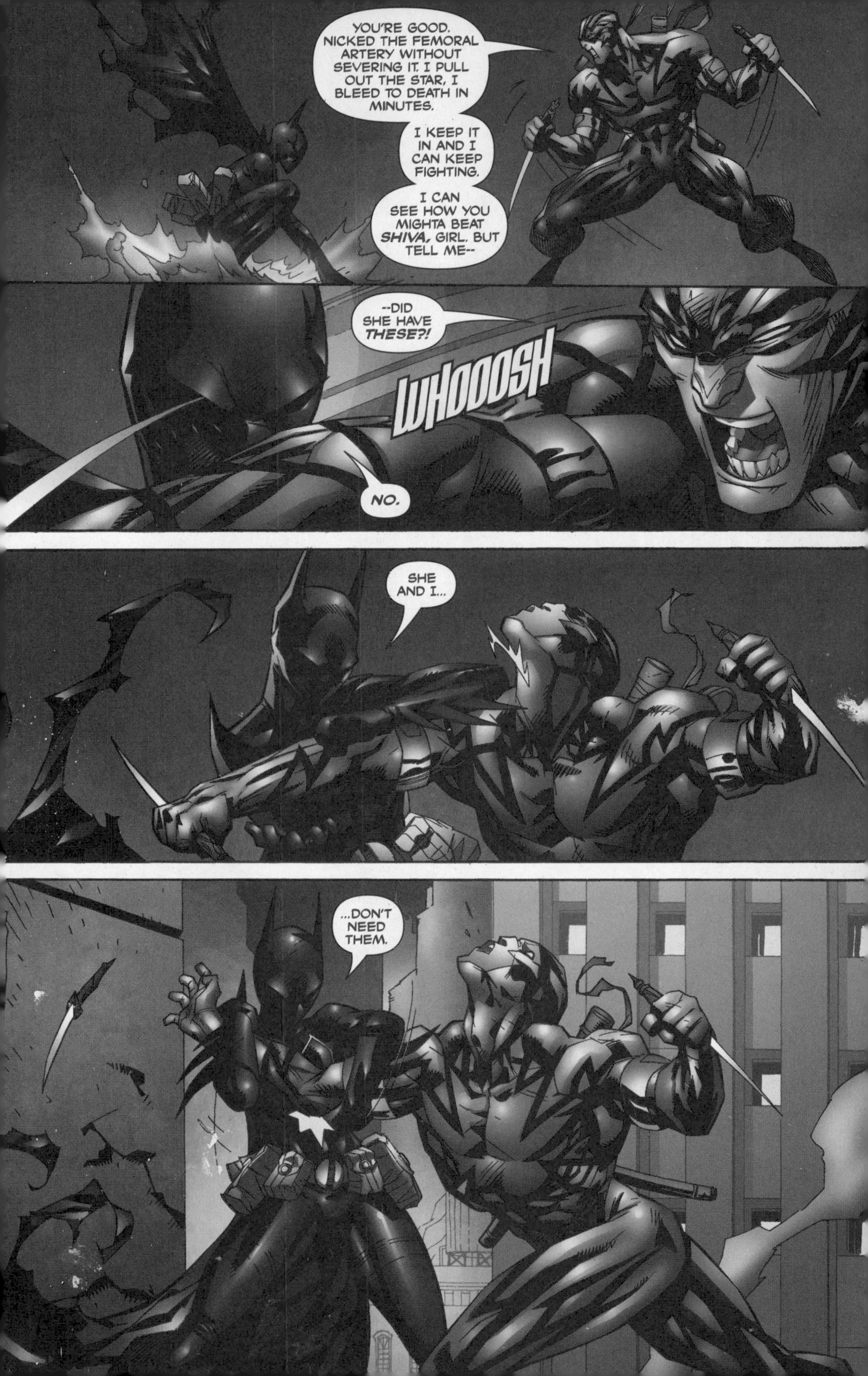
YOU'RE GOOD. NICKED THE FEMORAL ARTERY WITHOUT SEVERING IT. I PULL OUT THE STAR, I BLEED TO DEATH IN MINUTES.
I KEEP IT IN AND I CAN KEEP FIGHTING.
I CAN SEE HOW YOU MIGHTA BEAT SHIVA, GIRL. BUT TELL ME--
--DID SHE HAVE THESE?!
WHOOOSH
NO.
SHE AND I...
...DON'T NEED THEM.

YOU HURT ROBIN. FOR MONEY. WHY?

I AIN'T TELLIN YOU $#!%.

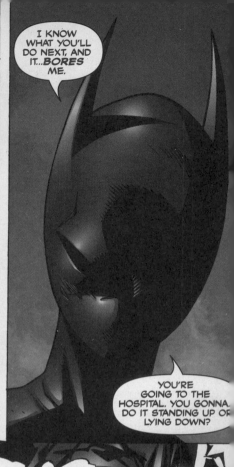

I KNOW WHAT YOU'LL DO NEXT, AND IT...BORES ME.

YOU'RE BLEEDING TO DEATH. YOUR ARM'S BROKEN.

I'M UNTOUCHED. HAVEN'T... BROKEN A SWEAT.

YOU'RE GOING TO THE HOSPITAL. YOU GONNA DO IT STANDING UP OR LYING DOWN?

RRARGH!!!

KRACK

HE CHOSE LYING DOWN.

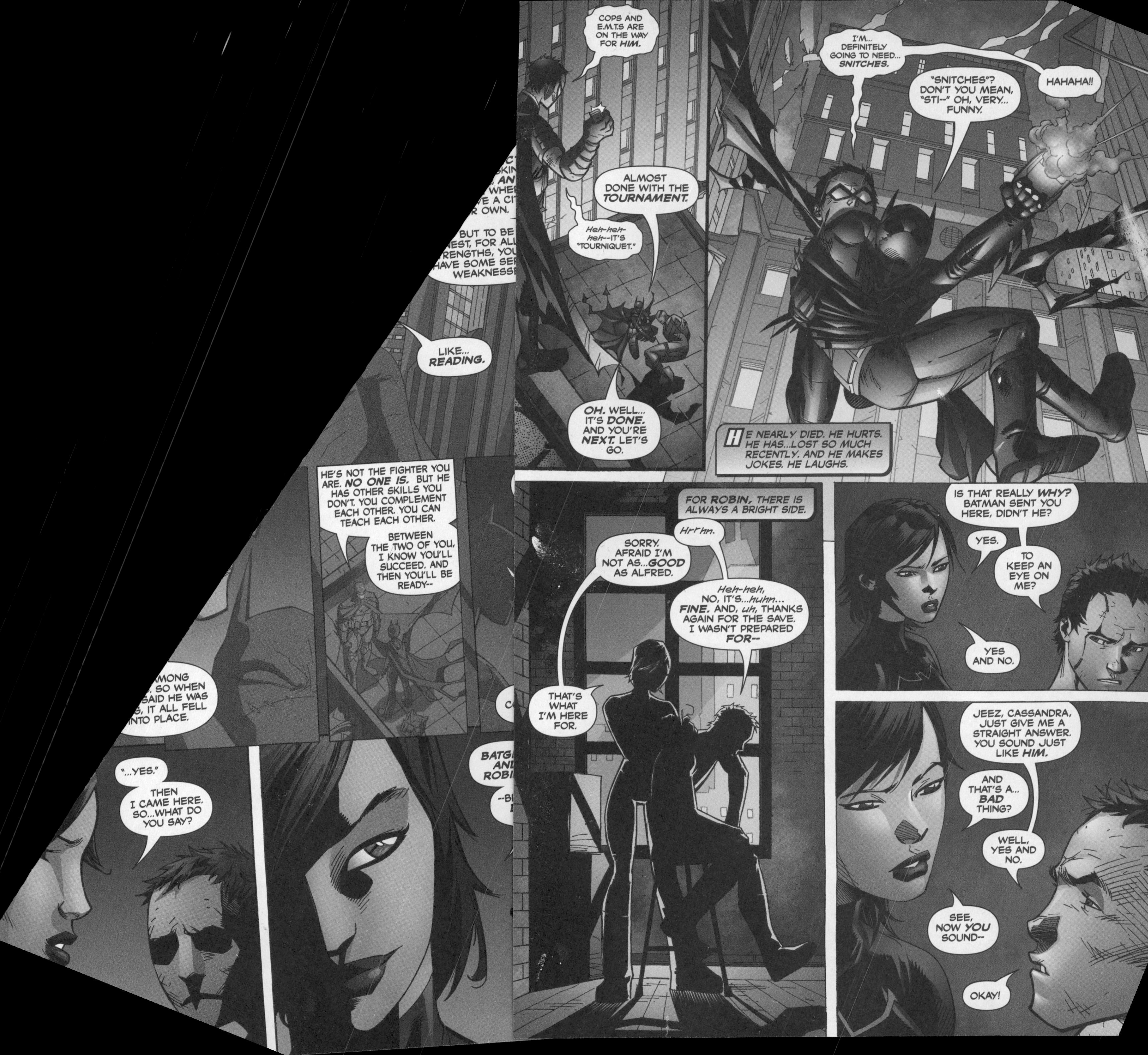
LIKE... READING.
HE'S NOT THE FIGHTER YOU ARE. NO ONE IS. BUT HE HAS OTHER SKILLS YOU DON'T. YOU COMPLEMENT EACH OTHER. YOU CAN TEACH EACH OTHER.
BETWEEN THE TWO OF YOU, I KNOW YOU'LL SUCCEED. AND THEN YOU'LL BE READY--
"...YES."
THEN I CAME HERE. SO...WHAT DO YOU SAY?
COPS AND E.M.T.S ARE ON THE WAY FOR HIM.
ALMOST DONE WITH THE TOURNAMENT.
Heh-heh-heh--IT'S "TOURNIQUET."
OH. WELL... IT'S DONE. AND YOU'RE NEXT. LET'S GO.
I'M... DEFINITELY GOING TO NEED... SNITCHES.
"SNITCHES"? DON'T YOU MEAN, "STI--" OH, VERY... FUNNY.
HAHAHA!!
HE NEARLY DIED. HE HURTS. HE HAS...LOST SO MUCH RECENTLY. AND HE MAKES JOKES. HE LAUGHS.
FOR ROBIN, THERE IS ALWAYS A BRIGHT SIDE.
Hrrhn.
SORRY. AFRAID I'M NOT AS...GOOD AS ALFRED.
Heh-heh, NO, IT'S...huhn... FINE. AND, uh, THANKS AGAIN FOR THE SAVE. I WASN'T PREPARED FOR--
THAT'S WHAT I'M HERE FOR.
IS THAT REALLY WHY? BATMAN SENT YOU HERE, DIDN'T HE?
YES.
TO KEEP AN EYE ON ME?
YES AND NO.
JEEZ, CASSANDRA, JUST GIVE ME A STRAIGHT ANSWER. YOU SOUND JUST LIKE HIM.
AND THAT'S A... BAD THING?
WELL, YES AND NO.
SEE, NOW YOU SOUND--
OKAY!

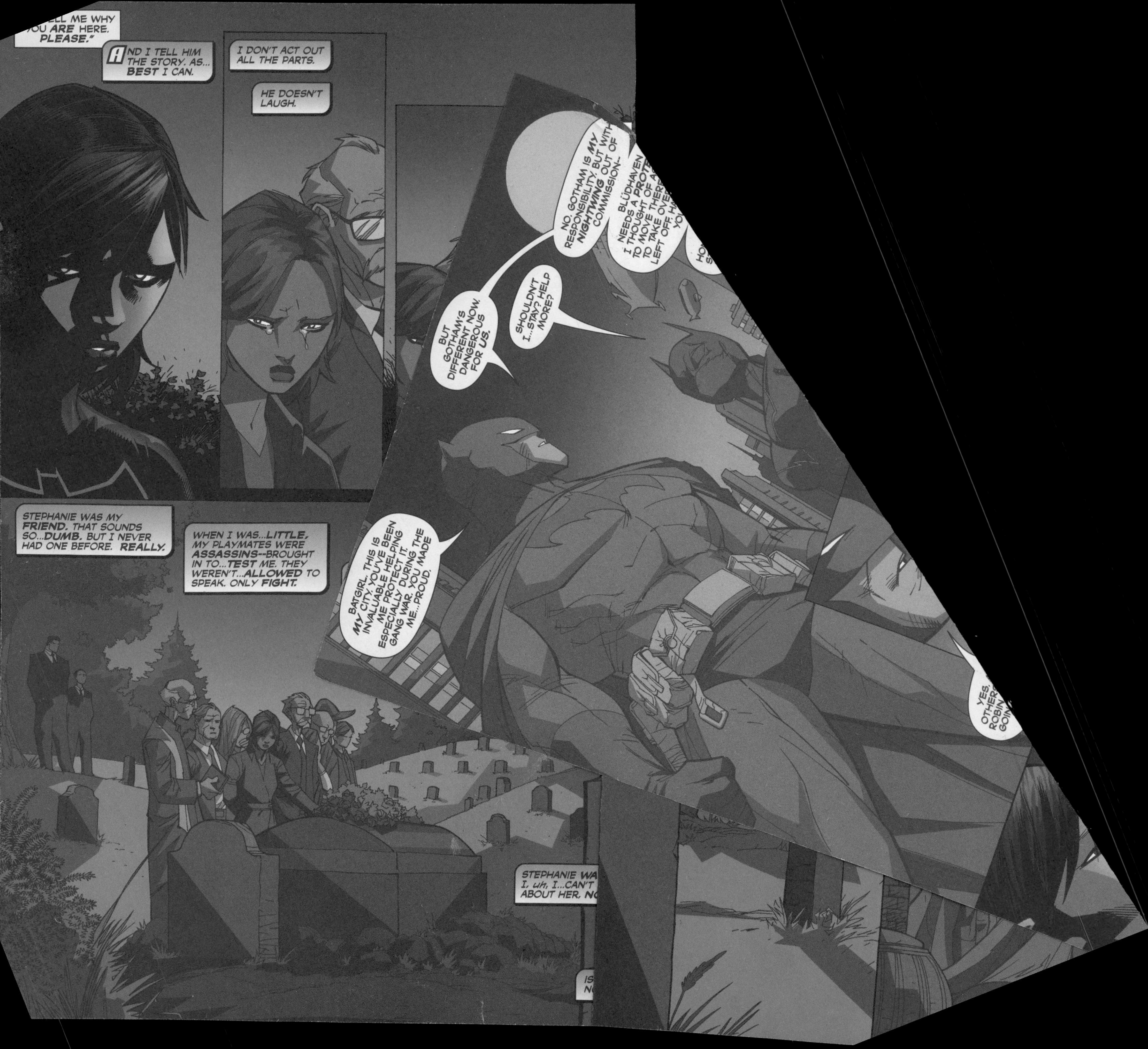
ELL ME WHY YOU ARE HERE. PLEASE."
AND I TELL HIM THE STORY. AS... BEST I CAN.
I DON'T ACT OUT ALL THE PARTS.
HE DOESN'T LAUGH.
STEPHANIE WAS MY FRIEND. THAT SOUNDS SO...DUMB. BUT I NEVER HAD ONE BEFORE. REALLY.
WHEN I WAS...LITTLE, MY PLAYMATES WERE ASSASSINS--BROUGHT IN TO...TEST ME. THEY WEREN'T...ALLOWED TO SPEAK. ONLY FIGHT.
NO. GOTHAM IS MY RESPONSIBILITY. BUT WITH NIGHTWING OUT OF COMMISSION--
BUT GOTHAM'S DIFFERENT NOW. DANGEROUS FOR US.
SHOULDN'T I...STAY? HELP MORE?
BATGIRL, THIS IS MY CITY. YOU'VE BEEN INVALUABLE HELPING ME PROTECT IT. ESPECIALLY DURING THE GANG WAR. YOU MADE ME...PROUD.

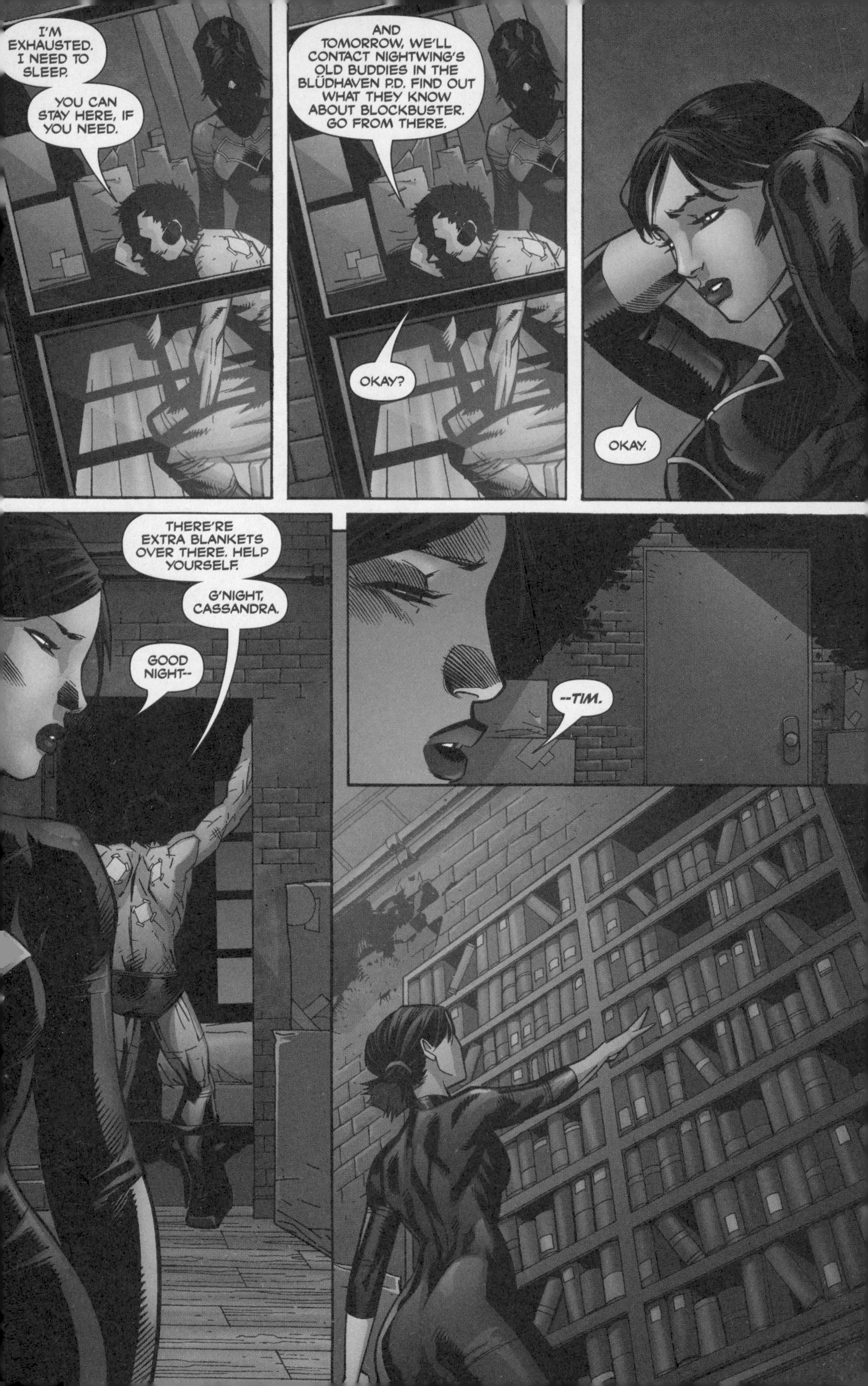
I'M EXHAUSTED. I NEED TO SLEEP.
YOU CAN STAY HERE, IF YOU NEED.
AND TOMORROW, WE'LL CONTACT NIGHTWING'S OLD BUDDIES IN THE BLÜDHAVEN P.D. FIND OUT WHAT THEY KNOW ABOUT BLOCKBUSTER. GO FROM THERE.
OKAY?
OKAY.
THERE'RE EXTRA BLANKETS OVER THERE. HELP YOURSELF.
G'NIGHT, CASSANDRA.
GOOD NIGHT--
--TIM.

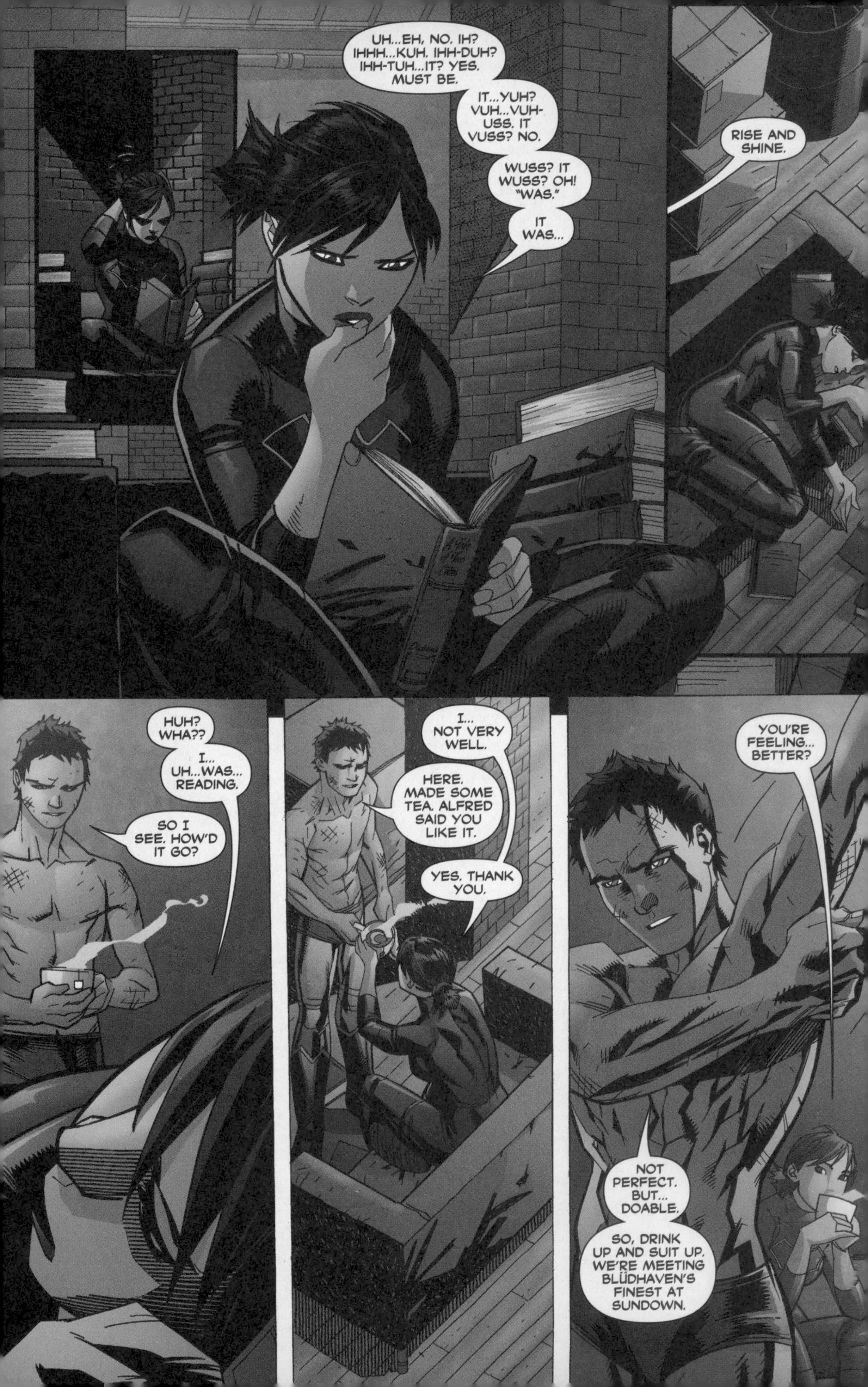
UH...EH, NO. IH? IHHH...KUH. IHH-DUH? IHH-TUH...IT? YES. MUST BE.
IT...YUH? VUH...VUH-USS. IT VUSS? NO.
WUSS? IT WUSS? OH! "WAS."
IT WAS...
RISE AND SHINE.
HUH? WHA??
I... UH...WAS... READING.
SO I SEE. HOW'D IT GO?
I... NOT VERY WELL.
HERE. MADE SOME TEA. ALFRED SAID YOU LIKE IT.
YES. THANK YOU.
YOU'RE FEELING... BETTER?
NOT PERFECT. BUT... DOABLE.
SO, DRINK UP AND SUIT UP. WE'RE MEETING BLÜDHAVEN'S FINEST AT SUNDOWN.

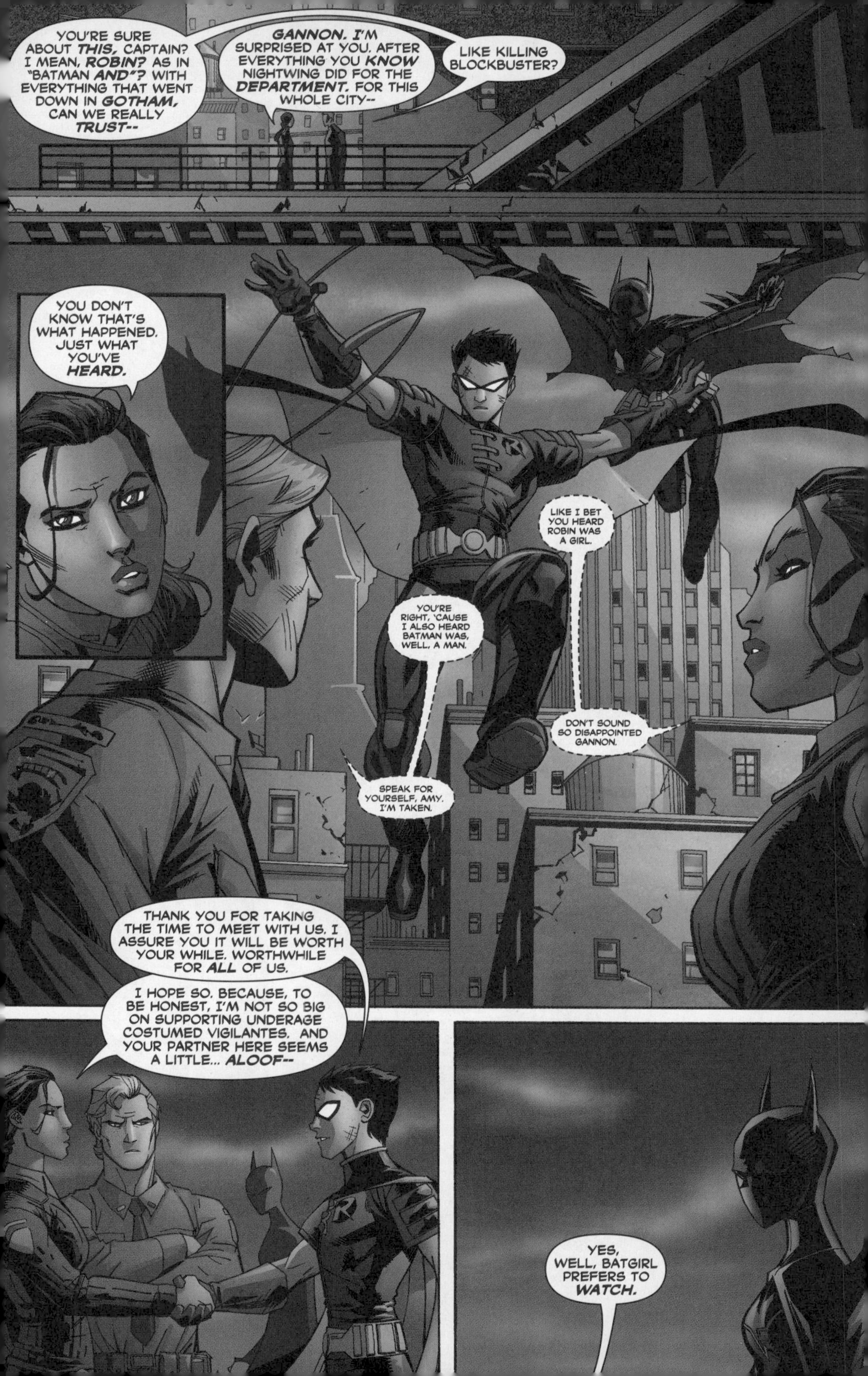
YOU'RE SURE ABOUT THIS, CAPTAIN? I MEAN, ROBIN? AS IN "BATMAN AND"? WITH EVERYTHING THAT WENT DOWN IN GOTHAM, CAN WE REALLY TRUST--
GANNON. I'M SURPRISED AT YOU. AFTER EVERYTHING YOU KNOW NIGHTWING DID FOR THE DEPARTMENT. FOR THIS WHOLE CITY--
LIKE KILLING BLOCKBUSTER?
YOU DON'T KNOW THAT'S WHAT HAPPENED. JUST WHAT YOU'VE HEARD.
LIKE I BET YOU HEARD ROBIN WAS A GIRL.
YOU'RE RIGHT, 'CAUSE I ALSO HEARD BATMAN WAS, WELL, A MAN.
DON'T SOUND SO DISAPPOINTED GANNON.
SPEAK FOR YOURSELF, AMY. I'M TAKEN.
THANK YOU FOR TAKING THE TIME TO MEET WITH US. I ASSURE YOU IT WILL BE WORTH YOUR WHILE. WORTHWHILE FOR ALL OF US.
I HOPE SO. BECAUSE, TO BE HONEST, I'M NOT SO BIG ON SUPPORTING UNDERAGE COSTUMED VIGILANTES. AND YOUR PARTNER HERE SEEMS A LITTLE... ALOOF--
YES, WELL, BATGIRL PREFERS TO WATCH.

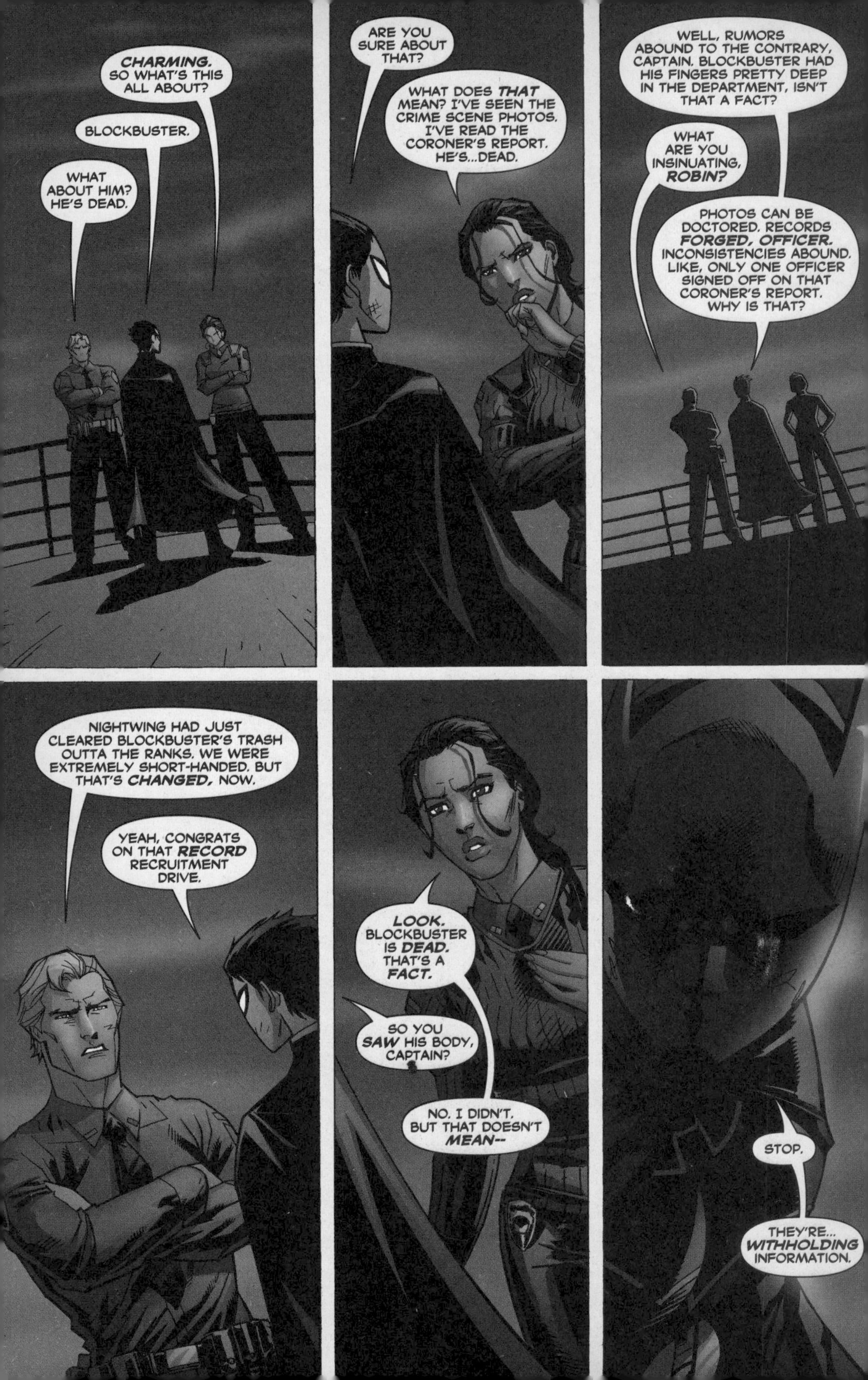
CHARMING. SO WHAT'S THIS ALL ABOUT?
BLOCKBUSTER.
WHAT ABOUT HIM? HE'S DEAD.
ARE YOU SURE ABOUT THAT?
WHAT DOES THAT MEAN? I'VE SEEN THE CRIME SCENE PHOTOS. I'VE READ THE CORONER'S REPORT. HE'S...DEAD.
WELL, RUMORS ABOUND TO THE CONTRARY, CAPTAIN. BLOCKBUSTER HAD HIS FINGERS PRETTY DEEP IN THE DEPARTMENT, ISN'T THAT A FACT?
WHAT ARE YOU INSINUATING, ROBIN?
PHOTOS CAN BE DOCTORED. RECORDS FORGED, OFFICER. INCONSISTENCIES ABOUND. LIKE, ONLY ONE OFFICER SIGNED OFF ON THAT CORONER'S REPORT. WHY IS THAT?
NIGHTWING HAD JUST CLEARED BLOCKBUSTER'S TRASH OUTTA THE RANKS. WE WERE EXTREMELY SHORT-HANDED. BUT THAT'S CHANGED, NOW.
YEAH, CONGRATS ON THAT RECORD RECRUITMENT DRIVE.
LOOK. BLOCKBUSTER IS DEAD. THAT'S A FACT.
SO YOU SAW HIS BODY, CAPTAIN?
NO. I DIDN'T. BUT THAT DOESN'T MEAN--
STOP.
THEY'RE... WITHHOLDING INFORMATION.

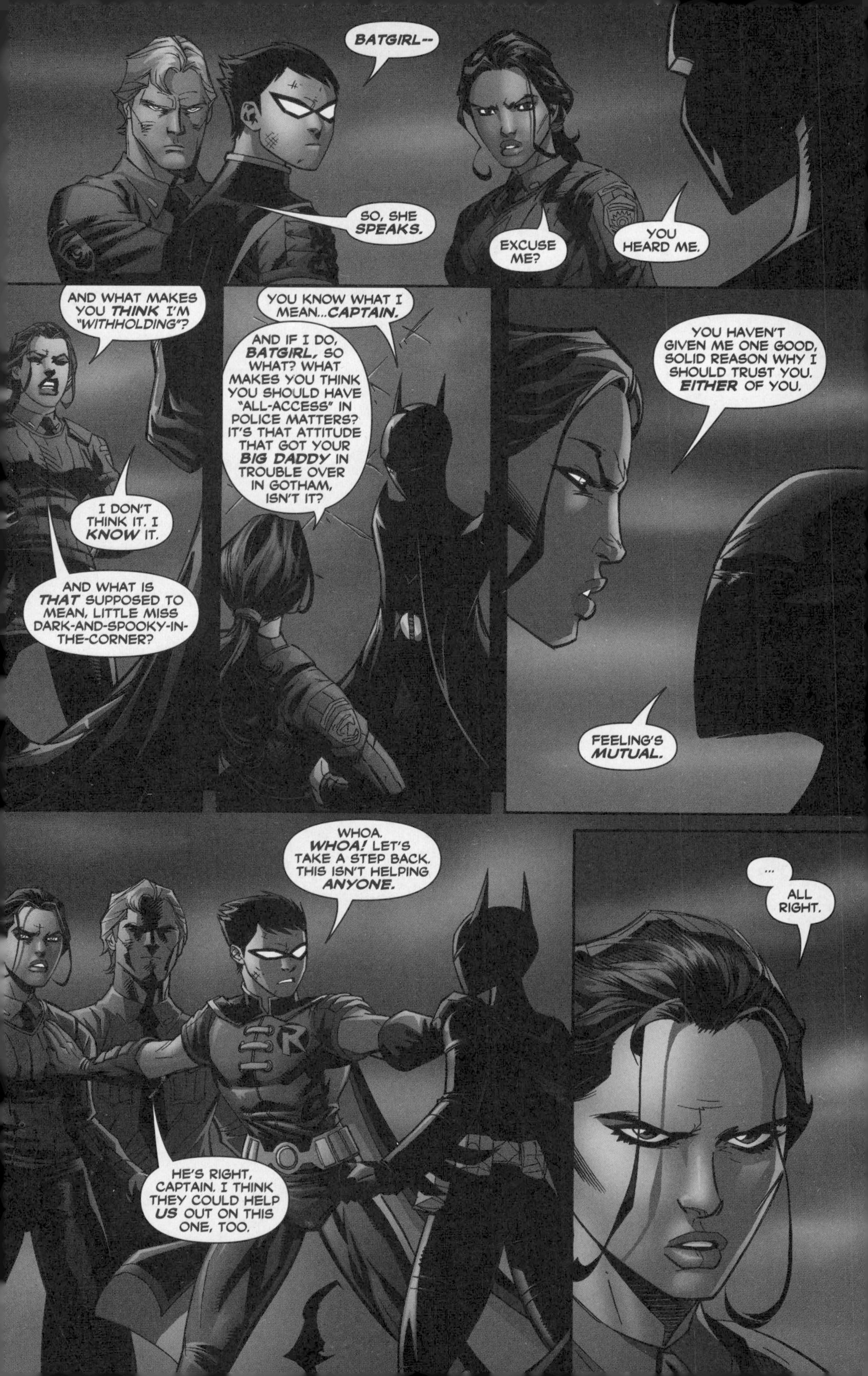
BATGIRL--
SO, SHE SPEAKS.
EXCUSE ME?
YOU HEARD ME.
AND WHAT MAKES YOU THINK I'M "WITHHOLDING"?
I DON'T THINK IT. I KNOW IT.
AND WHAT IS THAT SUPPOSED TO MEAN, LITTLE MISS DARK-AND-SPOOKY-IN-THE-CORNER?
YOU KNOW WHAT I MEAN...CAPTAIN.
AND IF I DO, BATGIRL, SO WHAT? WHAT MAKES YOU THINK YOU SHOULD HAVE "ALL-ACCESS" IN POLICE MATTERS? IT'S THAT ATTITUDE THAT GOT YOUR BIG DADDY IN TROUBLE OVER IN GOTHAM, ISN'T IT?
YOU HAVEN'T GIVEN ME ONE GOOD, SOLID REASON WHY I SHOULD TRUST YOU. EITHER OF YOU.
FEELING'S MUTUAL.
WHOA. WHOA! LET'S TAKE A STEP BACK. THIS ISN'T HELPING ANYONE.
HE'S RIGHT, CAPTAIN. I THINK THEY COULD HELP US OUT ON THIS ONE, TOO.
...
ALL RIGHT.

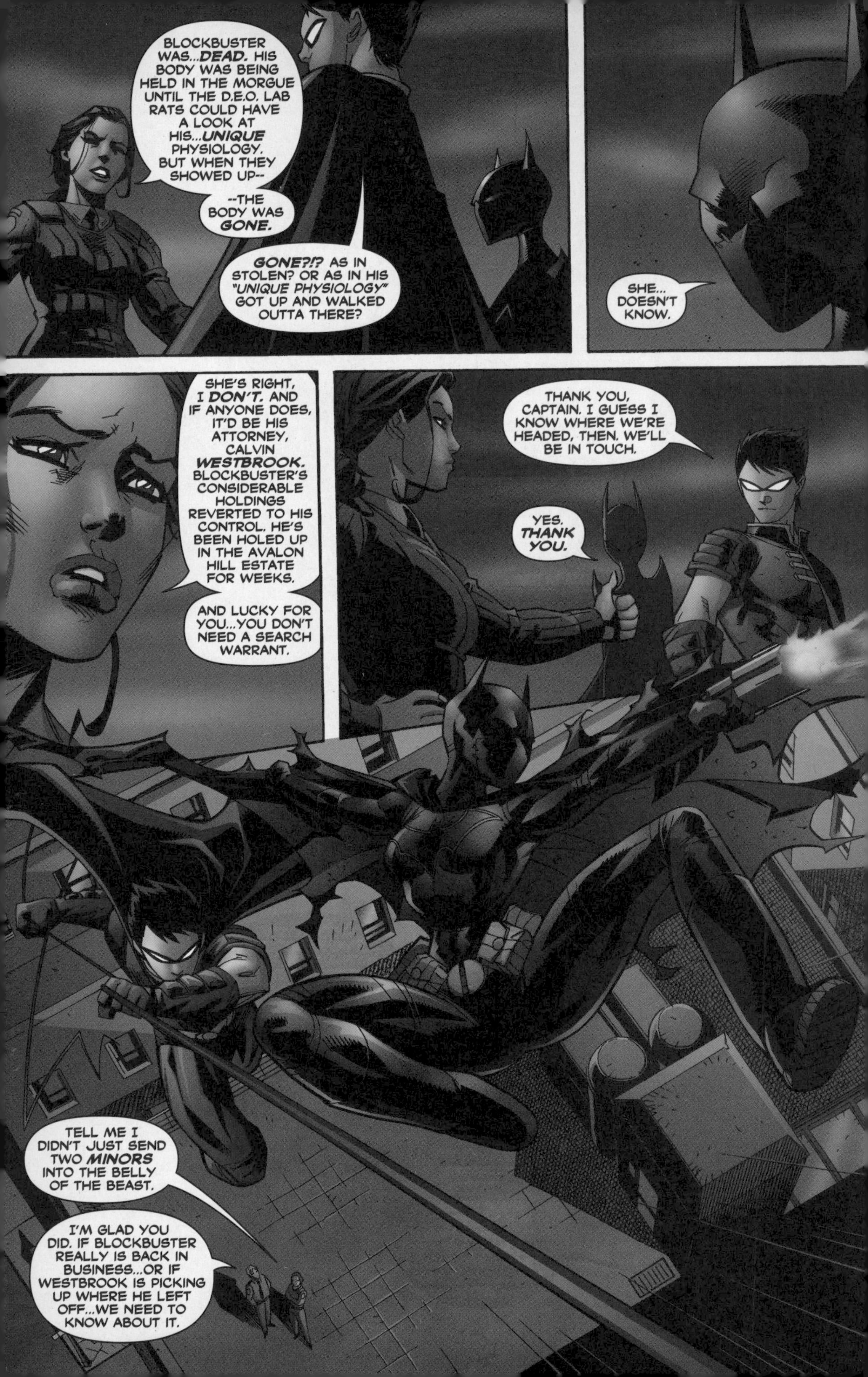
BLOCKBUSTER WAS...DEAD. HIS BODY WAS BEING HELD IN THE MORGUE UNTIL THE D.E.O. LAB RATS COULD HAVE A LOOK AT HIS...UNIQUE PHYSIOLOGY. BUT WHEN THEY SHOWED UP--
--THE BODY WAS GONE.
GONE?!? AS IN STOLEN? OR AS IN HIS "UNIQUE PHYSIOLOGY" GOT UP AND WALKED OUTTA THERE?
SHE... DOESN'T KNOW.
SHE'S RIGHT, I DON'T. AND IF ANYONE DOES, IT'D BE HIS ATTORNEY, CALVIN WESTBROOK. BLOCKBUSTER'S CONSIDERABLE HOLDINGS REVERTED TO HIS CONTROL. HE'S BEEN HOLED UP IN THE AVALON HILL ESTATE FOR WEEKS.
AND LUCKY FOR YOU...YOU DON'T NEED A SEARCH WARRANT.
THANK YOU, CAPTAIN. I GUESS I KNOW WHERE WE'RE HEADED, THEN. WE'LL BE IN TOUCH.
YES. THANK YOU.
TELL ME I DIDN'T JUST SEND TWO MINORS INTO THE BELLY OF THE BEAST.
I'M GLAD YOU DID. IF BLOCKBUSTER REALLY IS BACK IN BUSINESS...OR IF WESTBROOK IS PICKING UP WHERE HE LEFT OFF...WE NEED TO KNOW ABOUT IT.

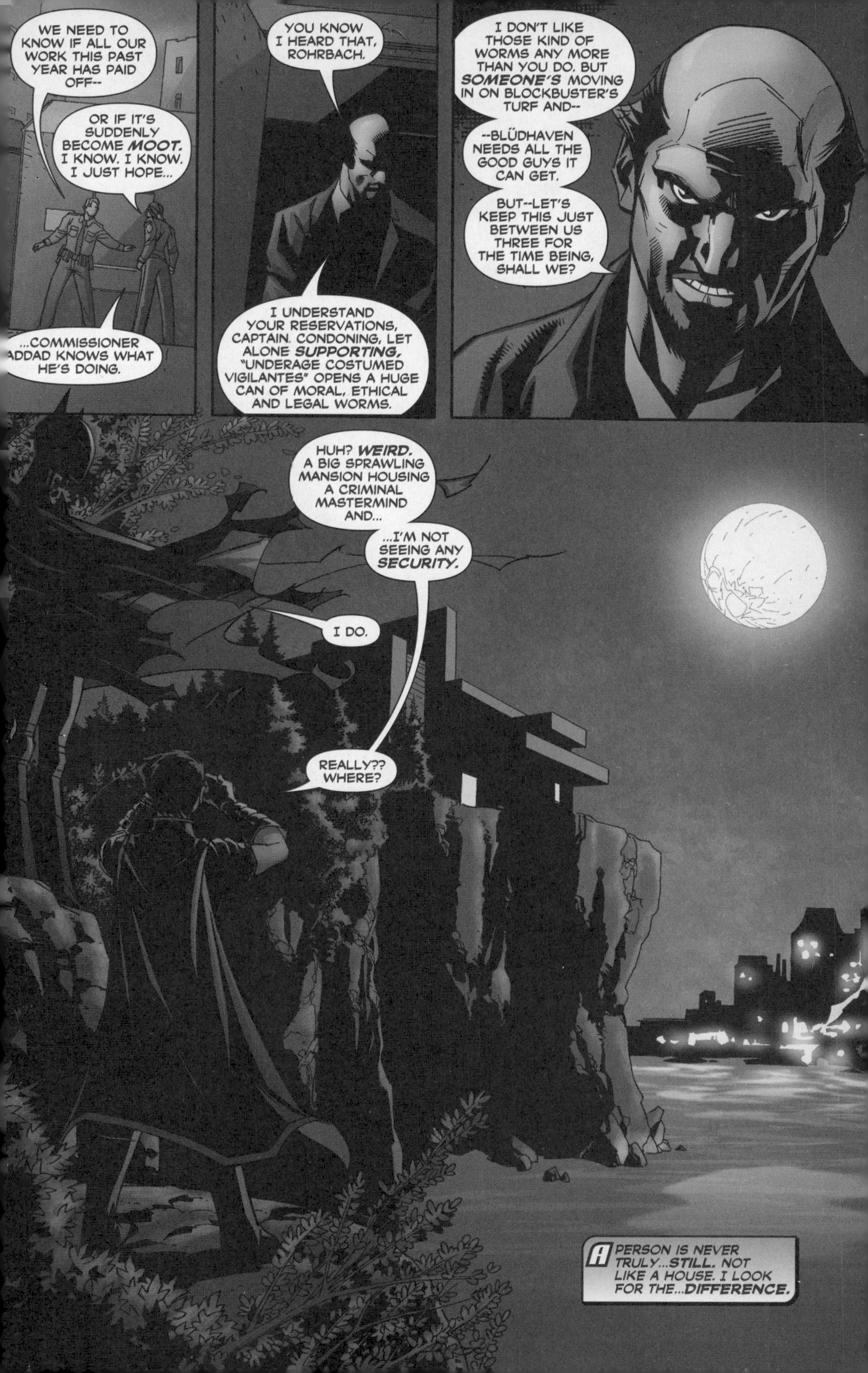
WE NEED TO KNOW IF ALL OUR WORK THIS PAST YEAR HAS PAID OFF--
OR IF IT'S SUDDENLY BECOME MOOT. I KNOW. I KNOW. I JUST HOPE...
...COMMISSIONER ADDAD KNOWS WHAT HE'S DOING.
YOU KNOW I HEARD THAT, ROHRBACH.
I UNDERSTAND YOUR RESERVATIONS, CAPTAIN. CONDONING, LET ALONE SUPPORTING, "UNDERAGE COSTUMED VIGILANTES" OPENS A HUGE CAN OF MORAL, ETHICAL AND LEGAL WORMS.
I DON'T LIKE THOSE KIND OF WORMS ANY MORE THAN YOU DO. BUT SOMEONE'S MOVING IN ON BLOCKBUSTER'S TURF AND--
--BLÜDHAVEN NEEDS ALL THE GOOD GUYS IT CAN GET.
BUT--LET'S KEEP THIS JUST BETWEEN US THREE FOR THE TIME BEING, SHALL WE?
HUH? WEIRD. A BIG SPRAWLING MANSION HOUSING A CRIMINAL MASTERMIND AND...
...I'M NOT SEEING ANY SECURITY.
I DO.
REALLY?? WHERE?
A PERSON IS NEVER TRULY...STILL. NOT LIKE A HOUSE. I LOOK FOR THE...DIFFERENCE.

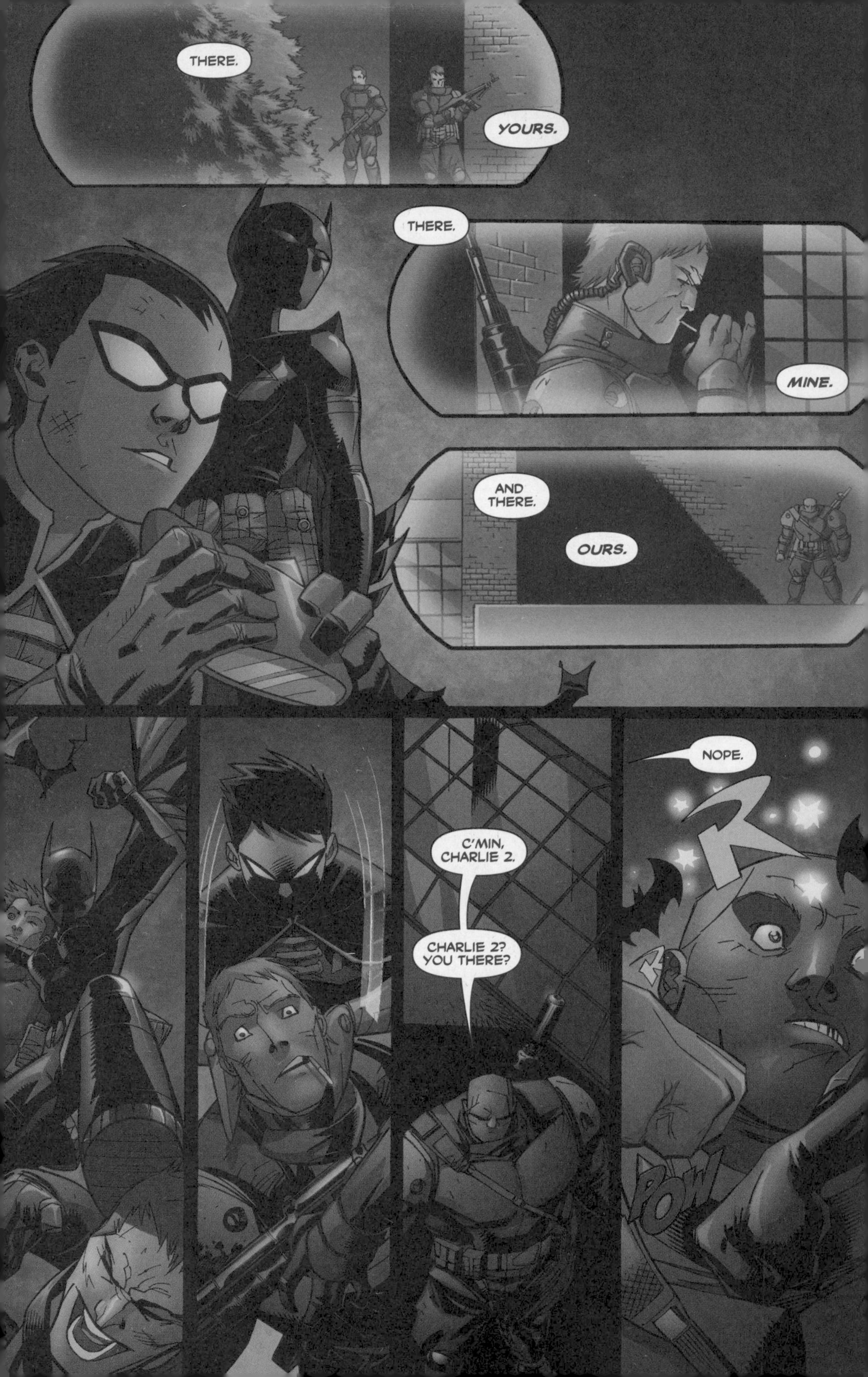
THERE.
YOURS.
THERE.
MINE.
AND THERE.
OURS.
C'MIN, CHARLIE 2.
CHARLIE 2? YOU THERE?
NOPE.
POW

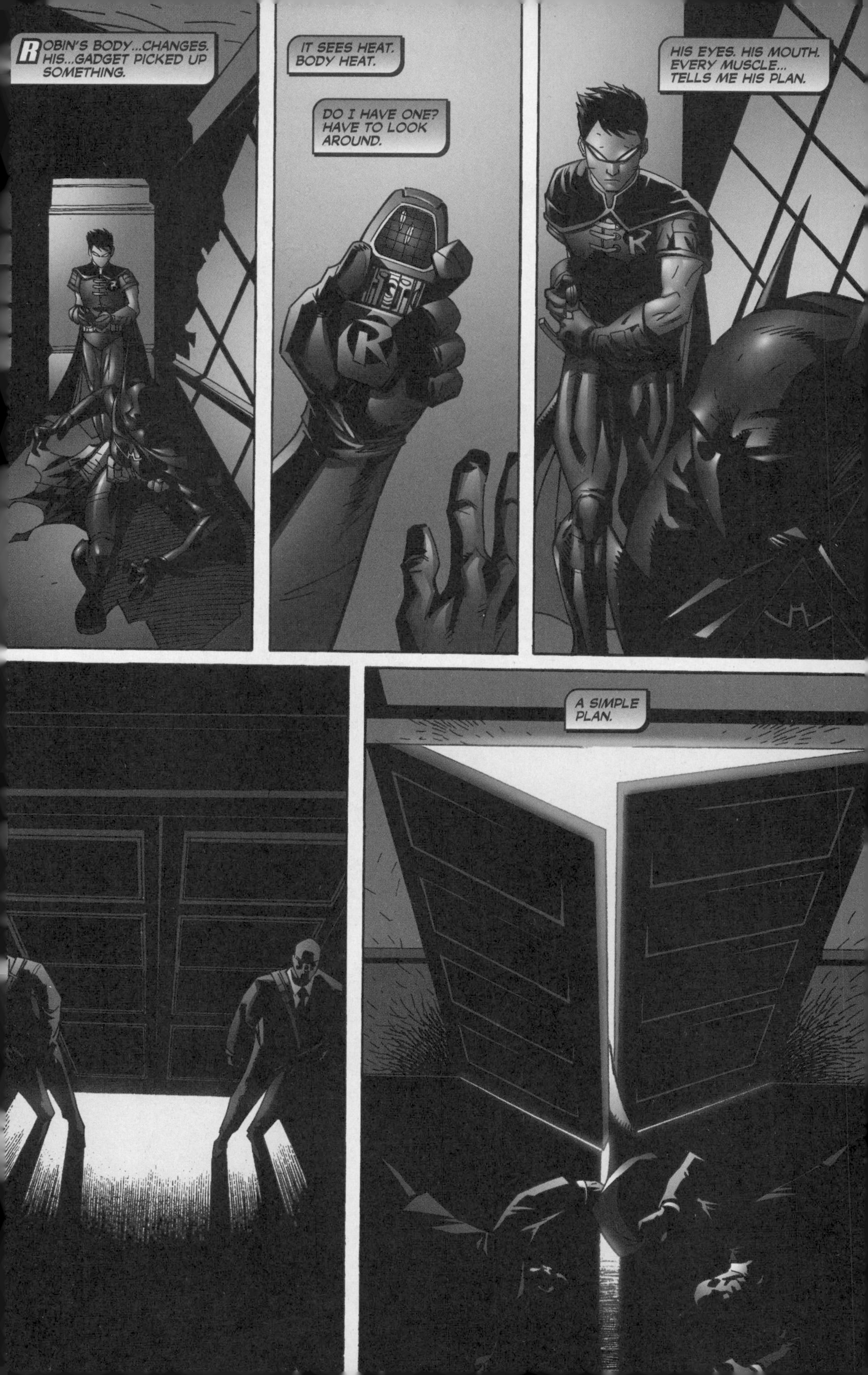
ROBIN'S BODY...CHANGES. HIS...GADGET PICKED UP SOMETHING.
IT SEES HEAT. BODY HEAT.
DO I HAVE ONE? HAVE TO LOOK AROUND.
HIS EYES. HIS MOUTH. EVERY MUSCLE... TELLS ME HIS PLAN.
A SIMPLE PLAN.

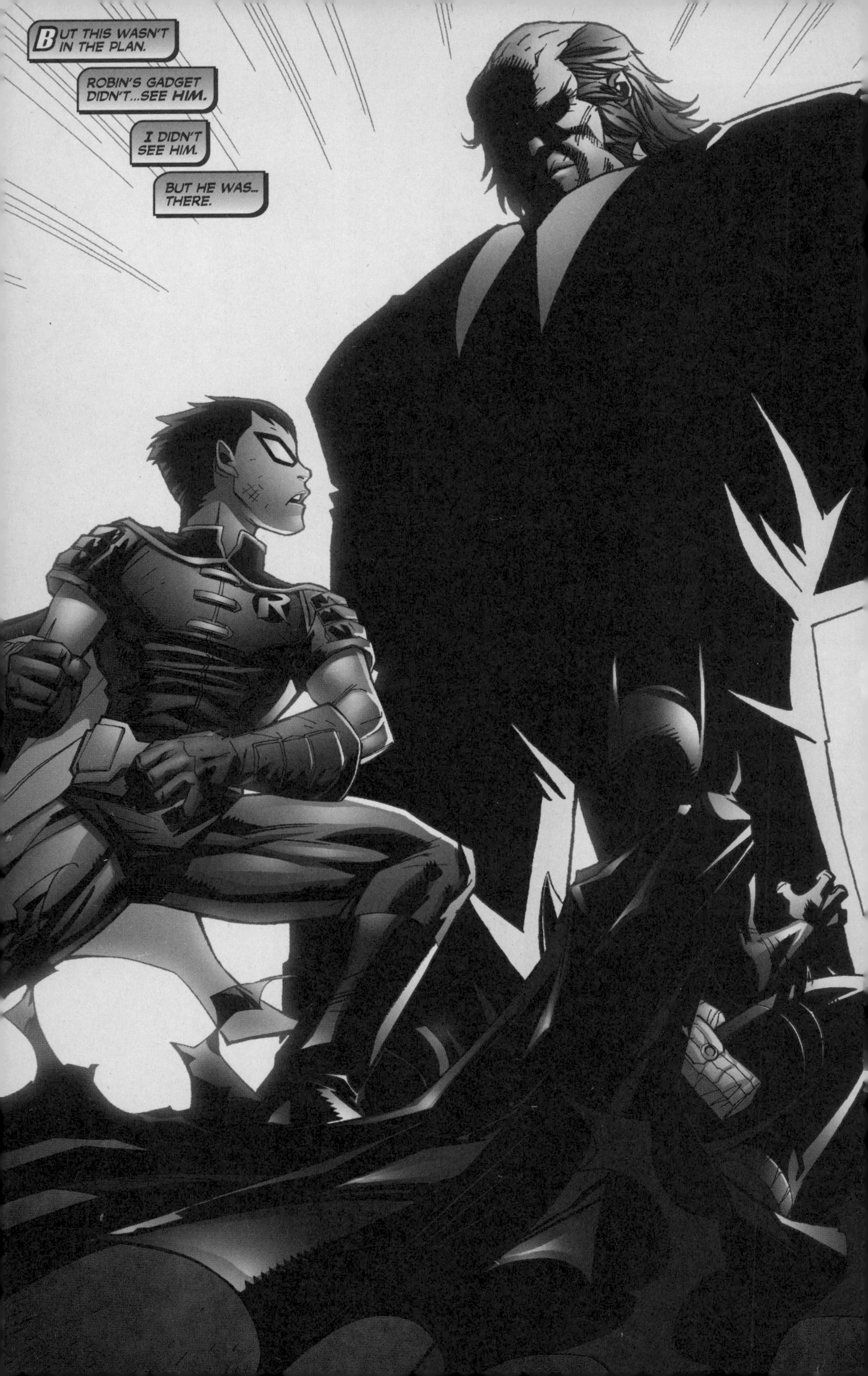
BUT THIS WASN'T IN THE PLAN.
ROBIN'S GADGET DIDN'T...SEE HIM.
I DIDN'T SEE HIM.
BUT HE WAS... THERE.

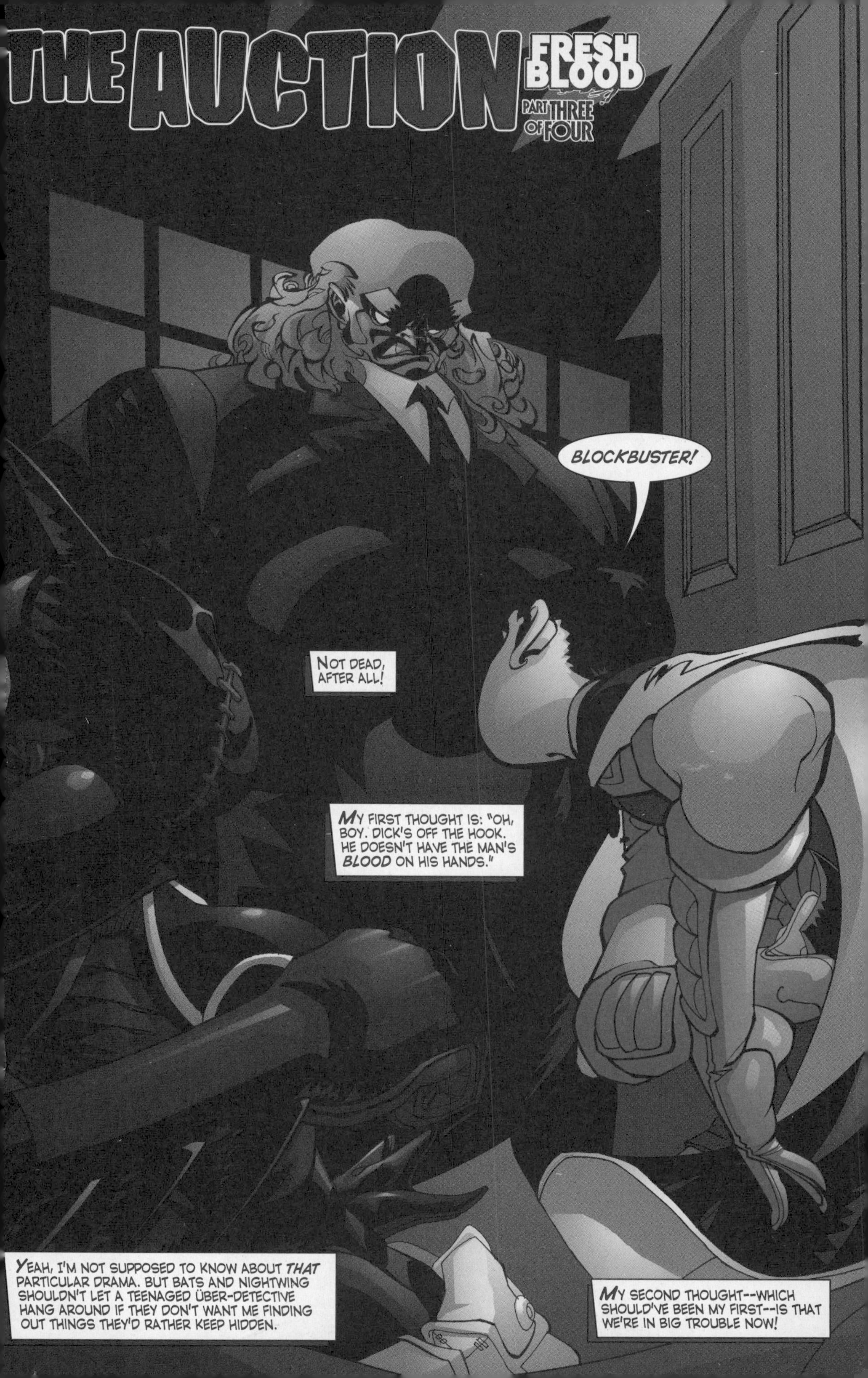
THE AUCTION
FRESH BLOOD
PART THREE OF FOUR
BLOCKBUSTER!
NOT DEAD, AFTER ALL!
MY FIRST THOUGHT IS: "OH, BOY. DICK'S OFF THE HOOK. HE DOESN'T HAVE THE MAN'S BLOOD ON HIS HANDS."
YEAH, I'M NOT SUPPOSED TO KNOW ABOUT THAT PARTICULAR DRAMA. BUT BATS AND NIGHTWING SHOULDN'T LET A TEENAGED ÜBER-DETECTIVE HANG AROUND IF THEY DON'T WANT ME FINDING OUT THINGS THEY'D RATHER KEEP HIDDEN.
MY SECOND THOUGHT--WHICH SHOULD'VE BEEN MY FIRST--IS THAT WE'RE IN BIG TROUBLE NOW!

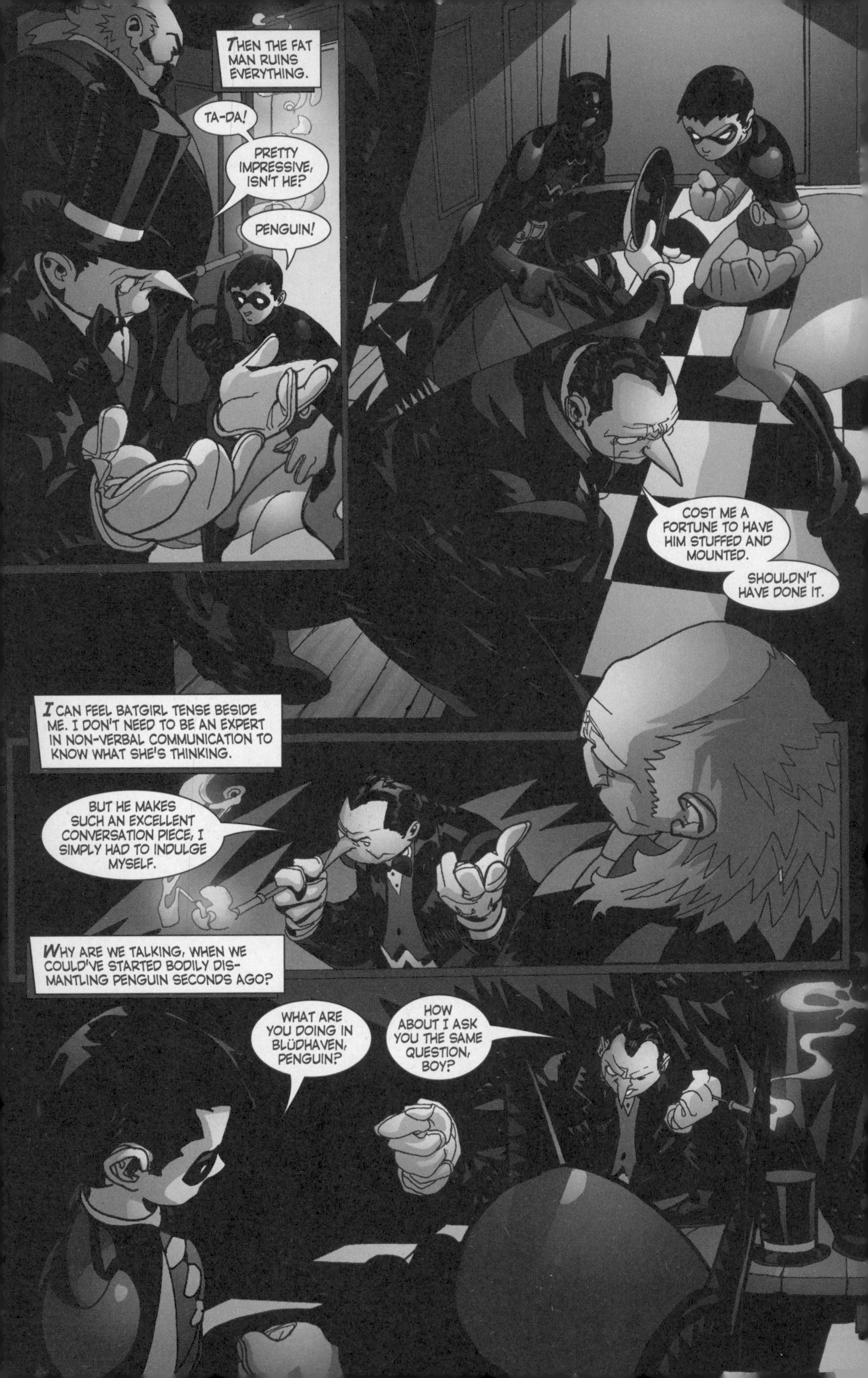
THEN THE FAT MAN RUINS EVERYTHING.
TA-DA!
PRETTY IMPRESSIVE, ISN'T HE?
PENGUIN!
COST ME A FORTUNE TO HAVE HIM STUFFED AND MOUNTED.
SHOULDN'T HAVE DONE IT.
I CAN FEEL BATGIRL TENSE BESIDE ME. I DON'T NEED TO BE AN EXPERT IN NON-VERBAL COMMUNICATION TO KNOW WHAT SHE'S THINKING.
BUT HE MAKES SUCH AN EXCELLENT CONVERSATION PIECE, I SIMPLY HAD TO INDULGE MYSELF.
WHY ARE WE TALKING, WHEN WE COULD'VE STARTED BODILY DIS-MANTLING PENGUIN SECONDS AGO?
WHAT ARE YOU DOING IN BLÜDHAVEN, PENGUIN?
HOW ABOUT I ASK YOU THE SAME QUESTION, BOY?

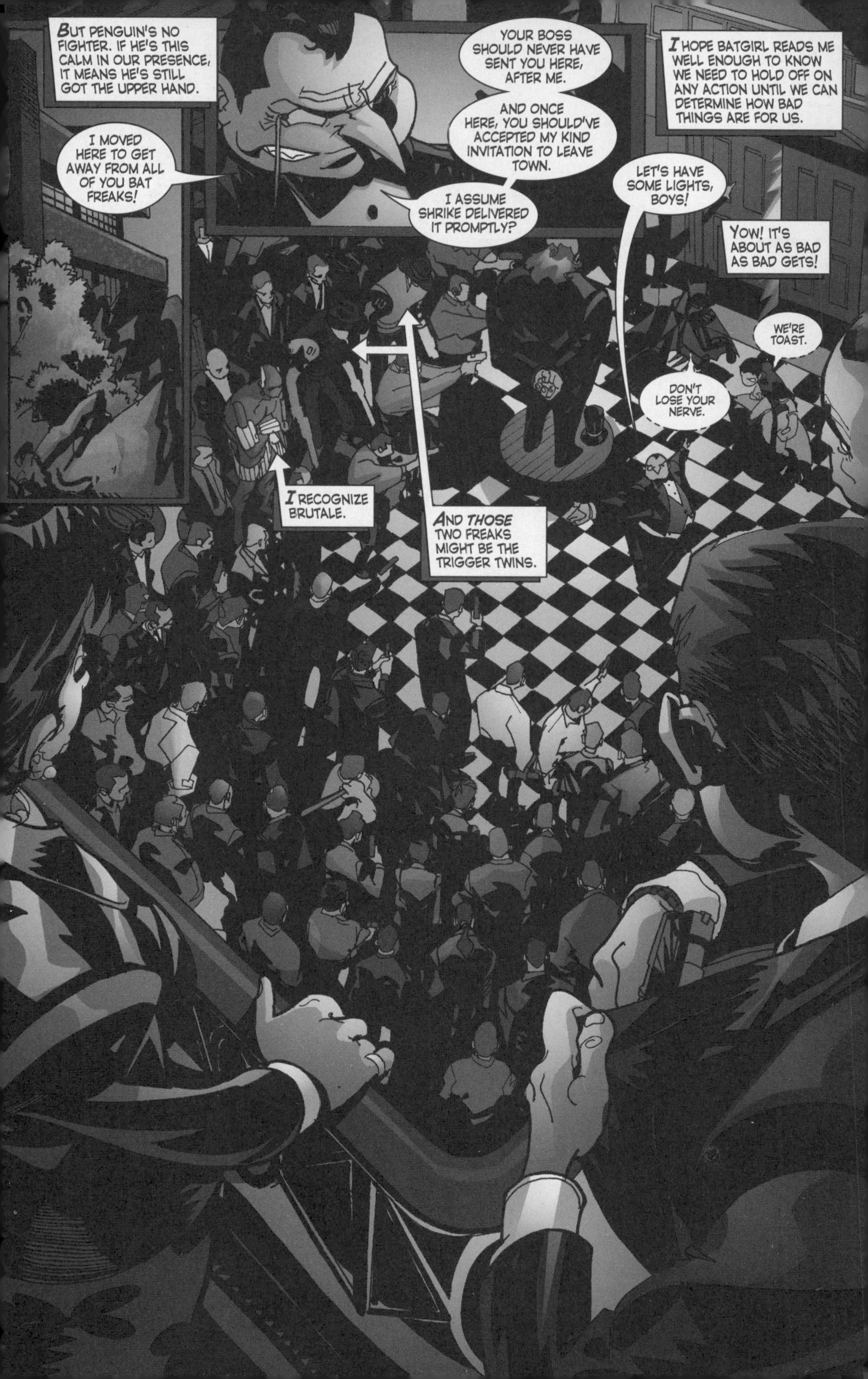
BUT PENGUIN'S NO FIGHTER. IF HE'S THIS CALM IN OUR PRESENCE, IT MEANS HE'S STILL GOT THE UPPER HAND.
I MOVED HERE TO GET AWAY FROM ALL OF YOU BAT FREAKS!
YOUR BOSS SHOULD NEVER HAVE SENT YOU HERE, AFTER ME.
AND ONCE HERE, YOU SHOULD'VE ACCEPTED MY KIND INVITATION TO LEAVE TOWN.
I ASSUME SHRIKE DELIVERED IT PROMPTLY?
I HOPE BATGIRL READS ME WELL ENOUGH TO KNOW WE NEED TO HOLD OFF ON ANY ACTION UNTIL WE CAN DETERMINE HOW BAD THINGS ARE FOR US.
LET'S HAVE SOME LIGHTS, BOYS!
YOW! IT'S ABOUT AS BAD AS BAD GETS!
WE'RE TOAST.
DON'T LOSE YOUR NERVE.
I RECOGNIZE BRUTALE.
AND THOSE TWO FREAKS MIGHT BE THE TRIGGER TWINS.

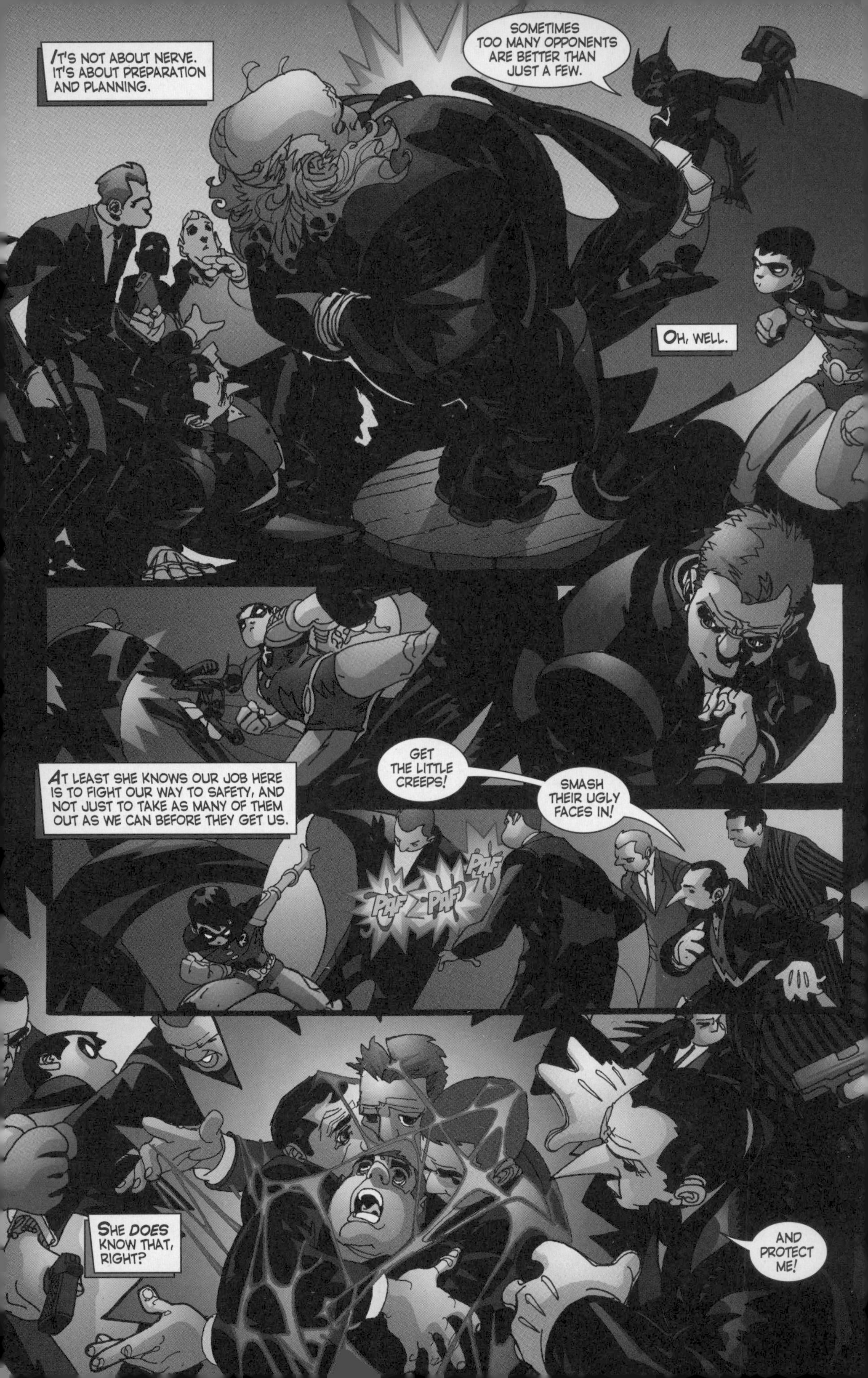

IT'S NOT ABOUT NERVE. IT'S ABOUT PREPARATION AND PLANNING.
SOMETIMES TOO MANY OPPONENTS ARE BETTER THAN JUST A FEW.
OH, WELL.
AT LEAST SHE KNOWS OUR JOB HERE IS TO FIGHT OUR WAY TO SAFETY, AND NOT JUST TO TAKE AS MANY OF THEM OUT AS WE CAN BEFORE THEY GET US.
GET THE LITTLE CREEPS!
SMASH THEIR UGLY FACES IN!
PAF
PAF
PAF
SHE DOES KNOW THAT, RIGHT?
AND PROTECT ME!

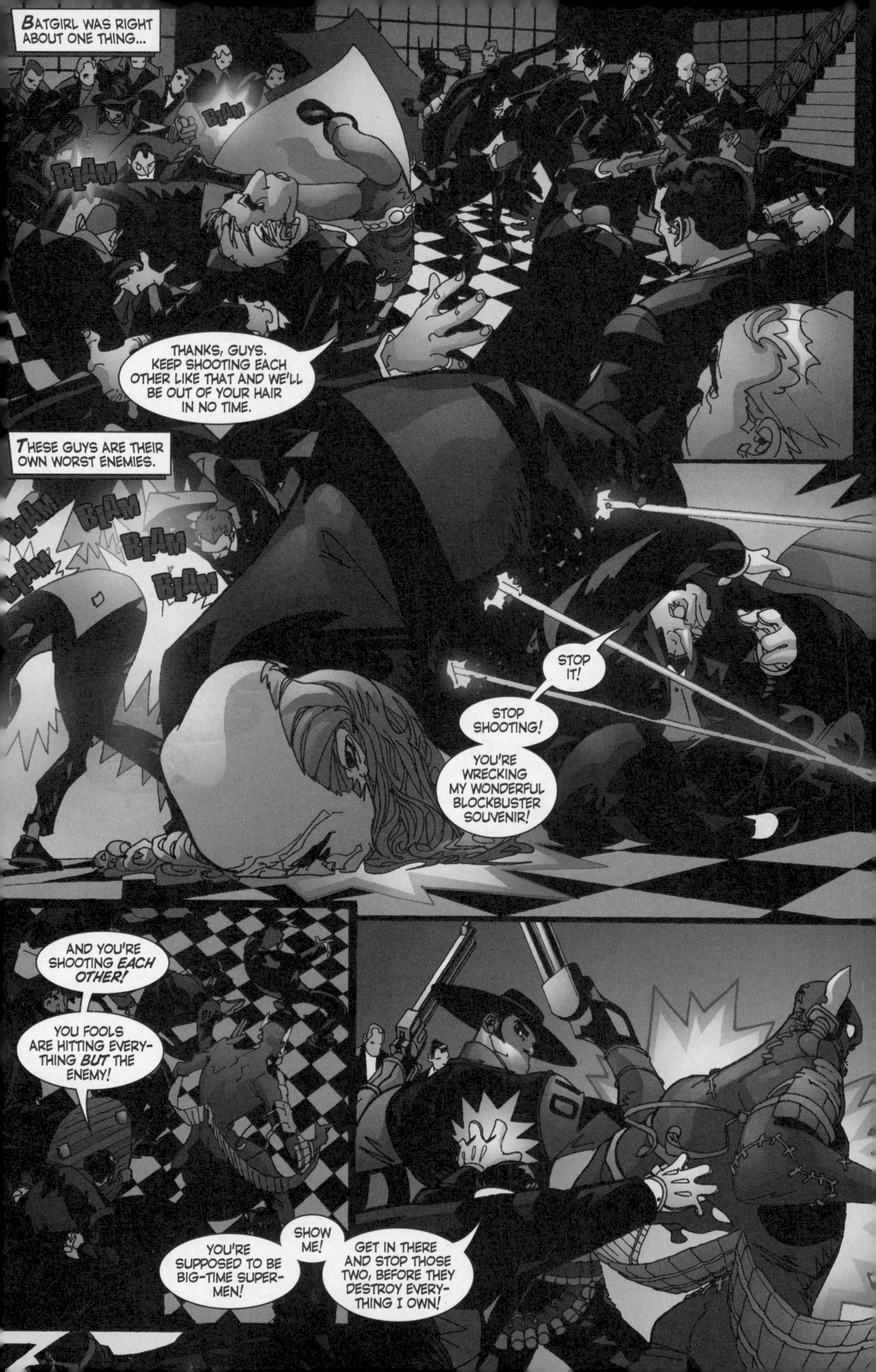
BATGIRL WAS RIGHT ABOUT ONE THING...
BLAM
BLAM
THANKS, GUYS. KEEP SHOOTING EACH OTHER LIKE THAT AND WE'LL BE OUT OF YOUR HAIR IN NO TIME.
THESE GUYS ARE THEIR OWN WORST ENEMIES.
BLAM
BLAM
BLAM
BLAM
BLAM
STOP IT!
STOP SHOOTING!
YOU'RE WRECKING MY WONDERFUL BLOCKBUSTER SOUVENIR!
AND YOU'RE SHOOTING *EACH OTHER!*
YOU FOOLS ARE HITTING EVERY-THING *BUT* THE ENEMY!
YOU'RE SUPPOSED TO BE BIG-TIME SUPER-MEN!
SHOW ME!
GET IN THERE AND STOP THOSE TWO, BEFORE THEY DESTROY EVERY-THING I OWN!

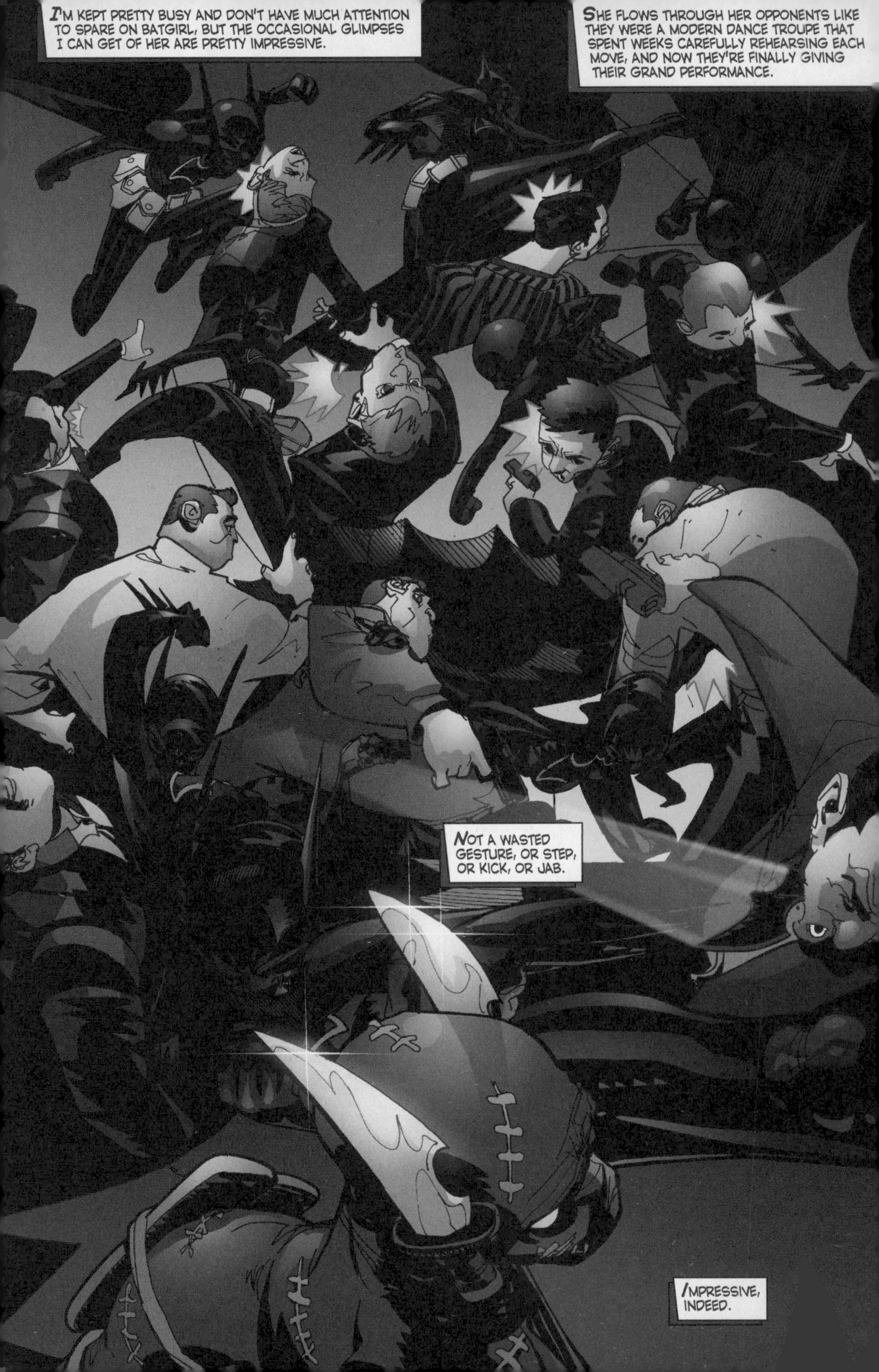
I'M KEPT PRETTY BUSY AND DON'T HAVE MUCH ATTENTION TO SPARE ON BATGIRL, BUT THE OCCASIONAL GLIMPSES I CAN GET OF HER ARE PRETTY IMPRESSIVE.
SHE FLOWS THROUGH HER OPPONENTS LIKE THEY WERE A MODERN DANCE TROUPE THAT SPENT WEEKS CAREFULLY REHEARSING EACH MOVE, AND NOW THEY'RE FINALLY GIVING THEIR GRAND PERFORMANCE.
NOT A WASTED GESTURE, OR STEP, OR KICK, OR JAB.
IMPRESSIVE, INDEED.

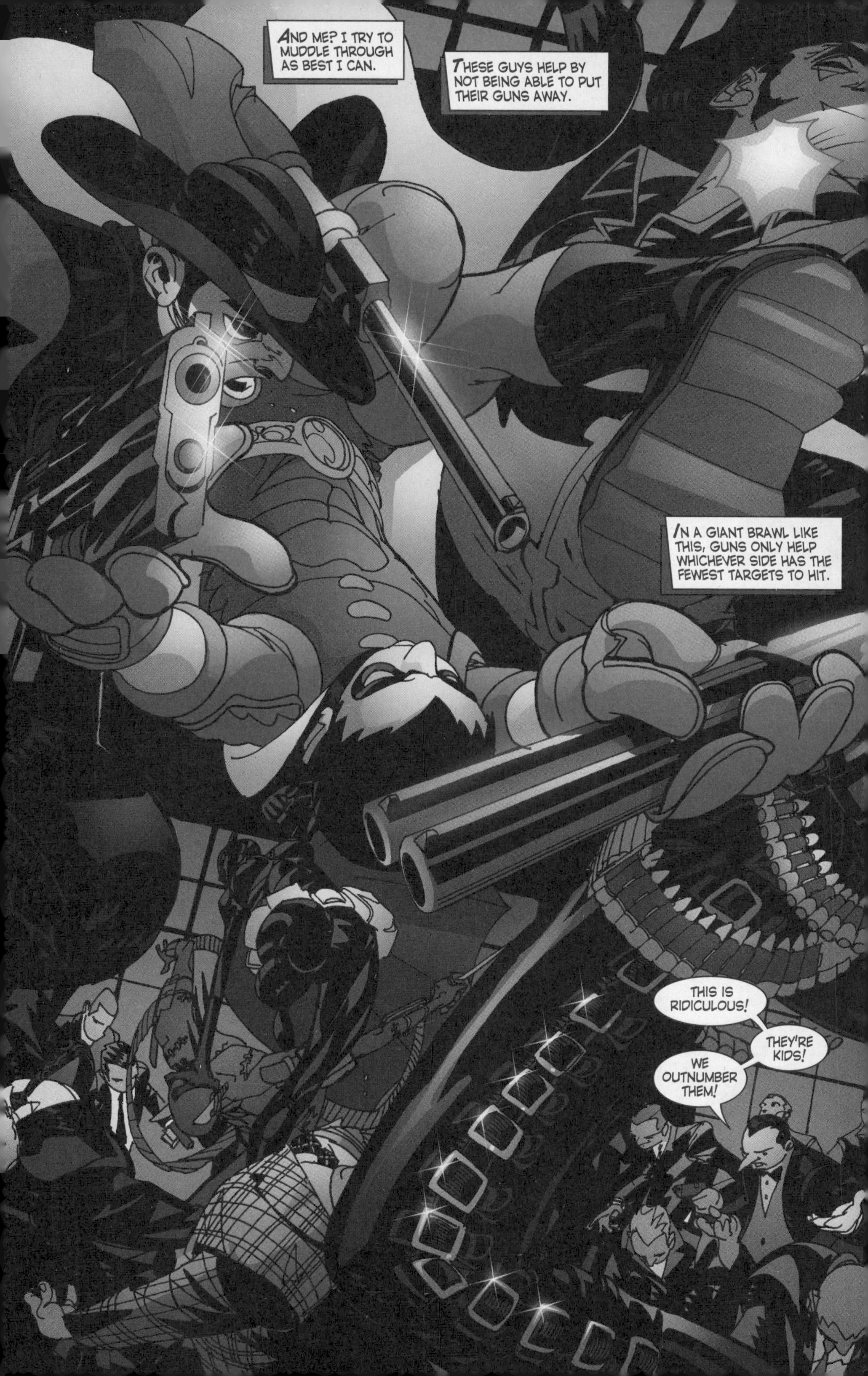
AND ME? I TRY TO MUDDLE THROUGH AS BEST I CAN.
THESE GUYS HELP BY NOT BEING ABLE TO PUT THEIR GUNS AWAY.
IN A GIANT BRAWL LIKE THIS, GUNS ONLY HELP WHICHEVER SIDE HAS THE FEWEST TARGETS TO HIT.
THIS IS RIDICULOUS!
THEY'RE KIDS!
WE OUTNUMBER THEM!

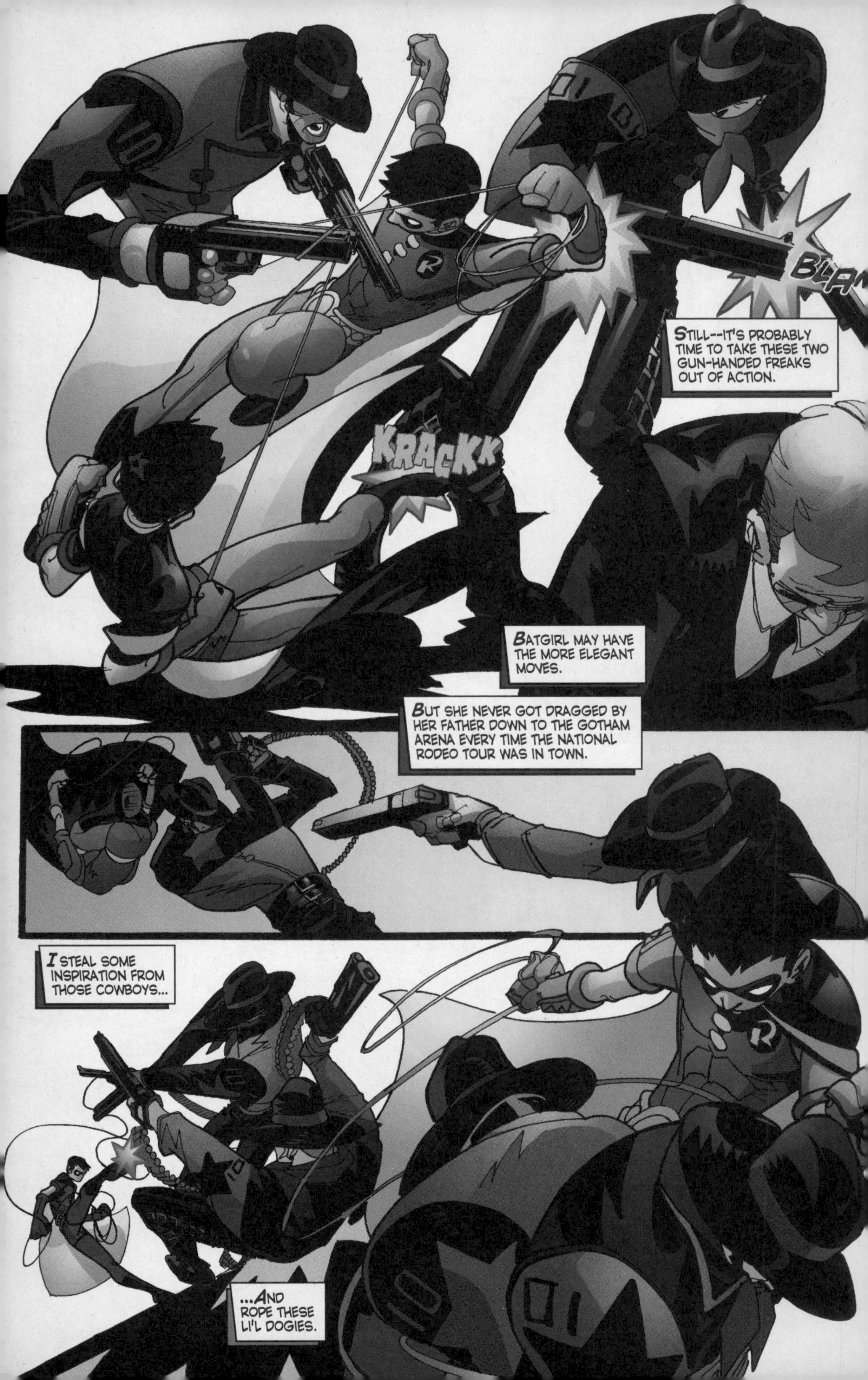
BLAM
STILL--IT'S PROBABLY TIME TO TAKE THESE TWO GUN-HANDED FREAKS OUT OF ACTION.
KRACKK
BATGIRL MAY HAVE THE MORE ELEGANT MOVES.
BUT SHE NEVER GOT DRAGGED BY HER FATHER DOWN TO THE GOTHAM ARENA EVERY TIME THE NATIONAL RODEO TOUR WAS IN TOWN.
I STEAL SOME INSPIRATION FROM THOSE COWBOYS...
...AND ROPE THESE LI'L DOGIES.

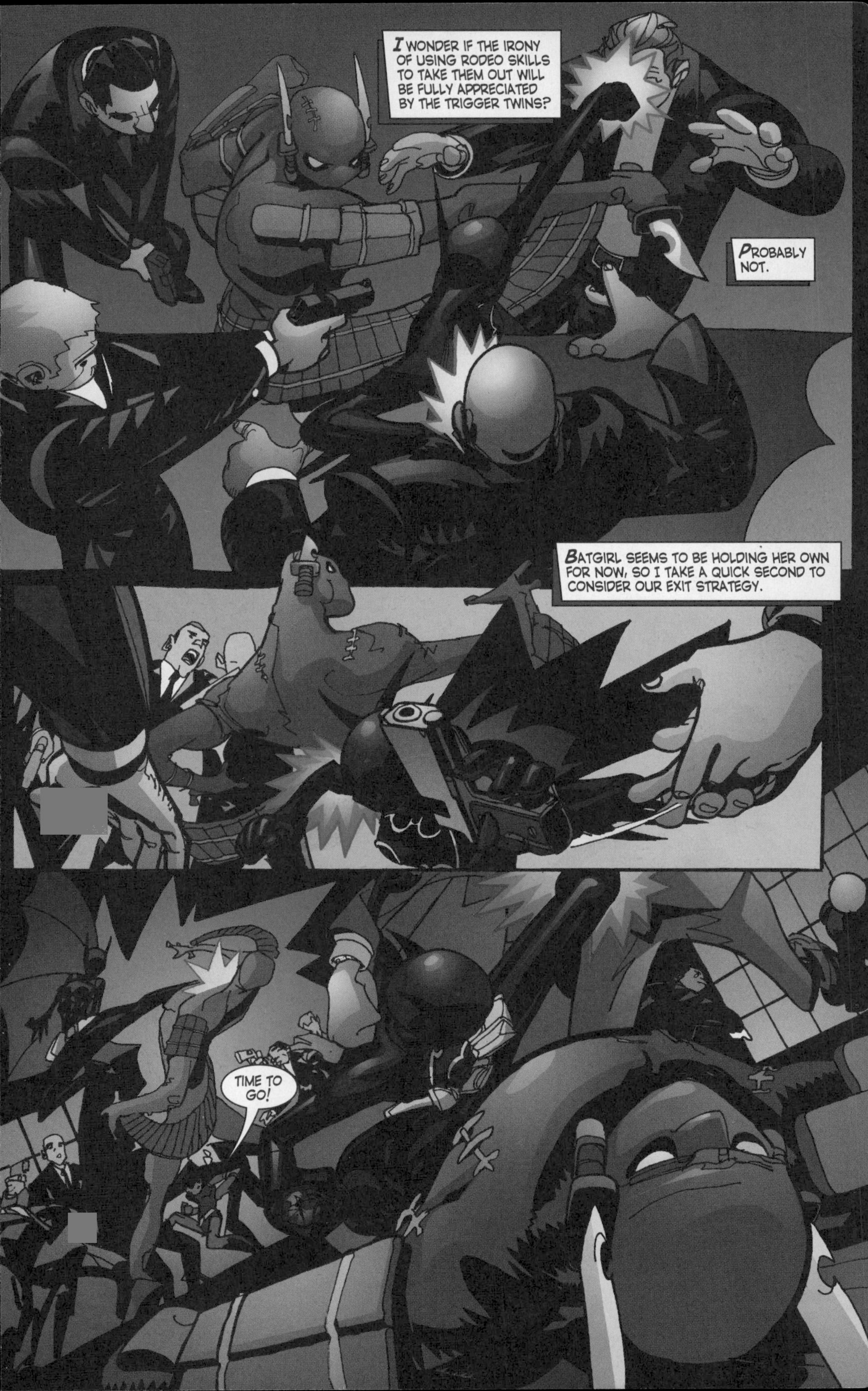
I WONDER IF THE IRONY OF USING RODEO SKILLS TO TAKE THEM OUT WILL BE FULLY APPRECIATED BY THE TRIGGER TWINS?
PROBABLY NOT.
BATGIRL SEEMS TO BE HOLDING HER OWN FOR NOW, SO I TAKE A QUICK SECOND TO CONSIDER OUR EXIT STRATEGY.
TIME TO GO!

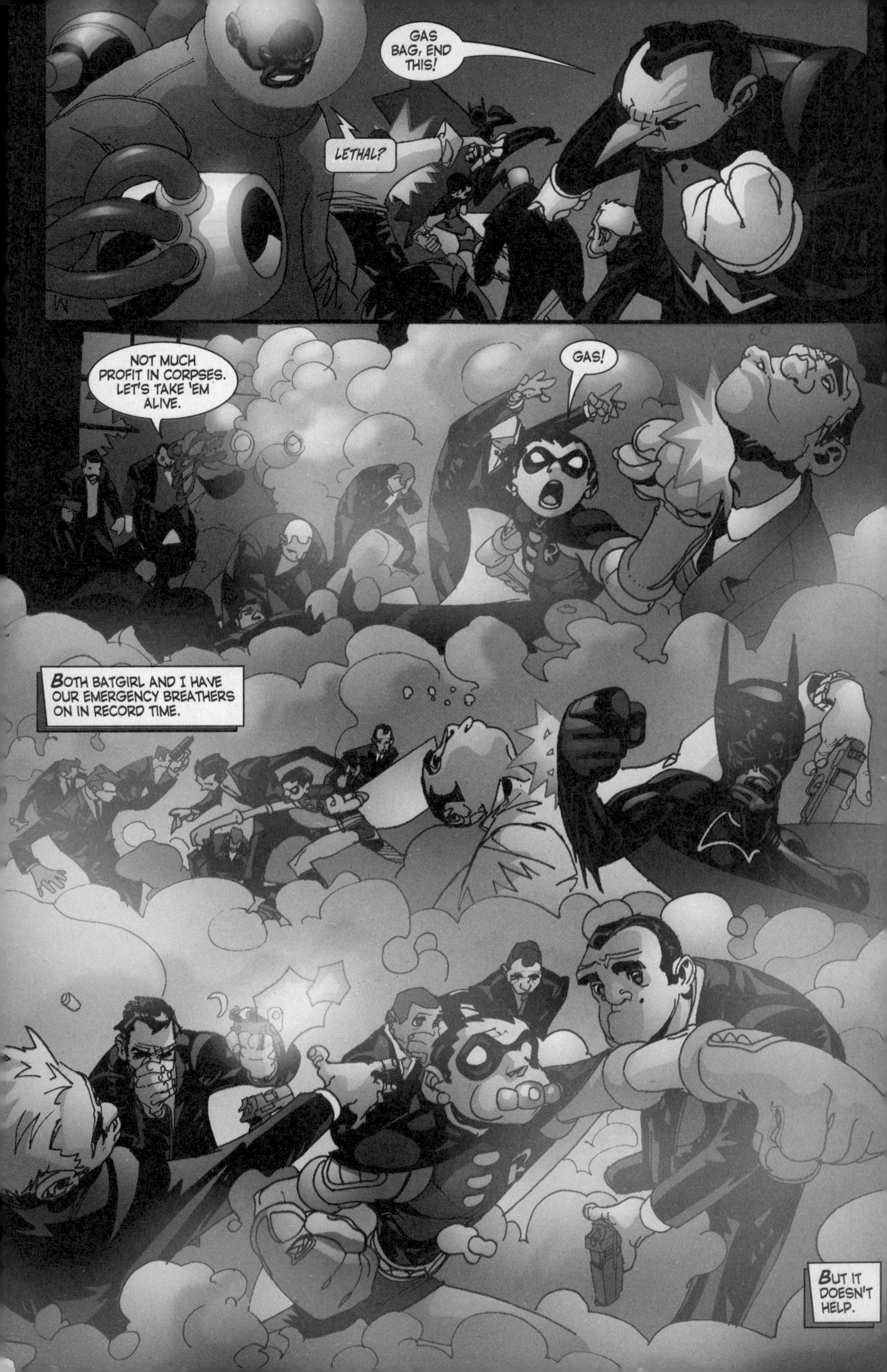
GAS BAG, END THIS!
LETHAL?
NOT MUCH PROFIT IN CORPSES. LET'S TAKE 'EM ALIVE.
GAS!
BOTH BATGIRL AND I HAVE OUR EMERGENCY BREATHERS ON IN RECORD TIME.
BUT IT DOESN'T HELP.

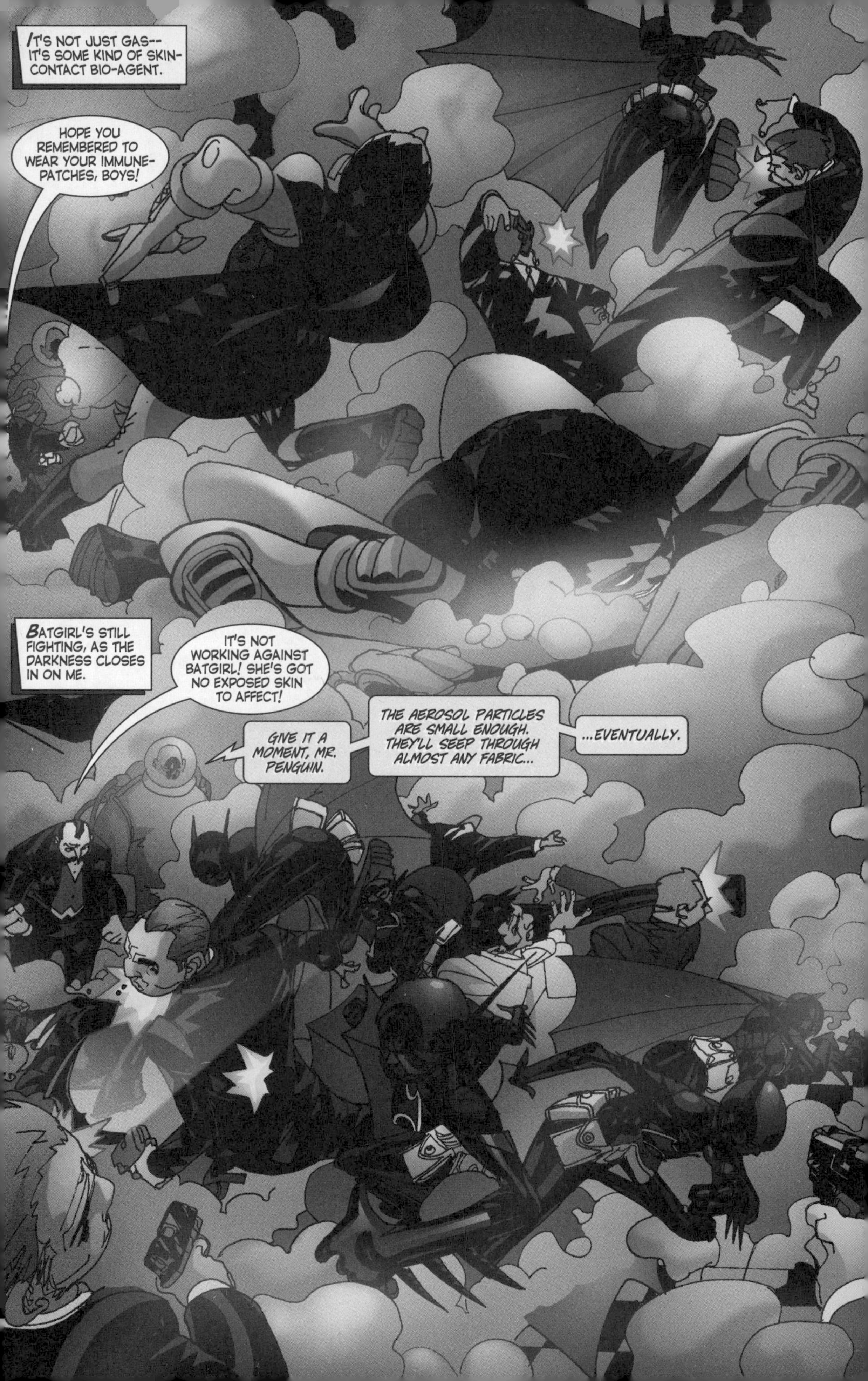

IT'S NOT JUST GAS-- IT'S SOME KIND OF SKIN-CONTACT BIO-AGENT.
HOPE YOU REMEMBERED TO WEAR YOUR IMMUNE-PATCHES, BOYS!
BATGIRL'S STILL FIGHTING, AS THE DARKNESS CLOSES IN ON ME.
IT'S NOT WORKING AGAINST BATGIRL! SHE'S GOT NO EXPOSED SKIN TO AFFECT!
GIVE IT A MOMENT, MR. PENGUIN.
THE AEROSOL PARTICLES ARE SMALL ENOUGH. THEY'LL SEEP THROUGH ALMOST ANY FABRIC...
...EVENTUALLY.

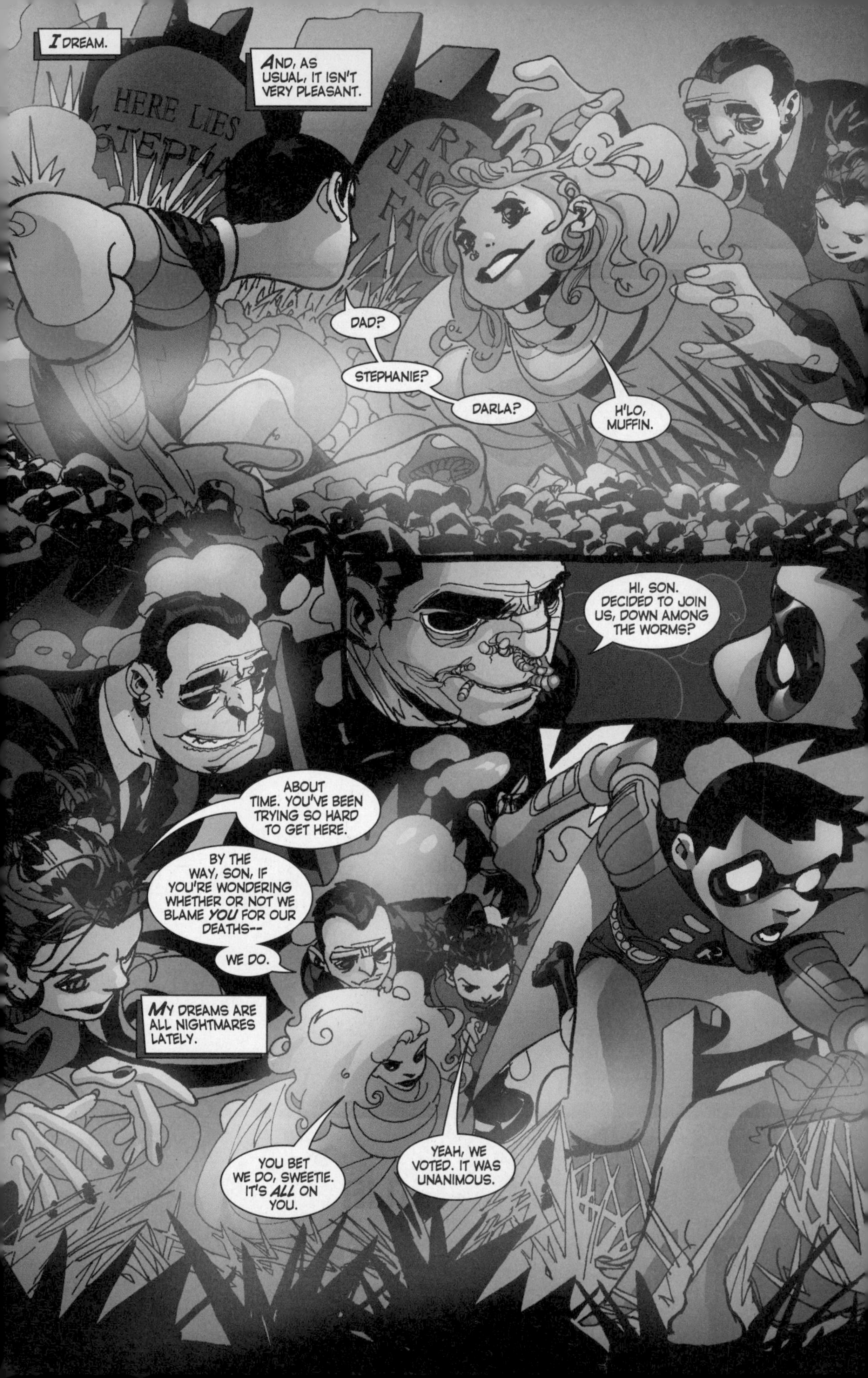

I DREAM.
AND, AS USUAL, IT ISN'T VERY PLEASANT.
HERE LIES STEPHA
DAD?
STEPHANIE?
DARLA?
H'LO, MUFFIN.
HI, SON. DECIDED TO JOIN US, DOWN AMONG THE WORMS?
ABOUT TIME. YOU'VE BEEN TRYING SO HARD TO GET HERE.
BY THE WAY, SON, IF YOU'RE WONDERING WHETHER OR NOT WE BLAME *YOU* FOR OUR DEATHS--
WE DO.
MY DREAMS ARE ALL NIGHTMARES LATELY.
YOU BET WE DO, SWEETIE. IT'S *ALL* ON YOU.
YEAH, WE VOTED. IT WAS UNANIMOUS.

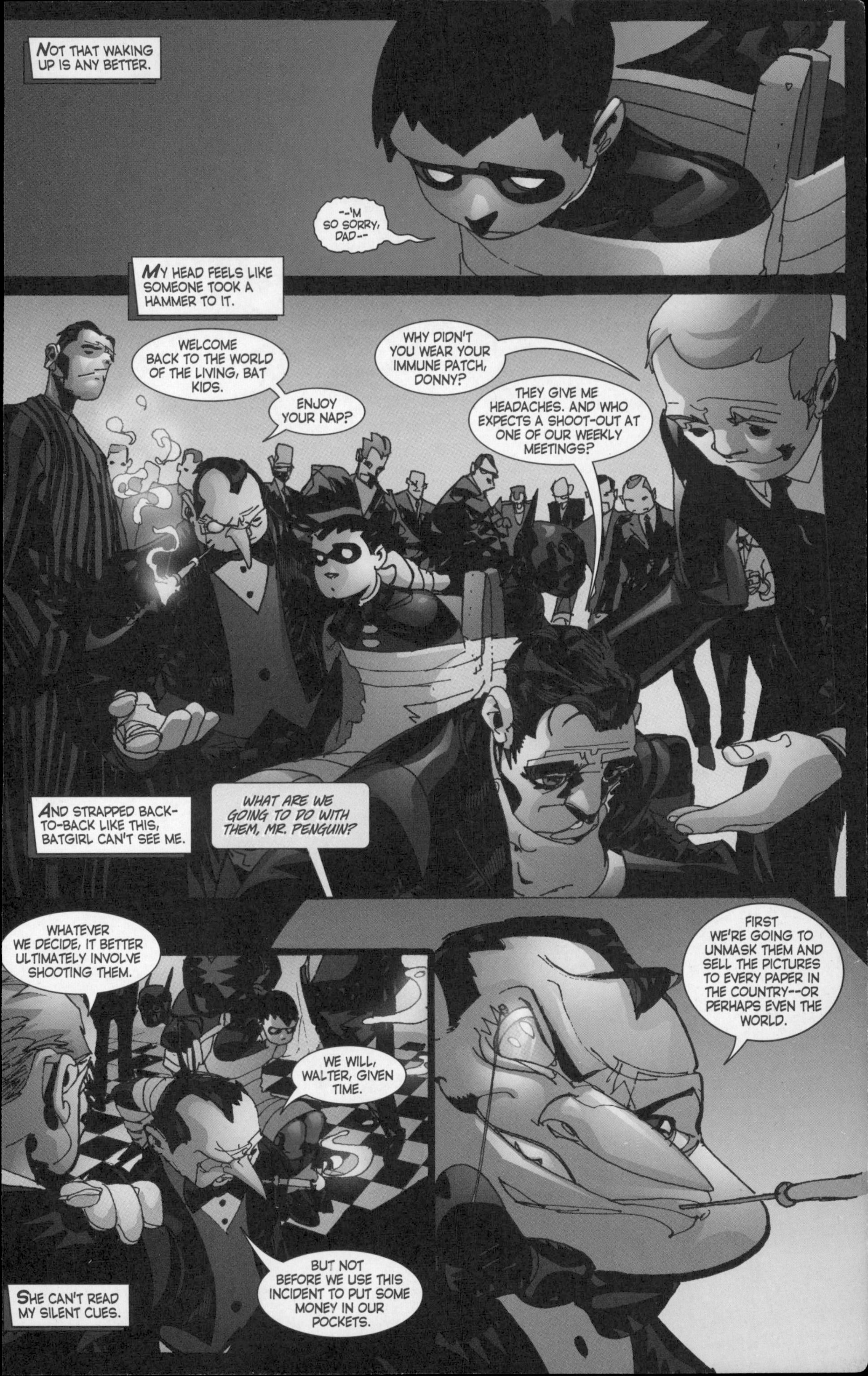
NOT THAT WAKING UP IS ANY BETTER.
--'M SO SORRY, DAD--
MY HEAD FEELS LIKE SOMEONE TOOK A HAMMER TO IT.
WELCOME BACK TO THE WORLD OF THE LIVING, BAT KIDS.
ENJOY YOUR NAP?
WHY DIDN'T YOU WEAR YOUR IMMUNE PATCH, DONNY?
THEY GIVE ME HEADACHES. AND WHO EXPECTS A SHOOT-OUT AT ONE OF OUR WEEKLY MEETINGS?
AND STRAPPED BACK-TO-BACK LIKE THIS, BATGIRL CAN'T SEE ME.
WHAT ARE WE GOING TO DO WITH THEM, MR. PENGUIN?
WHATEVER WE DECIDE, IT BETTER ULTIMATELY INVOLVE SHOOTING THEM.
WE WILL, WALTER, GIVEN TIME.
BUT NOT BEFORE WE USE THIS INCIDENT TO PUT SOME MONEY IN OUR POCKETS.
SHE CAN'T READ MY SILENT CUES.
FIRST WE'RE GOING TO UNMASK THEM AND SELL THE PICTURES TO EVERY PAPER IN THE COUNTRY--OR PERHAPS EVEN THE WORLD.

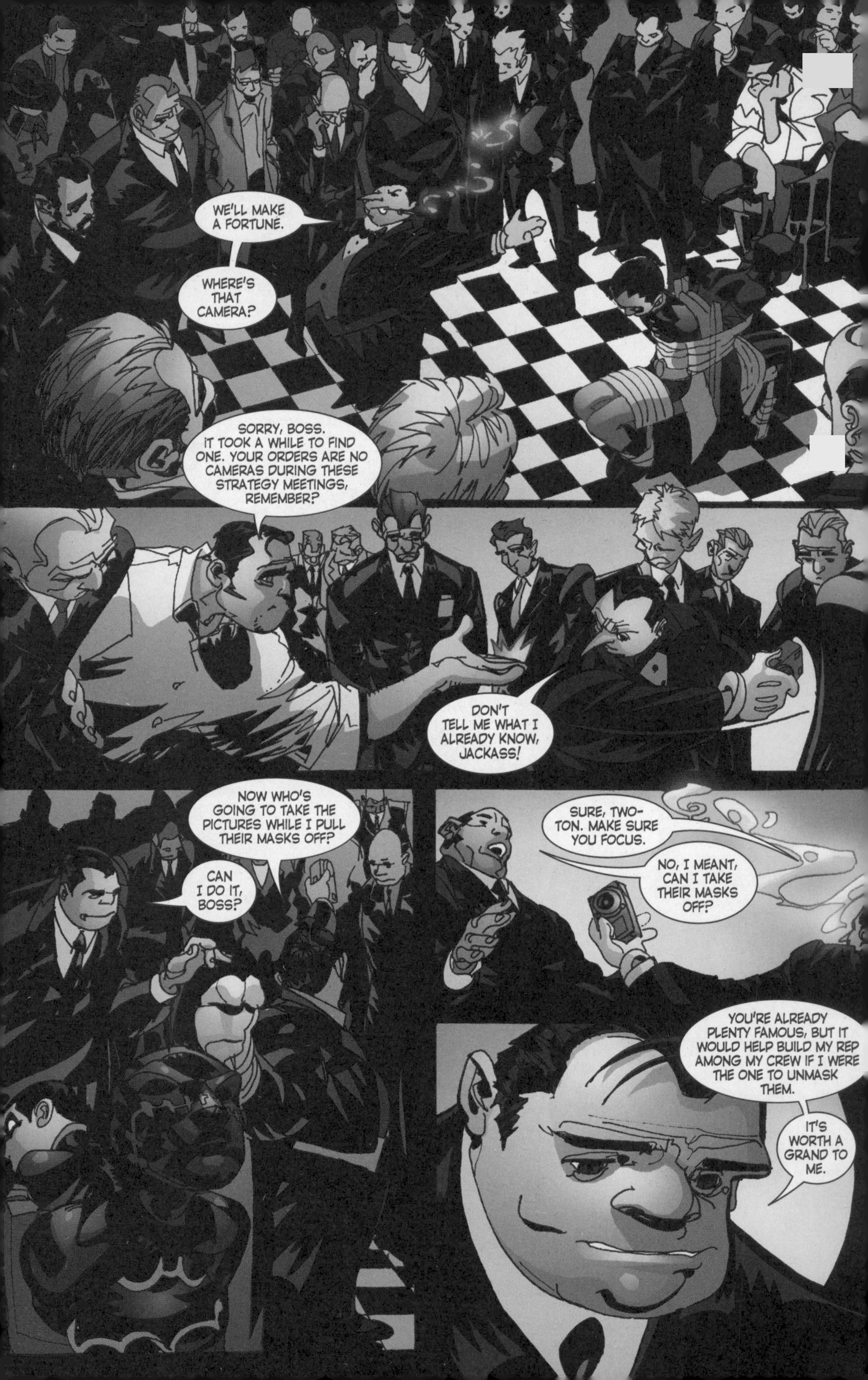
WE'LL MAKE A FORTUNE.
WHERE'S THAT CAMERA?
SORRY, BOSS. IT TOOK A WHILE TO FIND ONE. YOUR ORDERS ARE NO CAMERAS DURING THESE STRATEGY MEETINGS, REMEMBER?
DON'T TELL ME WHAT I ALREADY KNOW, JACKASS!
NOW WHO'S GOING TO TAKE THE PICTURES WHILE I PULL THEIR MASKS OFF?
CAN I DO IT, BOSS?
SURE, TWO-TON. MAKE SURE YOU FOCUS.
NO, I MEANT, CAN I TAKE THEIR MASKS OFF?
YOU'RE ALREADY PLENTY FAMOUS, BUT IT WOULD HELP BUILD MY REP AMONG MY CREW IF I WERE THE ONE TO UNMASK THEM.
IT'S WORTH A GRAND TO ME.

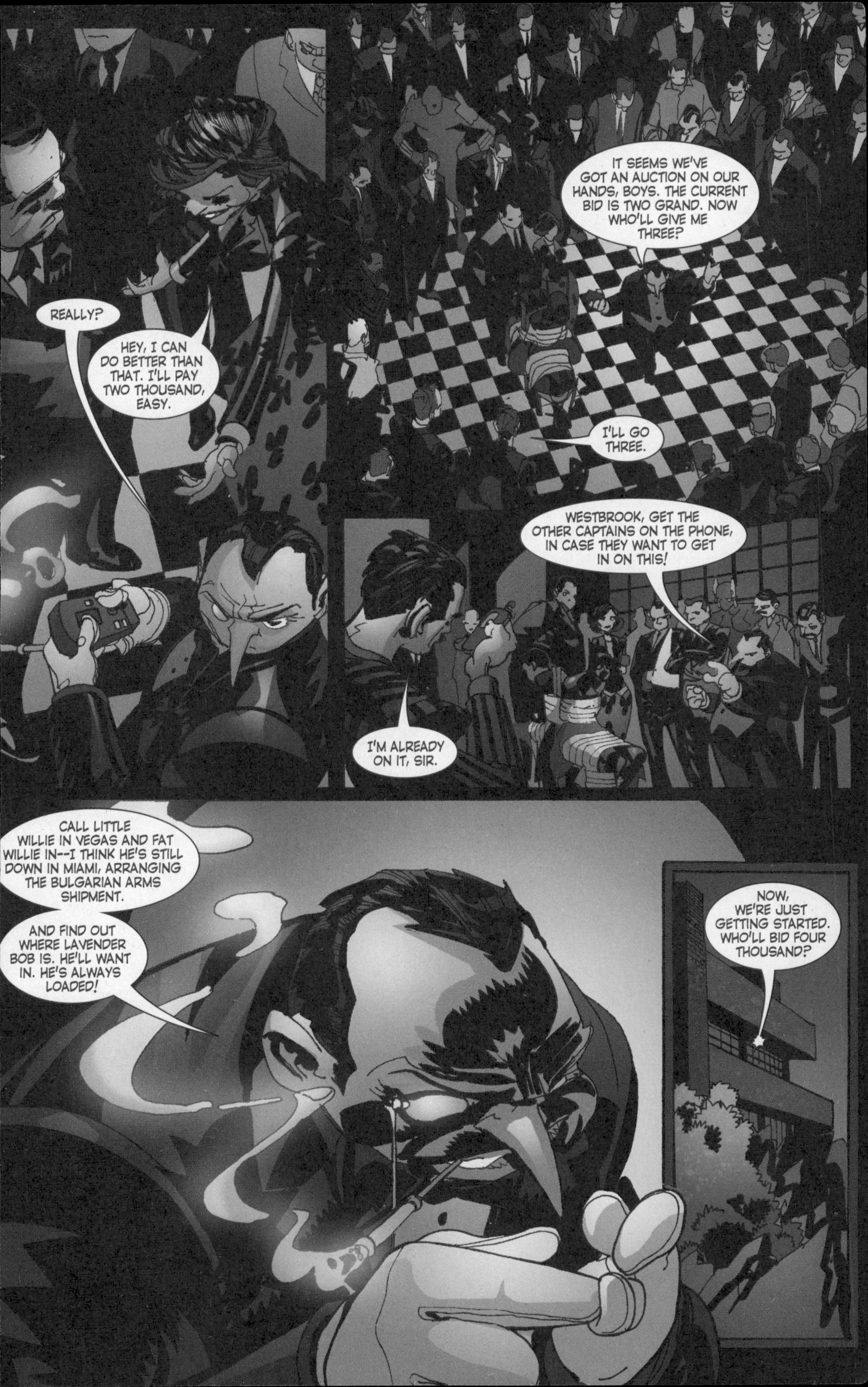
REALLY?
HEY, I CAN DO BETTER THAN THAT. I'LL PAY TWO THOUSAND, EASY.
IT SEEMS WE'VE GOT AN AUCTION ON OUR HANDS, BOYS. THE CURRENT BID IS TWO GRAND. NOW WHO'LL GIVE ME THREE?
I'LL GO THREE.
WESTBROOK, GET THE OTHER CAPTAINS ON THE PHONE, IN CASE THEY WANT TO GET IN ON THIS!
I'M ALREADY ON IT, SIR.
CALL LITTLE WILLIE IN VEGAS AND FAT WILLIE IN--I THINK HE'S STILL DOWN IN MIAMI, ARRANGING THE BULGARIAN ARMS SHIPMENT.
AND FIND OUT WHERE LAVENDER BOB IS. HE'LL WANT IN. HE'S ALWAYS LOADED!
NOW, WE'RE JUST GETTING STARTED. WHO'LL BID FOUR THOUSAND?

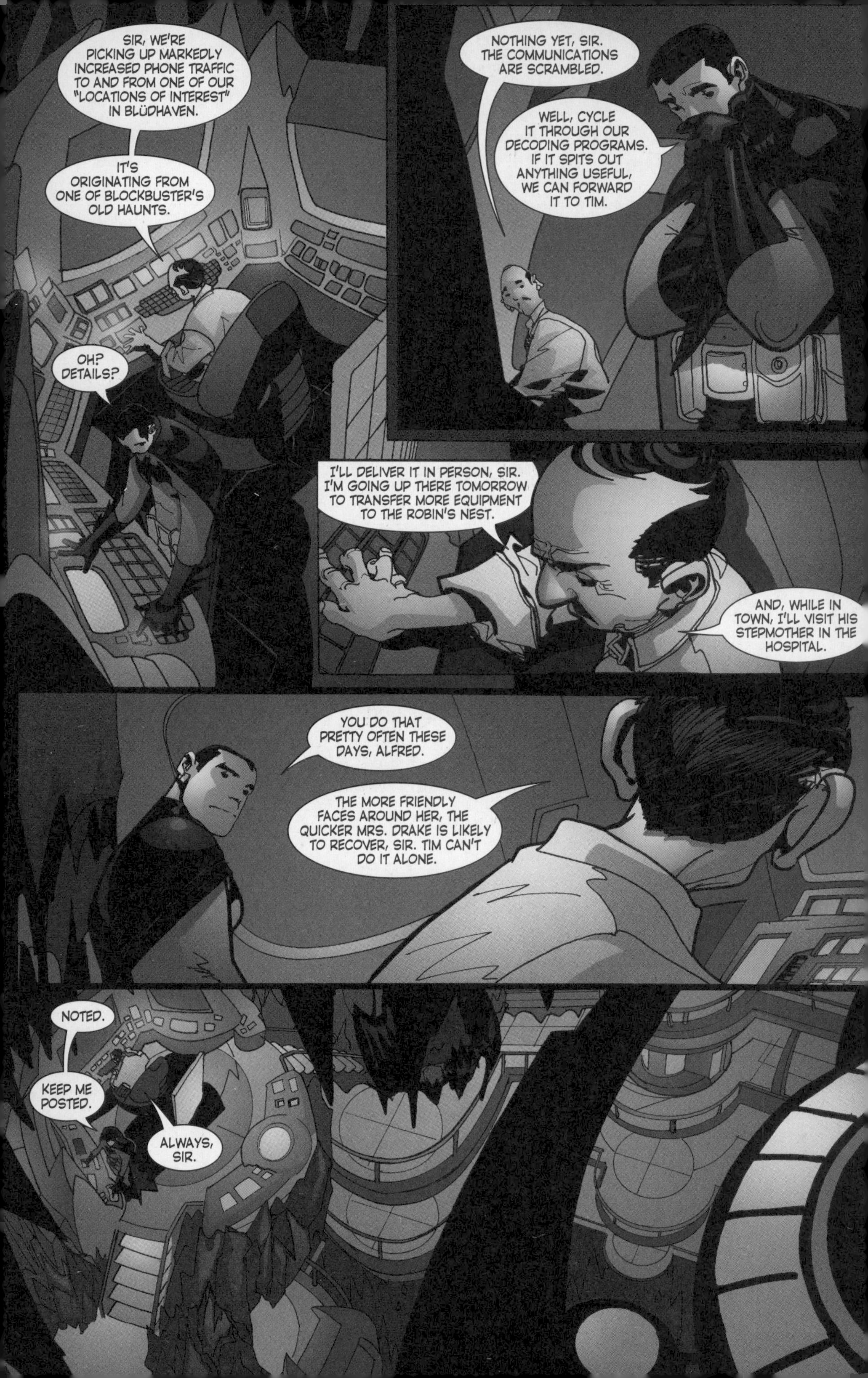
SIR, WE'RE PICKING UP MARKEDLY INCREASED PHONE TRAFFIC TO AND FROM ONE OF OUR "LOCATIONS OF INTEREST" IN BLÜDHAVEN.
IT'S ORIGINATING FROM ONE OF BLOCKBUSTER'S OLD HAUNTS.
OH? DETAILS?
NOTHING YET, SIR. THE COMMUNICATIONS ARE SCRAMBLED.
WELL, CYCLE IT THROUGH OUR DECODING PROGRAMS. IF IT SPITS OUT ANYTHING USEFUL, WE CAN FORWARD IT TO TIM.
I'LL DELIVER IT IN PERSON, SIR. I'M GOING UP THERE TOMORROW TO TRANSFER MORE EQUIPMENT TO THE ROBIN'S NEST.
AND, WHILE IN TOWN, I'LL VISIT HIS STEPMOTHER IN THE HOSPITAL.
YOU DO THAT PRETTY OFTEN THESE DAYS, ALFRED.
THE MORE FRIENDLY FACES AROUND HER, THE QUICKER MRS. DRAKE IS LIKELY TO RECOVER, SIR. TIM CAN'T DO IT ALONE.
NOTED.
KEEP ME POSTED.
ALWAYS, SIR.

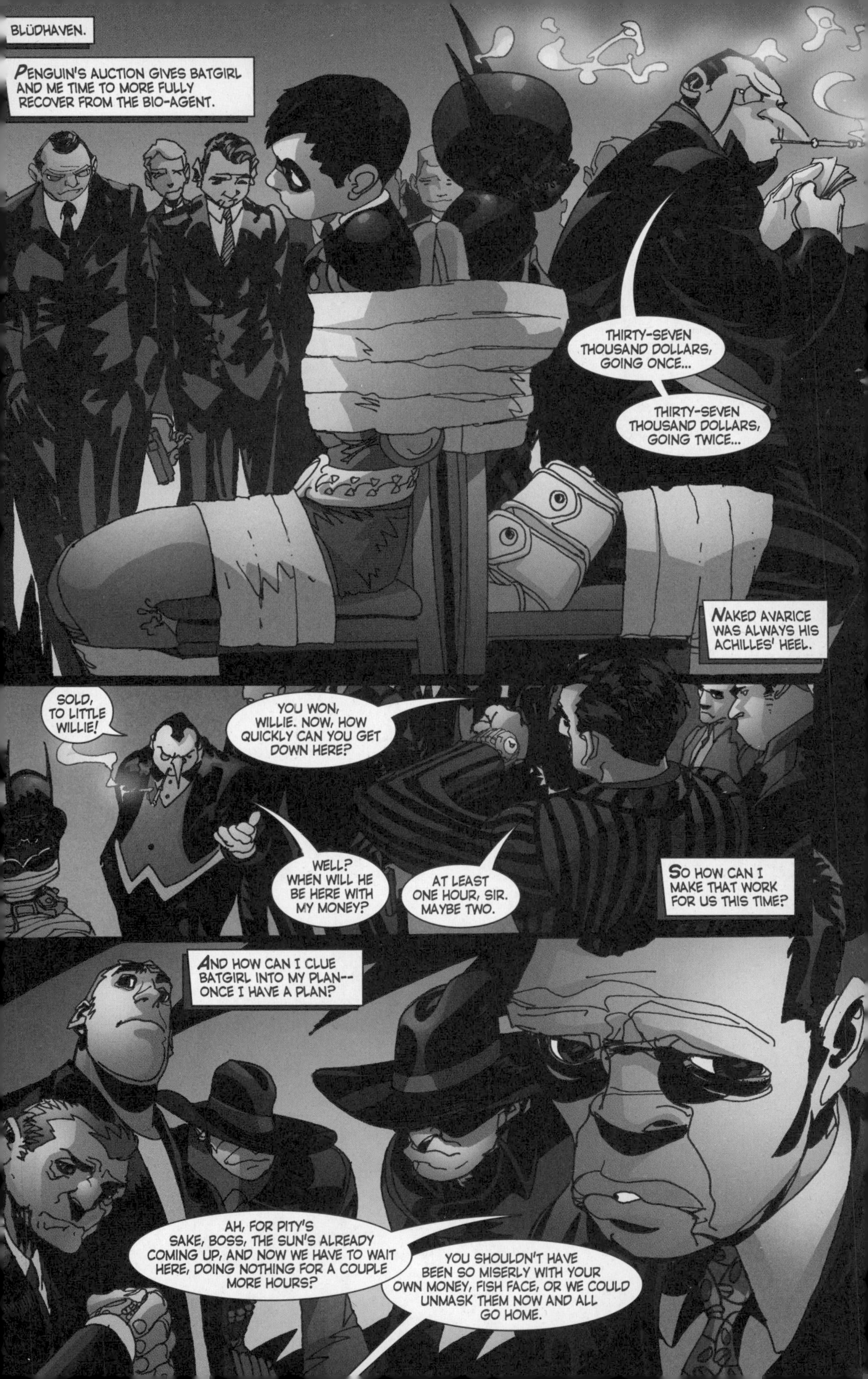
BLÜDHAVEN.
PENGUIN'S AUCTION GIVES BATGIRL AND ME TIME TO MORE FULLY RECOVER FROM THE BIO-AGENT.
THIRTY-SEVEN THOUSAND DOLLARS, GOING ONCE...
THIRTY-SEVEN THOUSAND DOLLARS, GOING TWICE...
NAKED AVARICE WAS ALWAYS HIS ACHILLES' HEEL.
SOLD, TO LITTLE WILLIE!
YOU WON, WILLIE. NOW, HOW QUICKLY CAN YOU GET DOWN HERE?
WELL? WHEN WILL HE BE HERE WITH MY MONEY?
AT LEAST ONE HOUR, SIR. MAYBE TWO.
SO HOW CAN I MAKE THAT WORK FOR US THIS TIME?
AND HOW CAN I CLUE BATGIRL INTO MY PLAN-- ONCE I HAVE A PLAN?
AH, FOR PITY'S SAKE, BOSS, THE SUN'S ALREADY COMING UP, AND NOW WE HAVE TO WAIT HERE, DOING NOTHING FOR A COUPLE MORE HOURS?
YOU SHOULDN'T HAVE BEEN SO MISERLY WITH YOUR OWN MONEY, FISH FACE, OR WE COULD UNMASK THEM NOW AND ALL GO HOME.

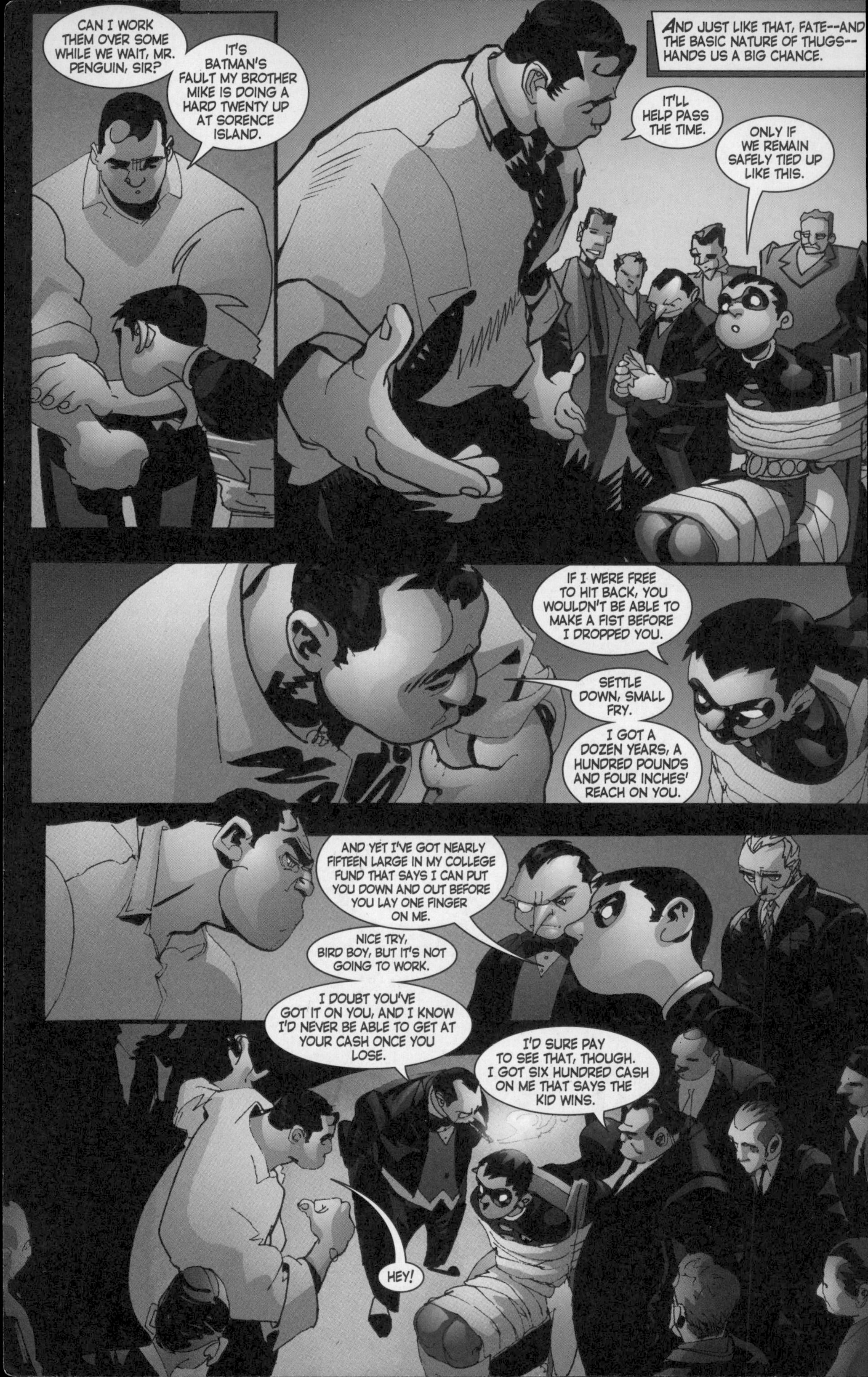
CAN I WORK THEM OVER SOME WHILE WE WAIT, MR. PENGUIN, SIR?
IT'S BATMAN'S FAULT MY BROTHER MIKE IS DOING A HARD TWENTY UP AT SORENCE ISLAND.
AND JUST LIKE THAT, FATE--AND THE BASIC NATURE OF THUGS--HANDS US A BIG CHANCE.
IT'LL HELP PASS THE TIME.
ONLY IF WE REMAIN SAFELY TIED UP LIKE THIS.
IF I WERE FREE TO HIT BACK, YOU WOULDN'T BE ABLE TO MAKE A FIST BEFORE I DROPPED YOU.
SETTLE DOWN, SMALL FRY.
I GOT A DOZEN YEARS, A HUNDRED POUNDS AND FOUR INCHES' REACH ON YOU.
AND YET I'VE GOT NEARLY FIFTEEN LARGE IN MY COLLEGE FUND THAT SAYS I CAN PUT YOU DOWN AND OUT BEFORE YOU LAY ONE FINGER ON ME.
NICE TRY, BIRD BOY, BUT IT'S NOT GOING TO WORK.
I DOUBT YOU'VE GOT IT ON YOU, AND I KNOW I'D NEVER BE ABLE TO GET AT YOUR CASH ONCE YOU LOSE.
I'D SURE PAY TO SEE THAT, THOUGH. I GOT SIX HUNDRED CASH ON ME THAT SAYS THE KID WINS.
HEY!

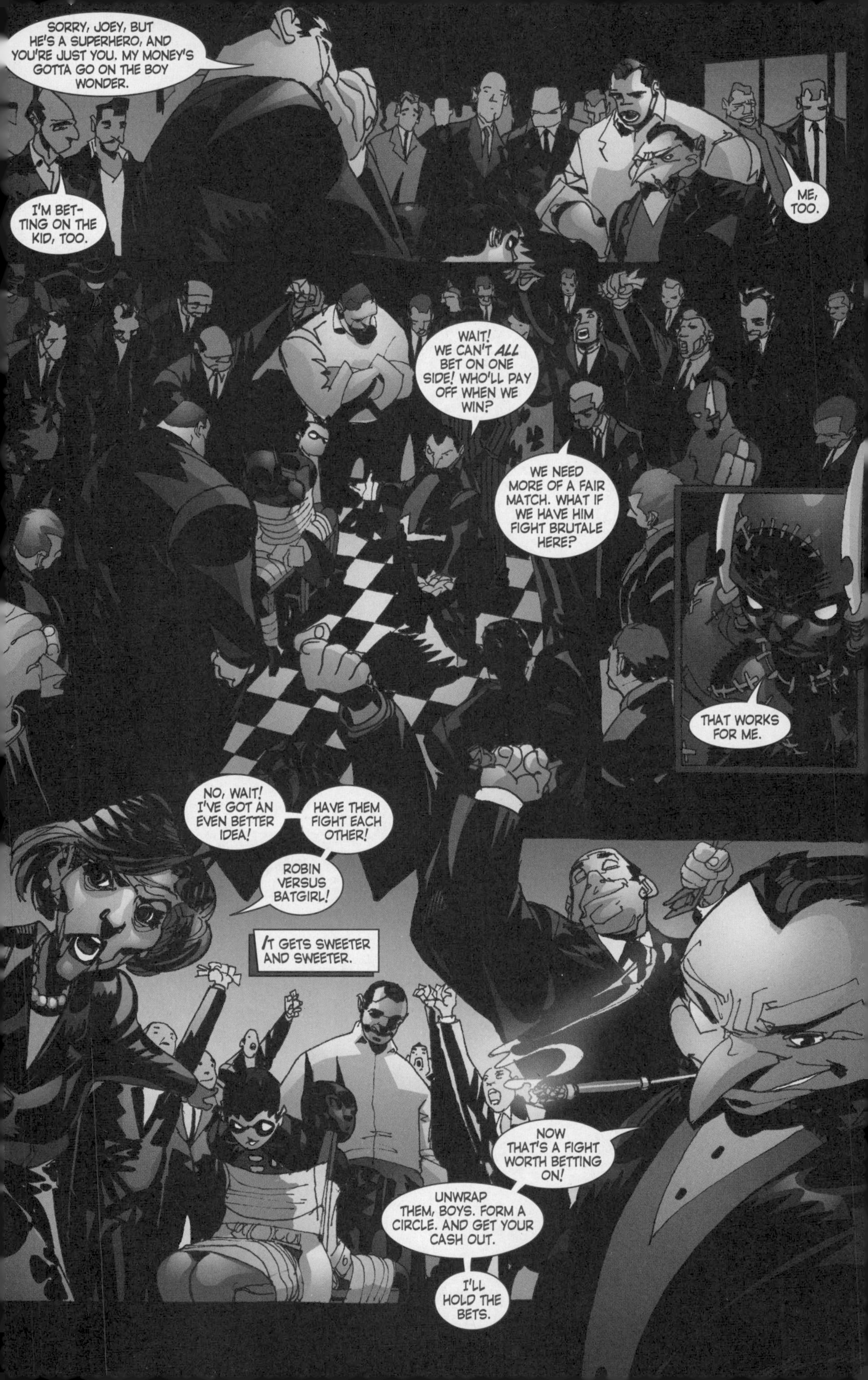
SORRY, JOEY, BUT HE'S A SUPERHERO, AND YOU'RE JUST YOU. MY MONEY'S GOTTA GO ON THE BOY WONDER.
I'M BETTING ON THE KID, TOO.
ME, TOO.
WAIT! WE CAN'T *ALL* BET ON ONE SIDE! WHO'LL PAY OFF WHEN WE WIN?
WE NEED MORE OF A FAIR MATCH. WHAT IF WE HAVE HIM FIGHT BRUTALE HERE?
THAT WORKS FOR ME.
NO, WAIT! I'VE GOT AN EVEN BETTER IDEA!
HAVE THEM FIGHT EACH OTHER!
ROBIN VERSUS BATGIRL!
IT GETS SWEETER AND SWEETER.
NOW THAT'S A FIGHT WORTH BETTING ON!
UNWRAP THEM, BOYS. FORM A CIRCLE. AND GET YOUR CASH OUT.
I'LL HOLD THE BETS.

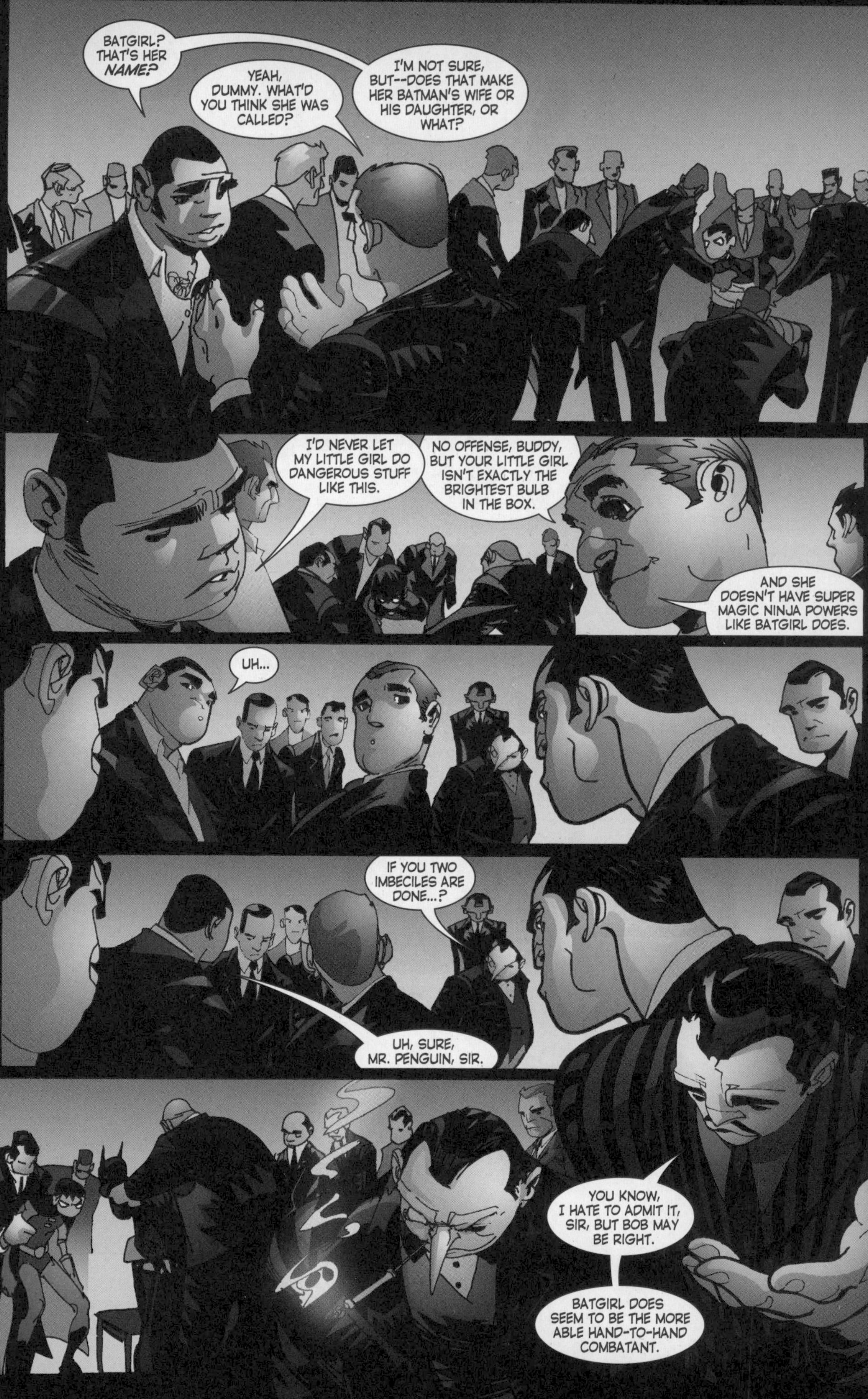
BATGIRL? THAT'S HER *NAME?*
YEAH, DUMMY. WHAT'D YOU THINK SHE WAS CALLED?
I'M NOT SURE, BUT--DOES THAT MAKE HER BATMAN'S WIFE OR HIS DAUGHTER, OR WHAT?
I'D NEVER LET MY LITTLE GIRL DO DANGEROUS STUFF LIKE THIS.
NO OFFENSE, BUDDY, BUT YOUR LITTLE GIRL ISN'T EXACTLY THE BRIGHTEST BULB IN THE BOX.
AND SHE DOESN'T HAVE SUPER MAGIC NINJA POWERS LIKE BATGIRL DOES.
UH...
IF YOU TWO IMBECILES ARE DONE...?
UH, SURE, MR. PENGUIN, SIR.
YOU KNOW, I HATE TO ADMIT IT, SIR, BUT BOB MAY BE RIGHT.
BATGIRL DOES SEEM TO BE THE MORE ABLE HAND-TO-HAND COMBATANT.

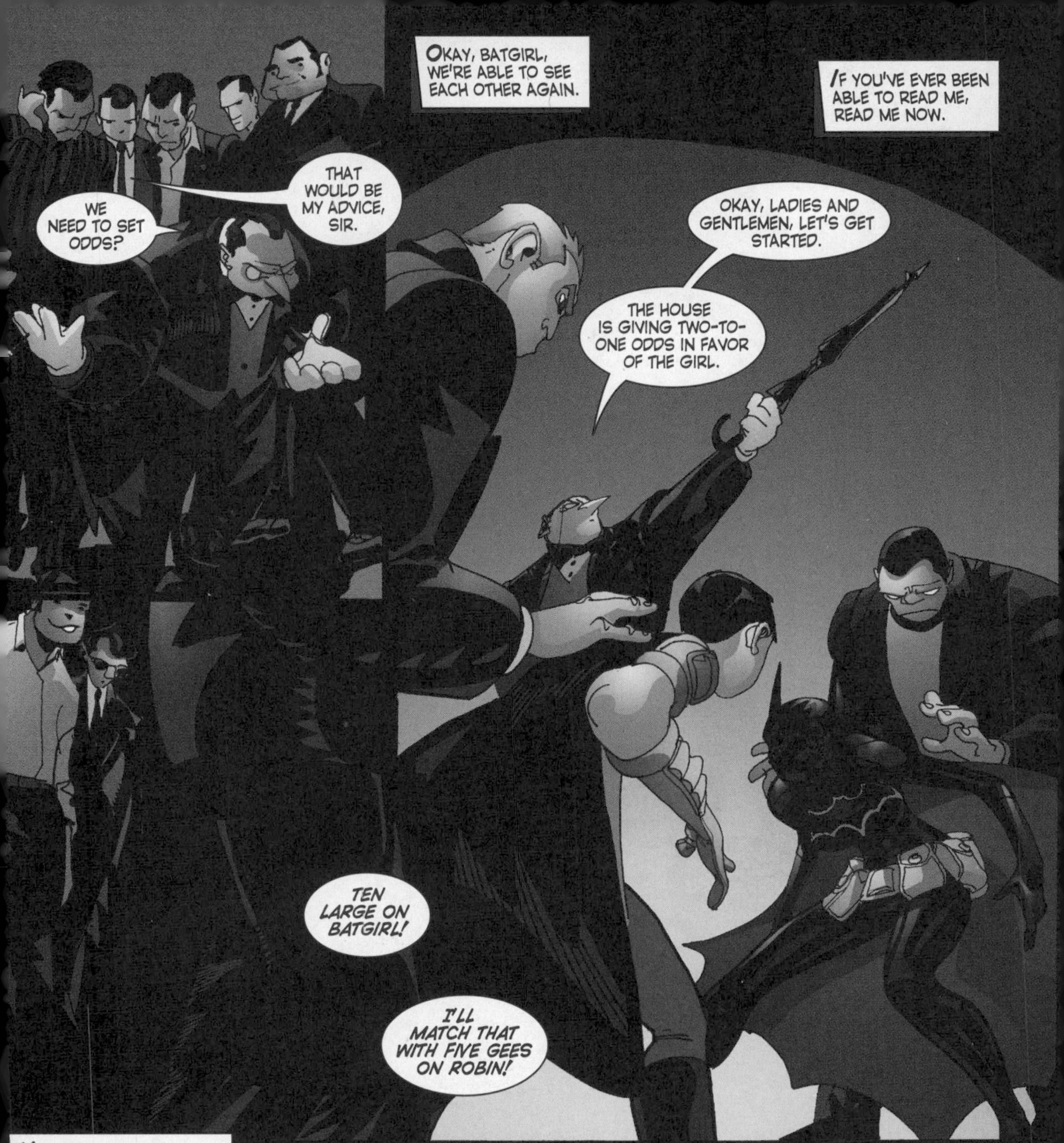
WE NEED TO SET ODDS?
THAT WOULD BE MY ADVICE, SIR.
OKAY, BATGIRL, WE'RE ABLE TO SEE EACH OTHER AGAIN.
IF YOU'VE EVER BEEN ABLE TO READ ME, READ ME NOW.
OKAY, LADIES AND GENTLEMEN, LET'S GET STARTED.
THE HOUSE IS GIVING TWO-TO-ONE ODDS IN FAVOR OF THE GIRL.
TEN LARGE ON BATGIRL!
I'LL MATCH THAT WITH FIVE GEES ON ROBIN!
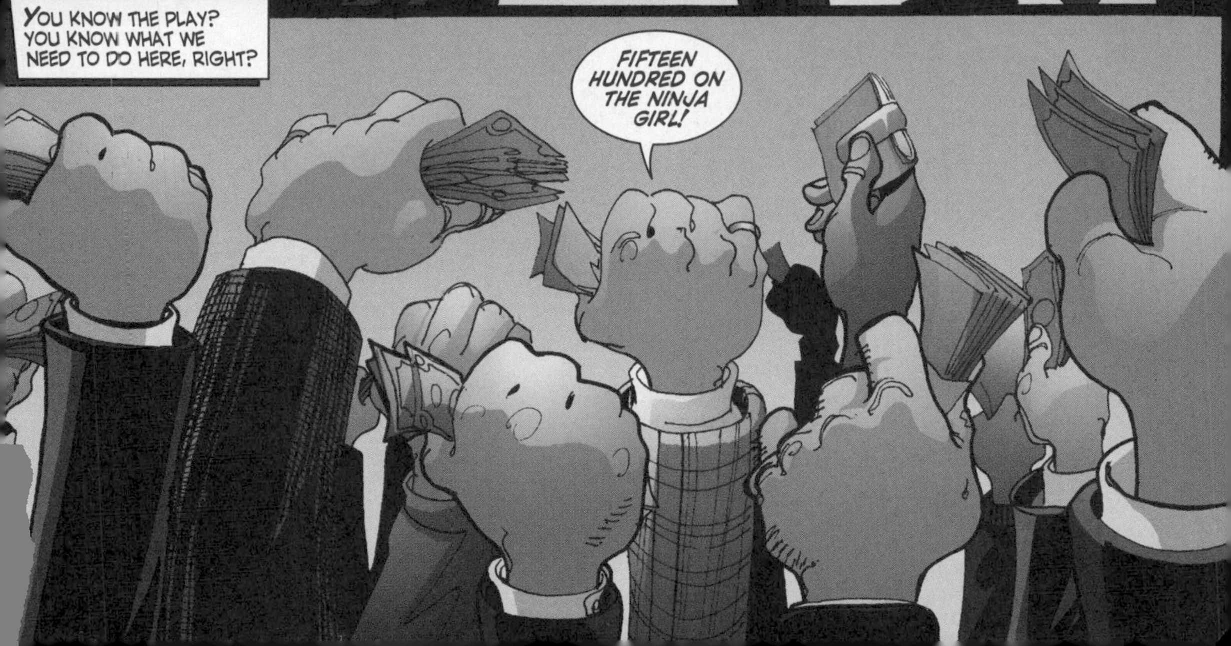
YOU KNOW THE PLAY? YOU KNOW WHAT WE NEED TO DO HERE, RIGHT?
FIFTEEN HUNDRED ON THE NINJA GIRL!

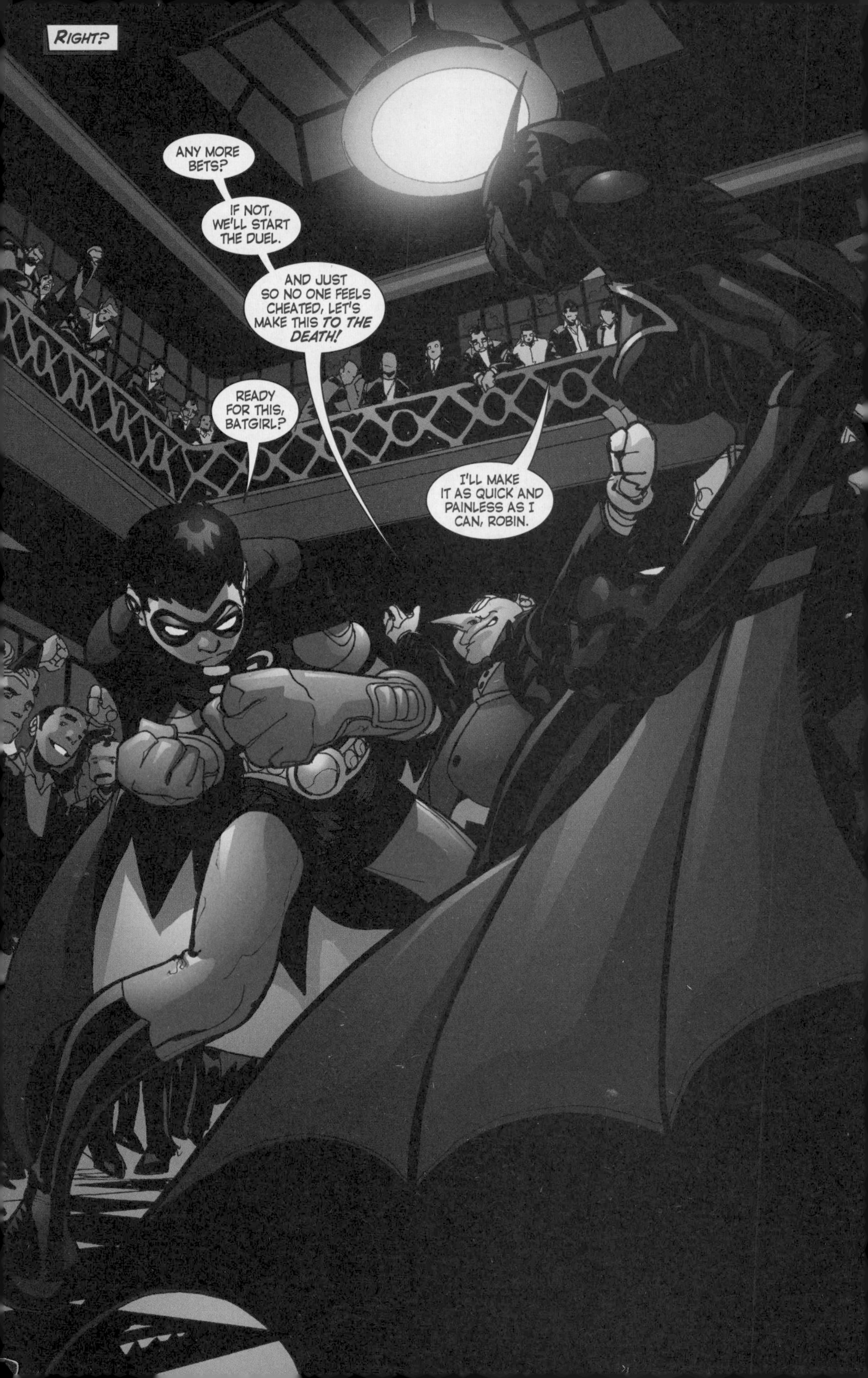
RIGHT?
ANY MORE BETS?
IF NOT, WE'LL START THE DUEL.
AND JUST SO NO ONE FEELS CHEATED, LET'S MAKE THIS *TO THE DEATH!*
READY FOR THIS, BATGIRL?
I'LL MAKE IT AS QUICK AND PAINLESS AS I CAN, ROBIN.

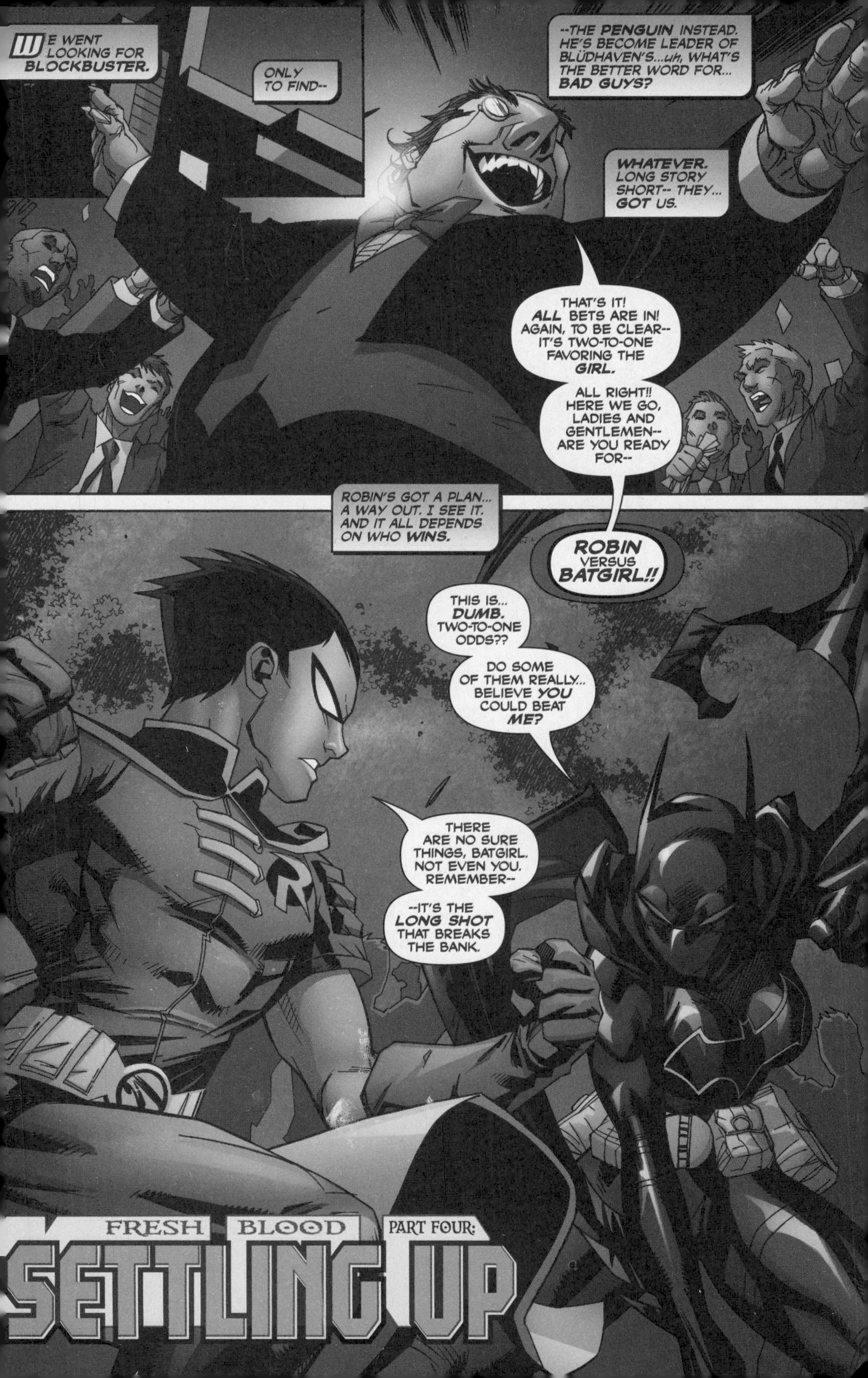
WE WENT LOOKING FOR BLOCKBUSTER.
ONLY TO FIND--
--THE PENGUIN INSTEAD. HE'S BECOME LEADER OF BLÜDHAVEN'S...uh, WHAT'S THE BETTER WORD FOR... BAD GUYS?
WHATEVER. LONG STORY SHORT-- THEY... GOT US.
THAT'S IT! ALL BETS ARE IN! AGAIN, TO BE CLEAR-- IT'S TWO-TO-ONE FAVORING THE GIRL.
ALL RIGHT!! HERE WE GO, LADIES AND GENTLEMEN-- ARE YOU READY FOR--
ROBIN'S GOT A PLAN... A WAY OUT. I SEE IT. AND IT ALL DEPENDS ON WHO WINS.
ROBIN VERSUS BATGIRL!!
THIS IS... DUMB. TWO-TO-ONE ODDS??
DO SOME OF THEM REALLY... BELIEVE YOU COULD BEAT ME?
THERE ARE NO SURE THINGS, BATGIRL. NOT EVEN YOU. REMEMBER--
--IT'S THE LONG SHOT THAT BREAKS THE BANK.
FRESH BLOOD PART FOUR:
SETTLING UP

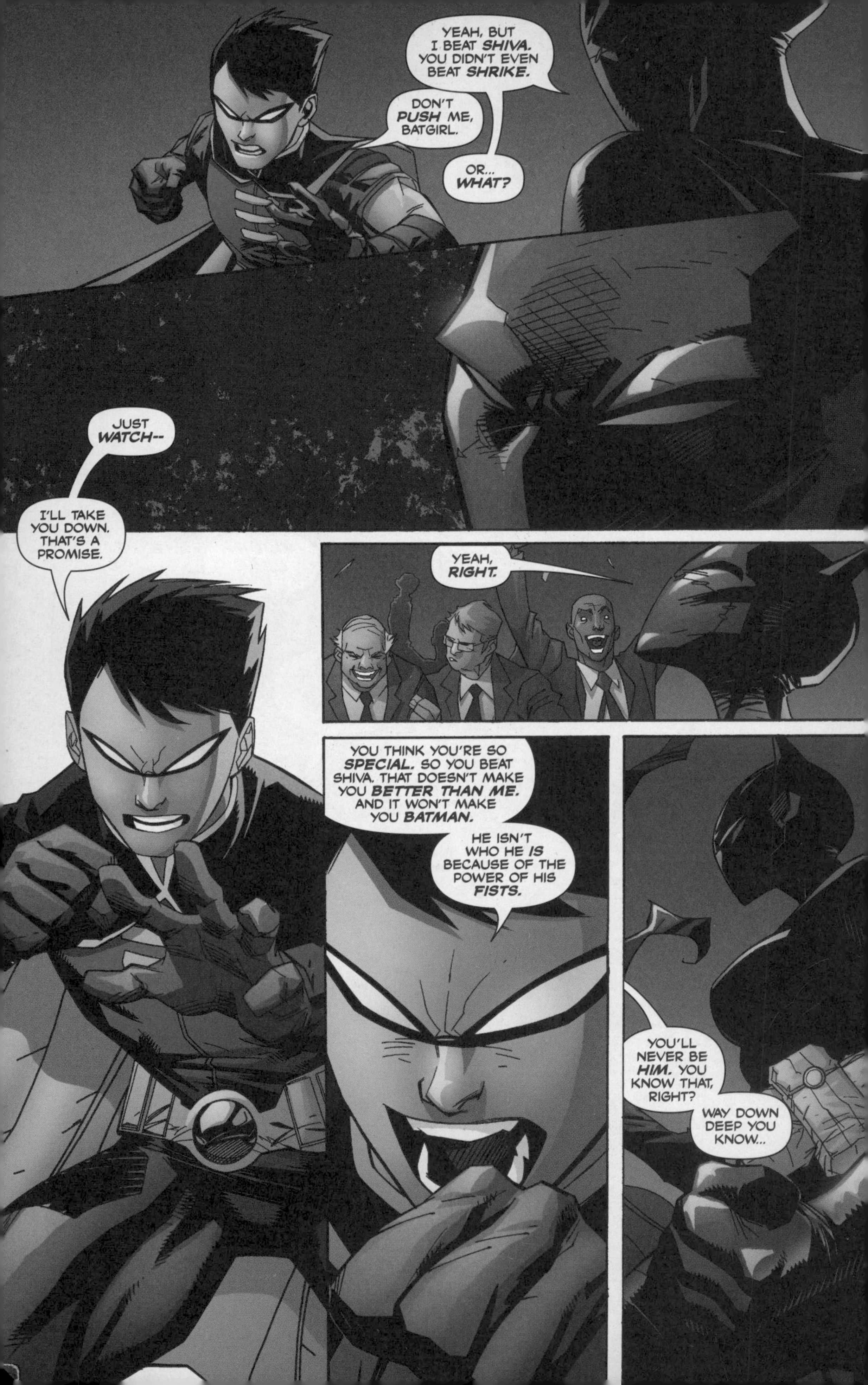
YEAH, BUT I BEAT SHIVA. YOU DIDN'T EVEN BEAT SHRIKE.
DON'T PUSH ME, BATGIRL.
OR... WHAT?
JUST WATCH--
I'LL TAKE YOU DOWN. THAT'S A PROMISE.
YEAH, RIGHT.
YOU THINK YOU'RE SO SPECIAL. SO YOU BEAT SHIVA. THAT DOESN'T MAKE YOU BETTER THAN ME. AND IT WON'T MAKE YOU BATMAN.
HE ISN'T WHO HE IS BECAUSE OF THE POWER OF HIS FISTS.
YOU'LL NEVER BE HIM. YOU KNOW THAT, RIGHT?
WAY DOWN DEEP YOU KNOW...

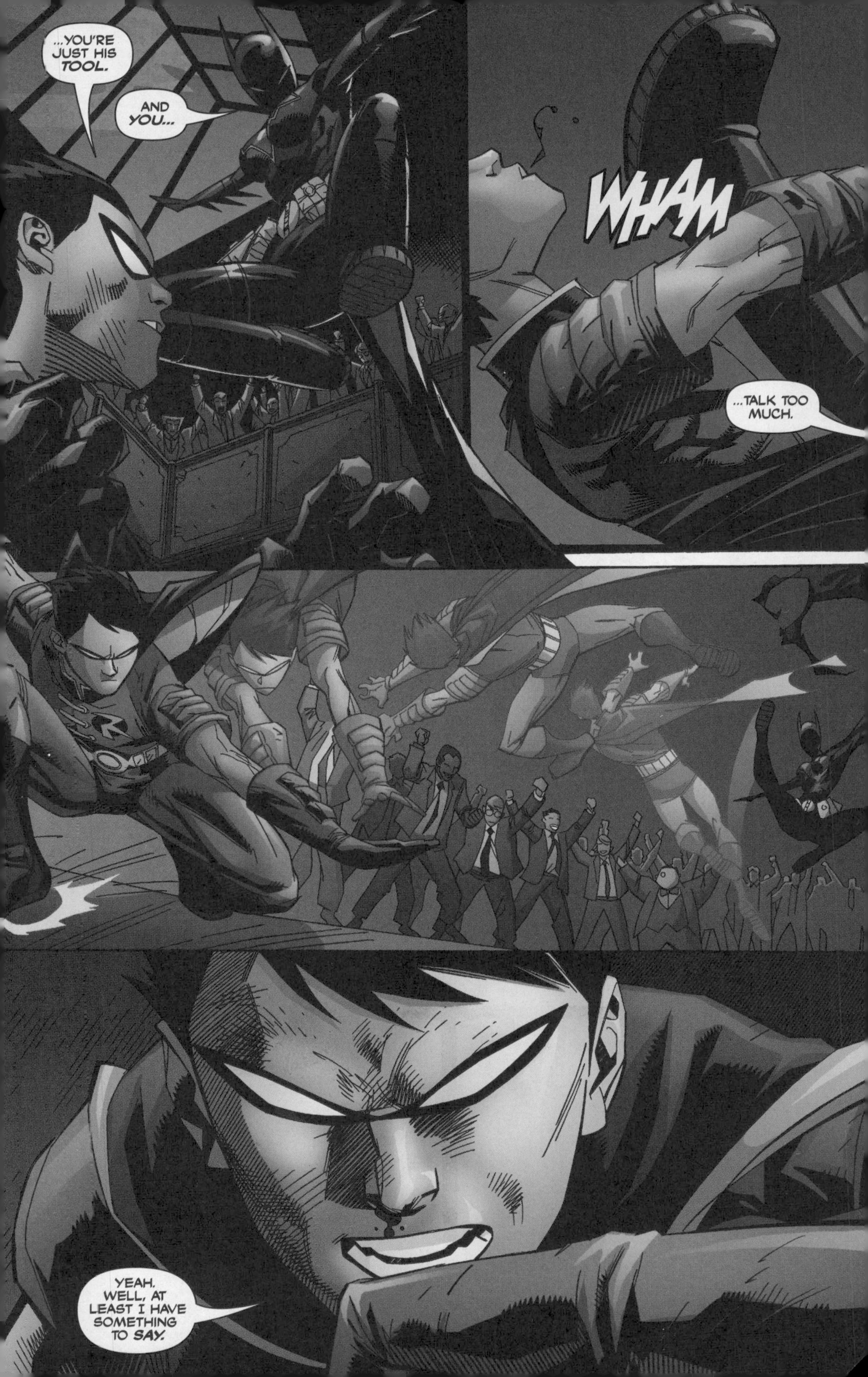
...YOU'RE JUST HIS TOOL.
AND YOU...
WHAM
...TALK TOO MUCH.
YEAH. WELL, AT LEAST I HAVE SOMETHING TO SAY.

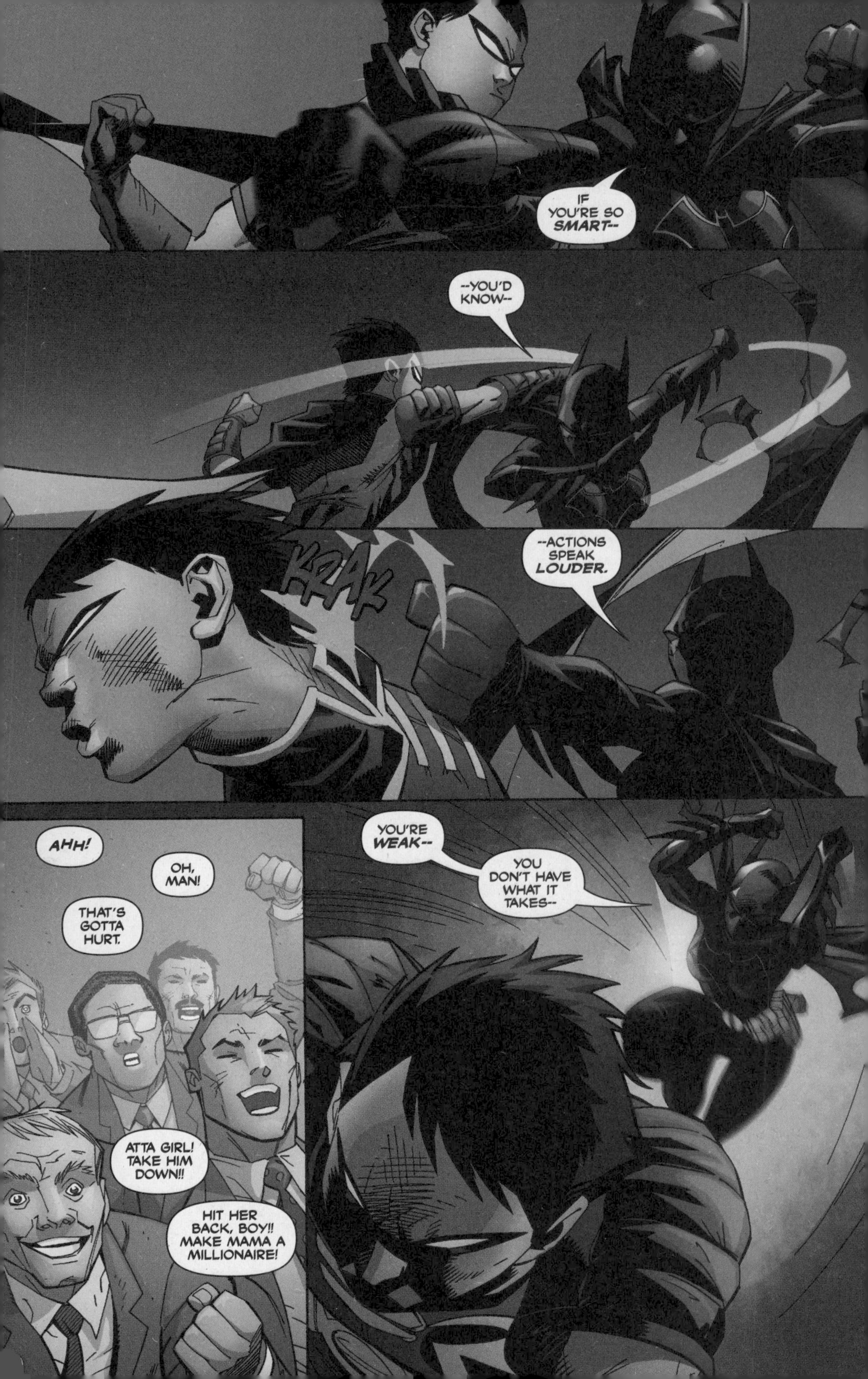
IF YOU'RE SO SMART--
--YOU'D KNOW--
KRAK
--ACTIONS SPEAK LOUDER.
AHH!
OH, MAN!
THAT'S GOTTA HURT.
ATTA GIRL! TAKE HIM DOWN!!
HIT HER BACK, BOY!! MAKE MAMA A MILLIONAIRE!
YOU'RE WEAK--
YOU DON'T HAVE WHAT IT TAKES--

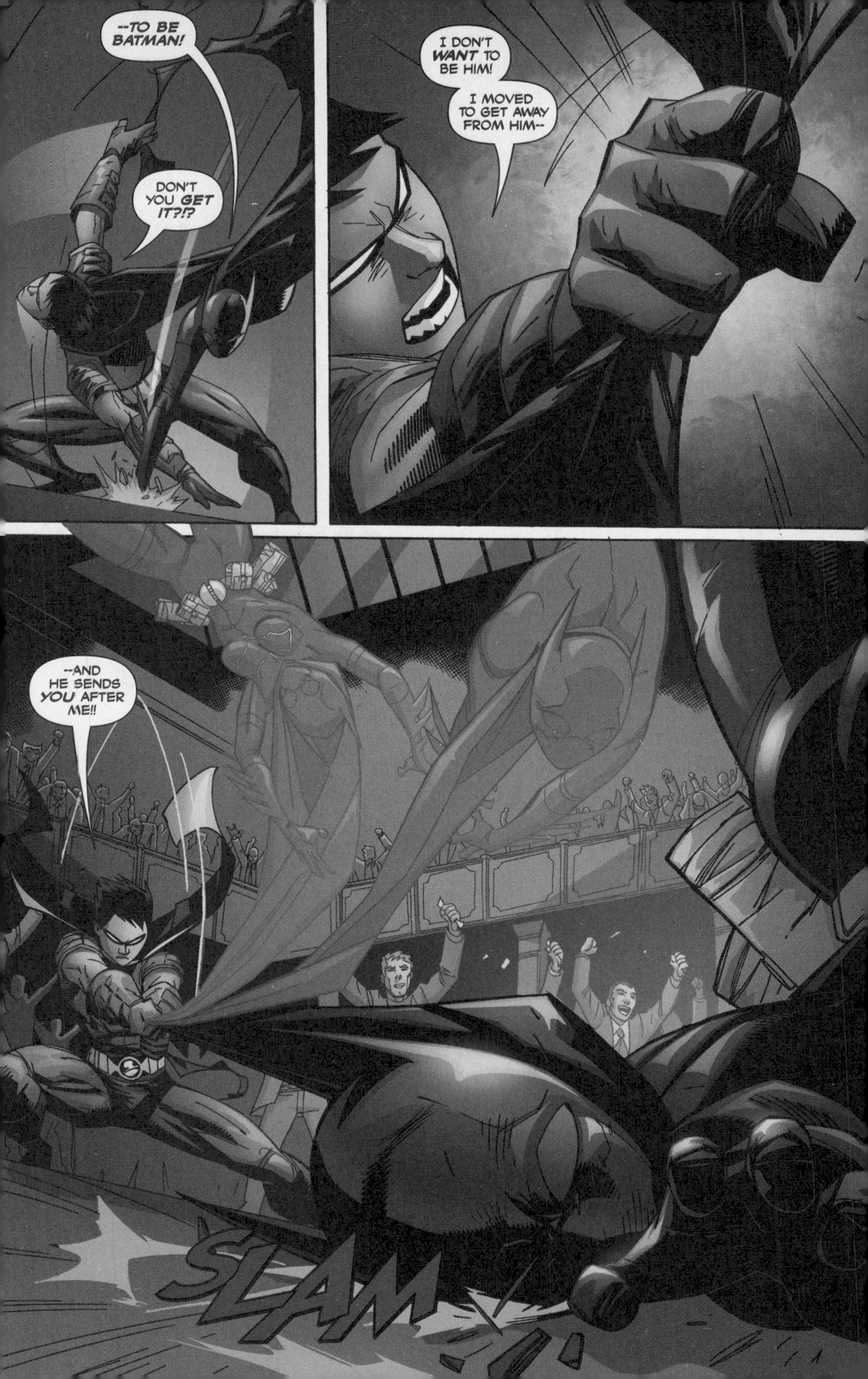
--TO BE BATMAN!
DON'T YOU GET IT?!?
I DON'T WANT TO BE HIM!
I MOVED TO GET AWAY FROM HIM--
--AND HE SENDS YOU AFTER ME!!
SLAM

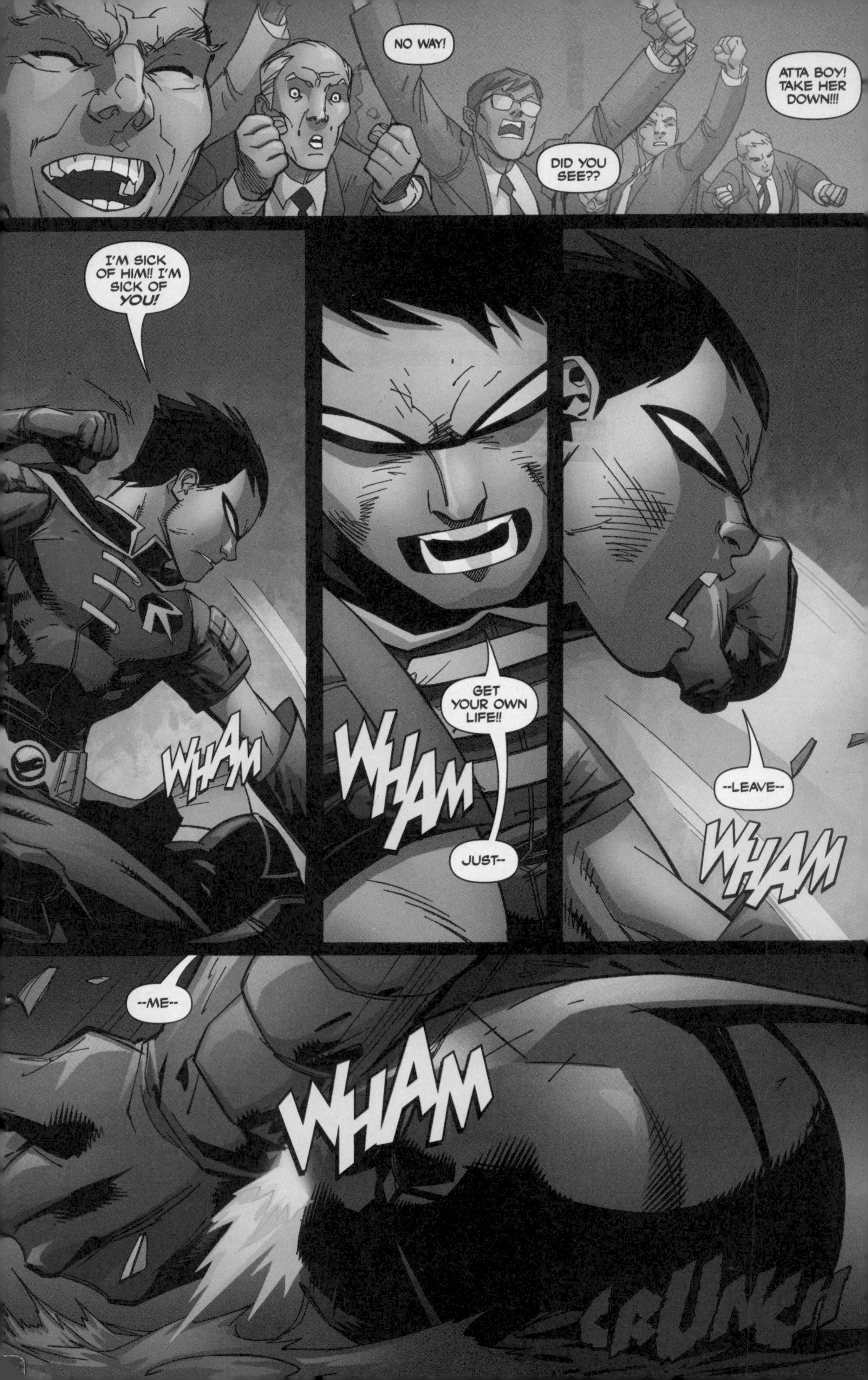
NO WAY!
ATTA BOY! TAKE HER DOWN!!!
DID YOU SEE??
I'M SICK OF HIM!! I'M SICK OF *YOU!*
WHAM
GET YOUR OWN LIFE!!
WHAM
JUST--
--LEAVE--
WHAM
--ME--
WHAM
CRUNCH

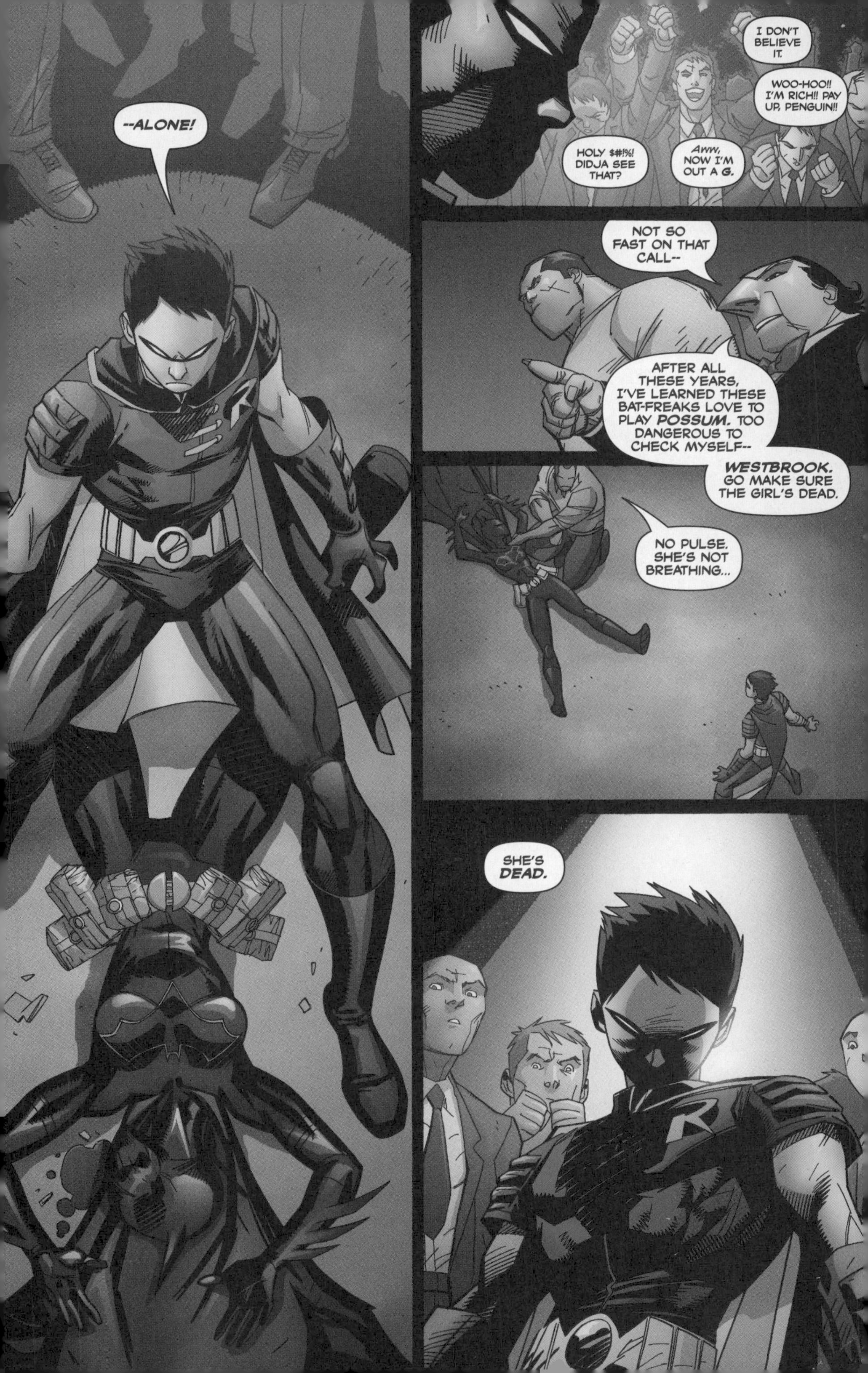
--ALONE!
I DON'T BELIEVE IT.
WOO-HOO!! I'M RICH!! PAY UP, PENGUIN!!
HOLY $#!%! DIDJA SEE THAT?
AWW, NOW I'M OUT A G.
NOT SO FAST ON THAT CALL--
AFTER ALL THESE YEARS, I'VE LEARNED THESE BAT-FREAKS LOVE TO PLAY POSSUM. TOO DANGEROUS TO CHECK MYSELF--
WESTBROOK. GO MAKE SURE THE GIRL'S DEAD.
NO PULSE. SHE'S NOT BREATHING...
SHE'S DEAD.

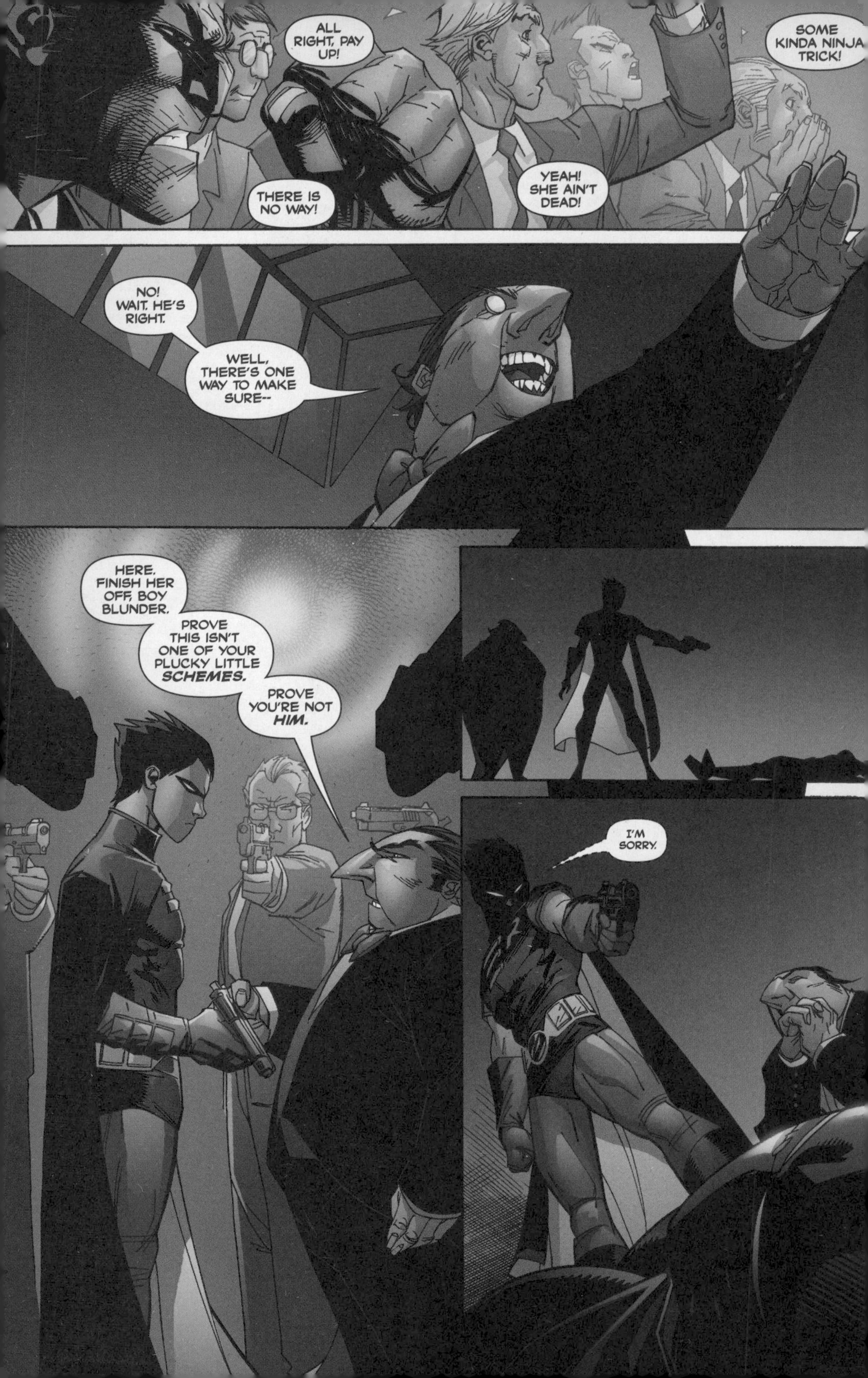
ALL RIGHT, PAY UP!
SOME KINDA NINJA TRICK!
THERE IS NO WAY!
YEAH! SHE AIN'T DEAD!
NO! WAIT. HE'S RIGHT.
WELL, THERE'S ONE WAY TO MAKE SURE--
HERE. FINISH HER OFF, BOY BLUNDER.
PROVE THIS ISN'T ONE OF YOUR PLUCKY LITTLE SCHEMES.
PROVE YOU'RE NOT HIM.
I'M SORRY.

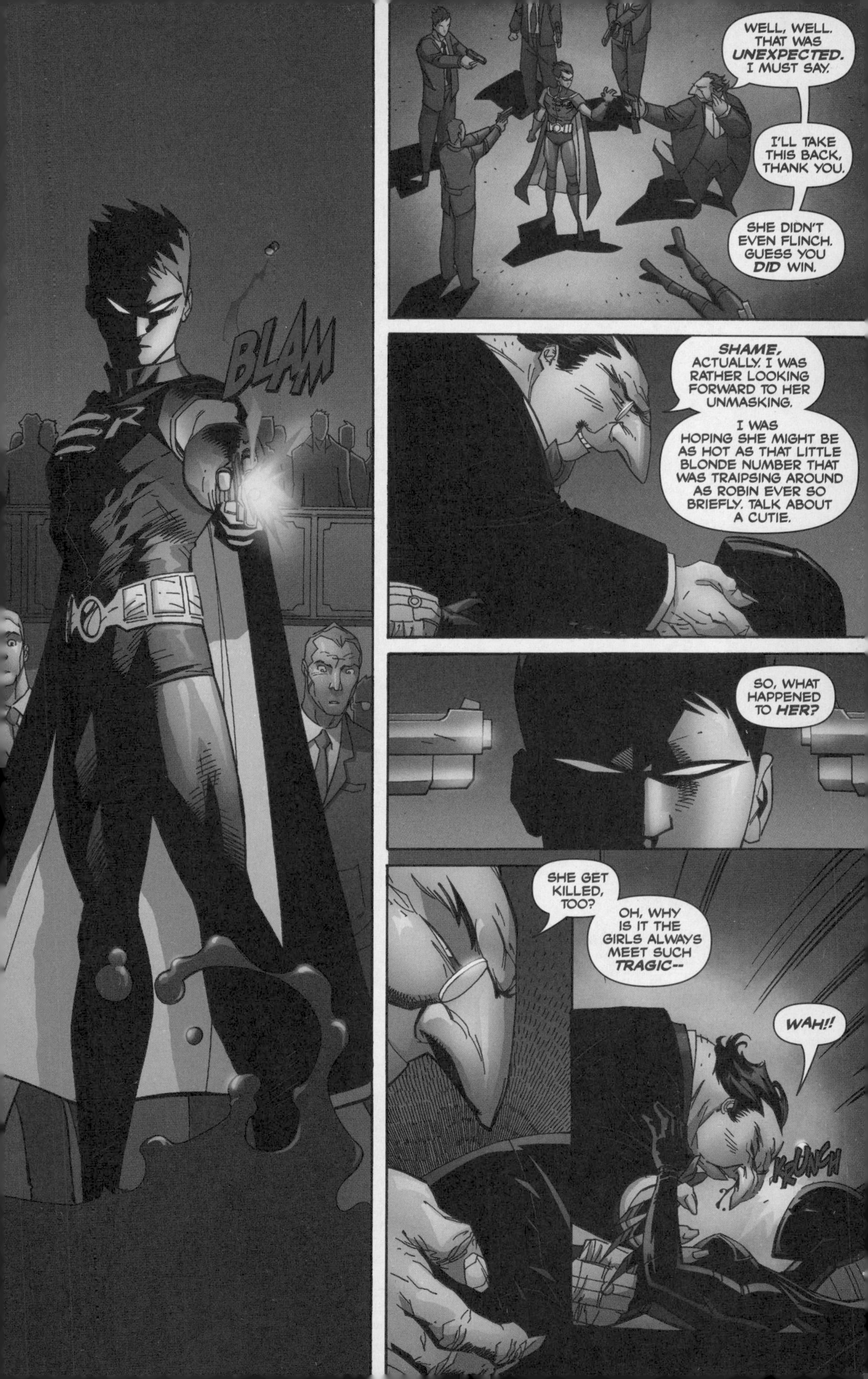
BLAM
WELL, WELL. THAT WAS UNEXPECTED. I MUST SAY.
I'LL TAKE THIS BACK, THANK YOU.
SHE DIDN'T EVEN FLINCH. GUESS YOU DID WIN.
SHAME, ACTUALLY. I WAS RATHER LOOKING FORWARD TO HER UNMASKING.
I WAS HOPING SHE MIGHT BE AS HOT AS THAT LITTLE BLONDE NUMBER THAT WAS TRAIPSING AROUND AS ROBIN EVER SO BRIEFLY. TALK ABOUT A CUTIE.
SO, WHAT HAPPENED TO HER?
SHE GET KILLED, TOO?
OH, WHY IS IT THE GIRLS ALWAYS MEET SUCH TRAGIC--
WAH!!
KRUNCH

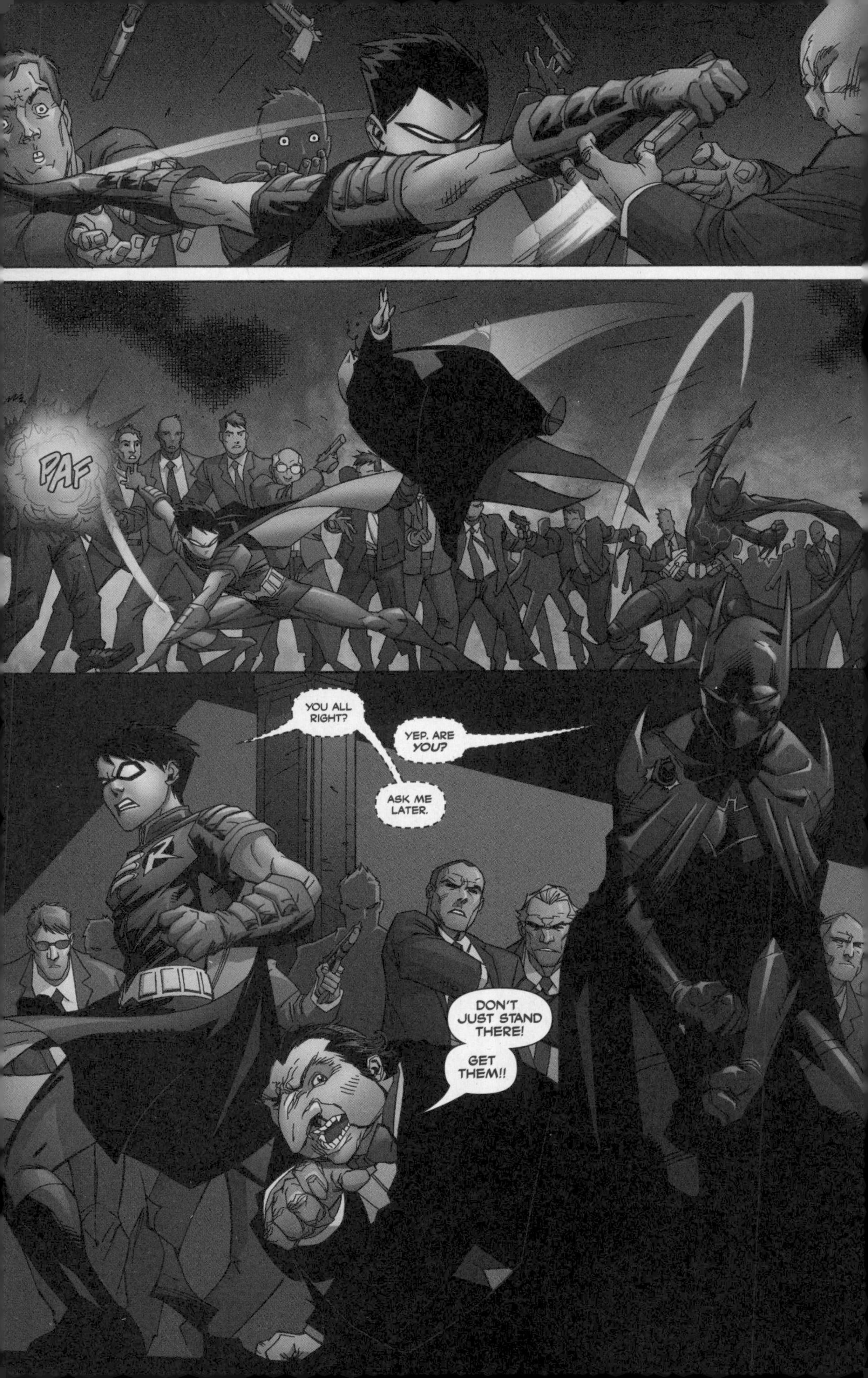
PAF
YOU ALL RIGHT?
YEP. ARE YOU?
ASK ME LATER.
DON'T JUST STAND THERE!
GET THEM!!

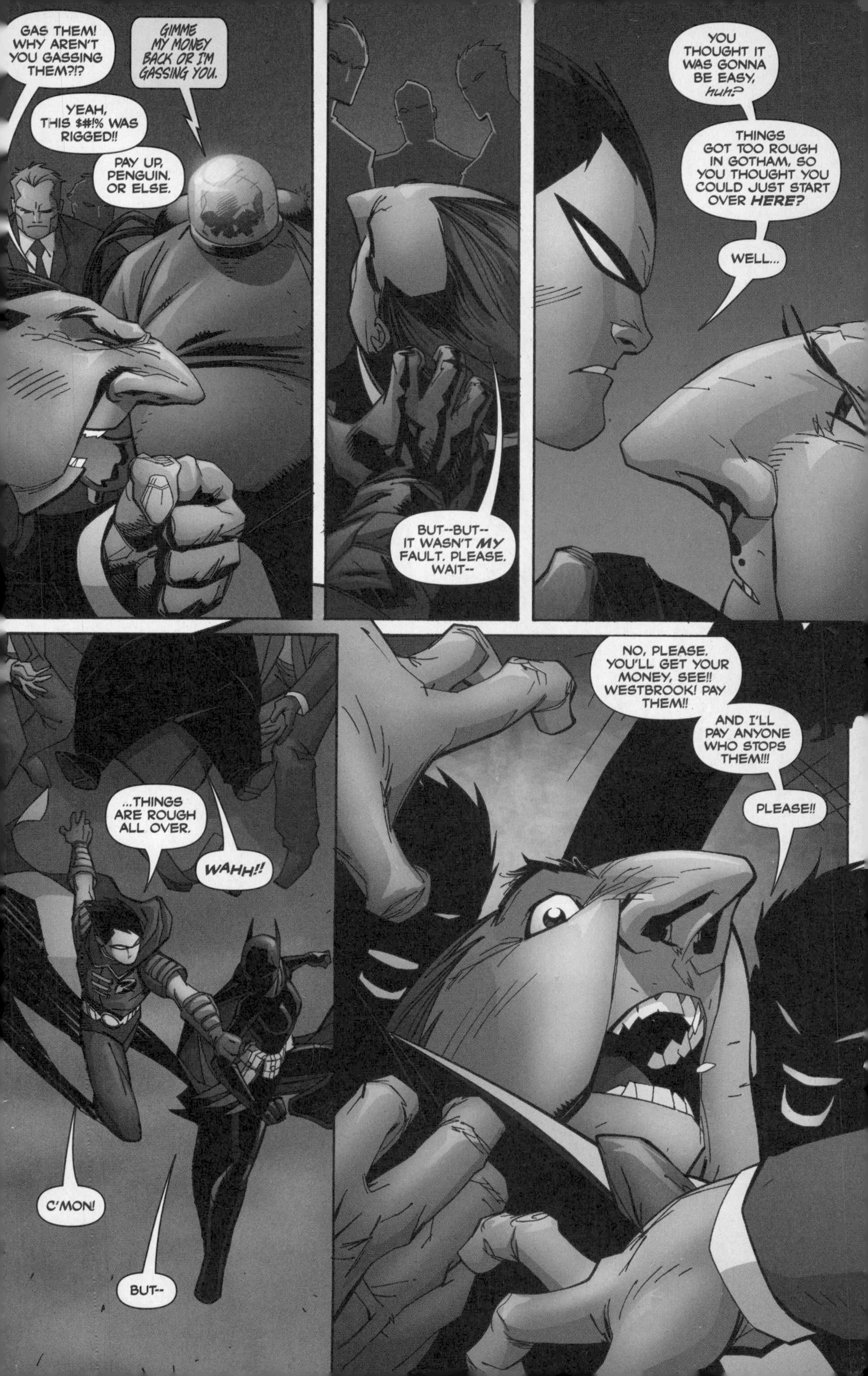
GAS THEM! WHY AREN'T YOU GASSING THEM?!?
GIMME MY MONEY BACK OR I'M GASSING YOU.
YEAH, THIS $#!% WAS RIGGED!!
PAY UP, PENGUIN. OR ELSE.
BUT--BUT-- IT WASN'T MY FAULT. PLEASE. WAIT--
YOU THOUGHT IT WAS GONNA BE EASY, huh?
THINGS GOT TOO ROUGH IN GOTHAM, SO YOU THOUGHT YOU COULD JUST START OVER HERE?
WELL...
...THINGS ARE ROUGH ALL OVER.
WAHH!!
C'MON!
BUT--
NO, PLEASE. YOU'LL GET YOUR MONEY, SEE!! WESTBROOK! PAY THEM!!
AND I'LL PAY ANYONE WHO STOPS THEM!!!
PLEASE!!

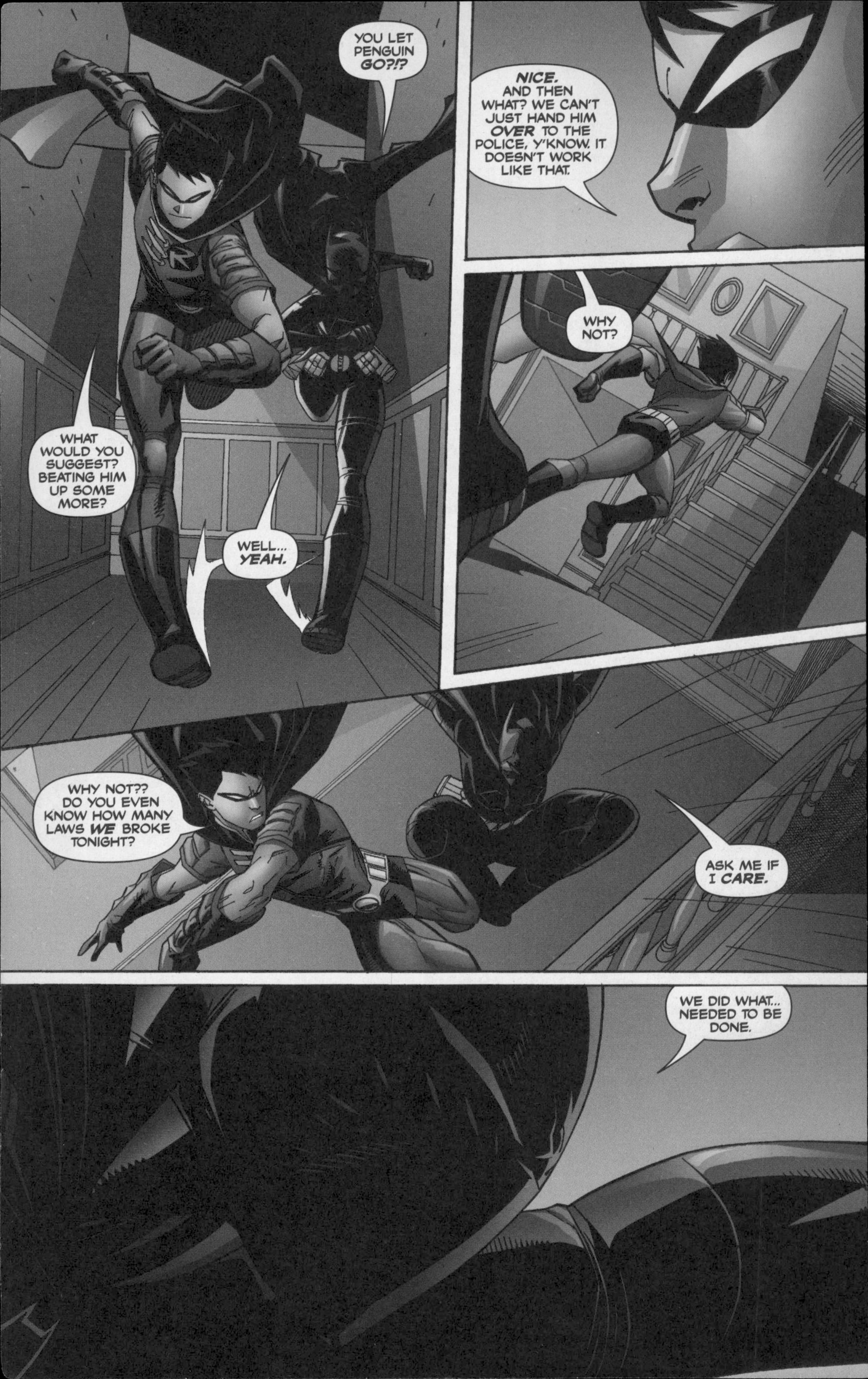
YOU LET PENGUIN GO?!?
NICE. AND THEN WHAT? WE CAN'T JUST HAND HIM OVER TO THE POLICE, Y'KNOW. IT DOESN'T WORK LIKE THAT.
WHY NOT?
WHAT WOULD YOU SUGGEST? BEATING HIM UP SOME MORE?
WELL... YEAH.
WHY NOT?? DO YOU EVEN KNOW HOW MANY LAWS WE BROKE TONIGHT?
ASK ME IF I CARE.
WE DID WHAT... NEEDED TO BE DONE.

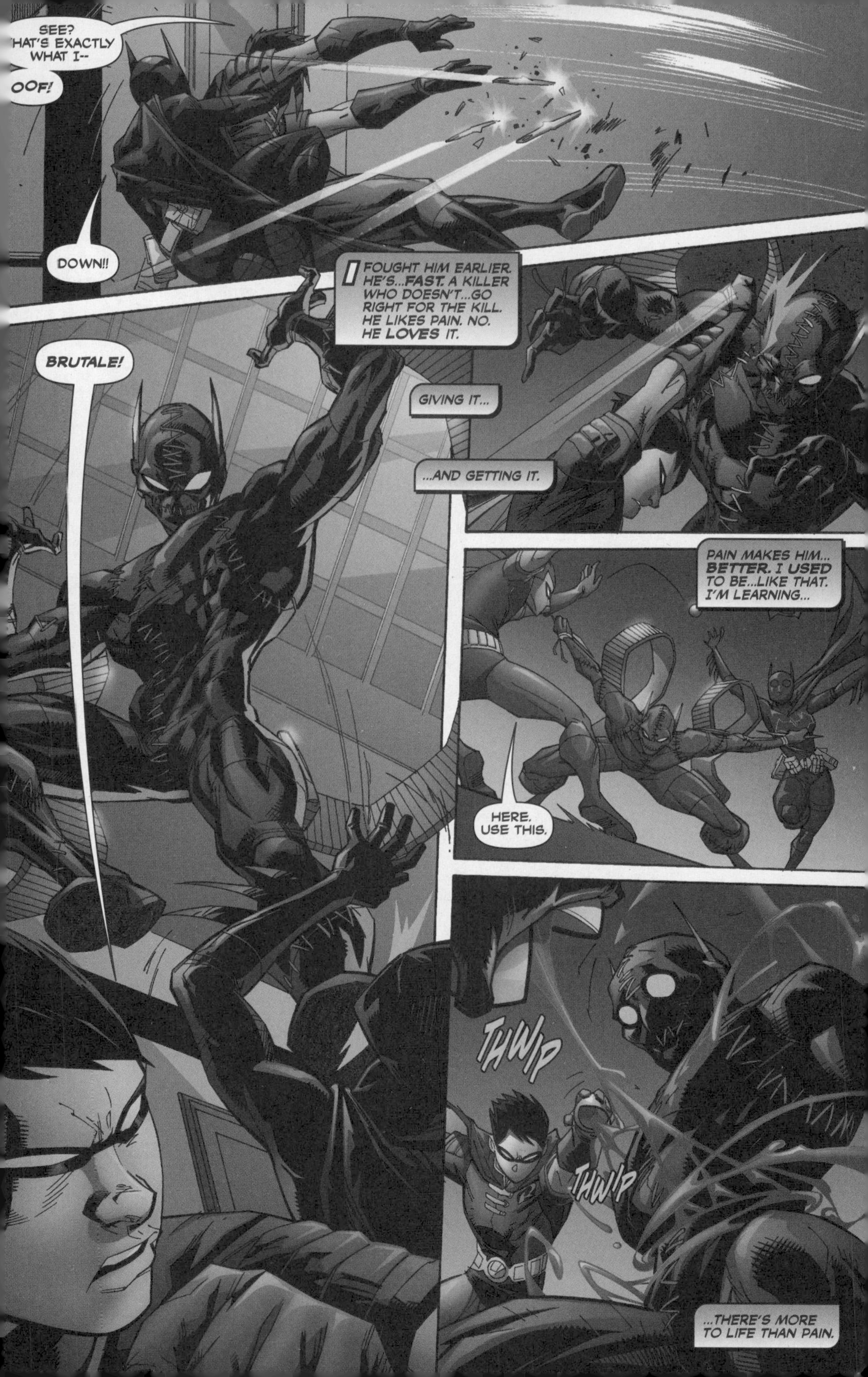
SEE? THAT'S EXACTLY WHAT I--
OOF!
DOWN!!
I FOUGHT HIM EARLIER. HE'S...FAST. A KILLER WHO DOESN'T...GO RIGHT FOR THE KILL. HE LIKES PAIN. NO. HE LOVES IT.
BRUTALE!
GIVING IT...
...AND GETTING IT.
PAIN MAKES HIM... BETTER. I USED TO BE...LIKE THAT. I'M LEARNING...
HERE. USE THIS.
THWIP
THWIP
...THERE'S MORE TO LIFE THAN PAIN.

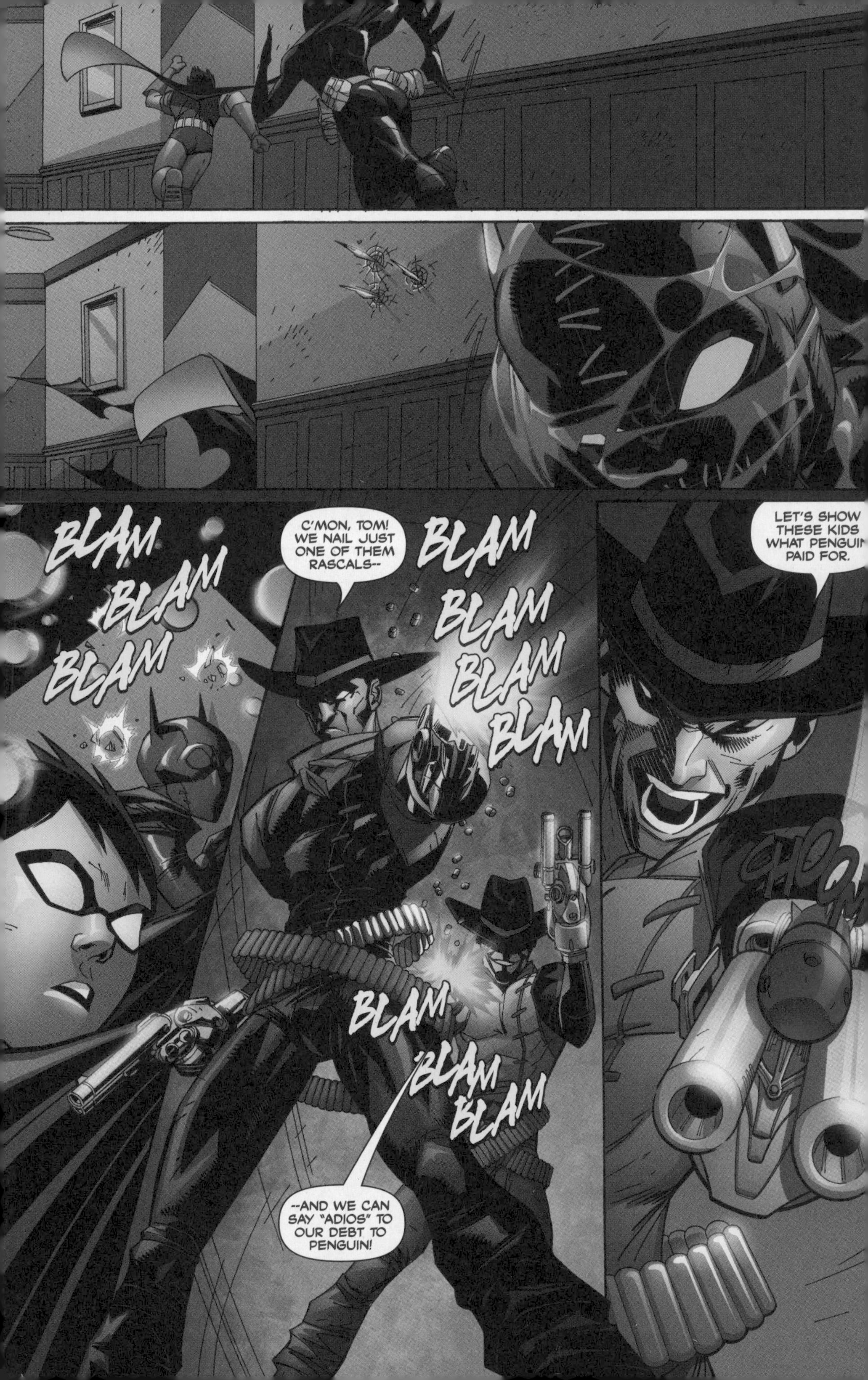
BLAM
BLAM
BLAM
C'MON, TOM! WE NAIL JUST ONE OF THEM RASCALS--
BLAM
BLAM
BLAM
BLAM
BLAM
BLAM
BLAM
--AND WE CAN SAY "ADIOS" TO OUR DEBT TO PENGUIN!
LET'S SHOW THESE KIDS WHAT PENGUIN PAID FOR.

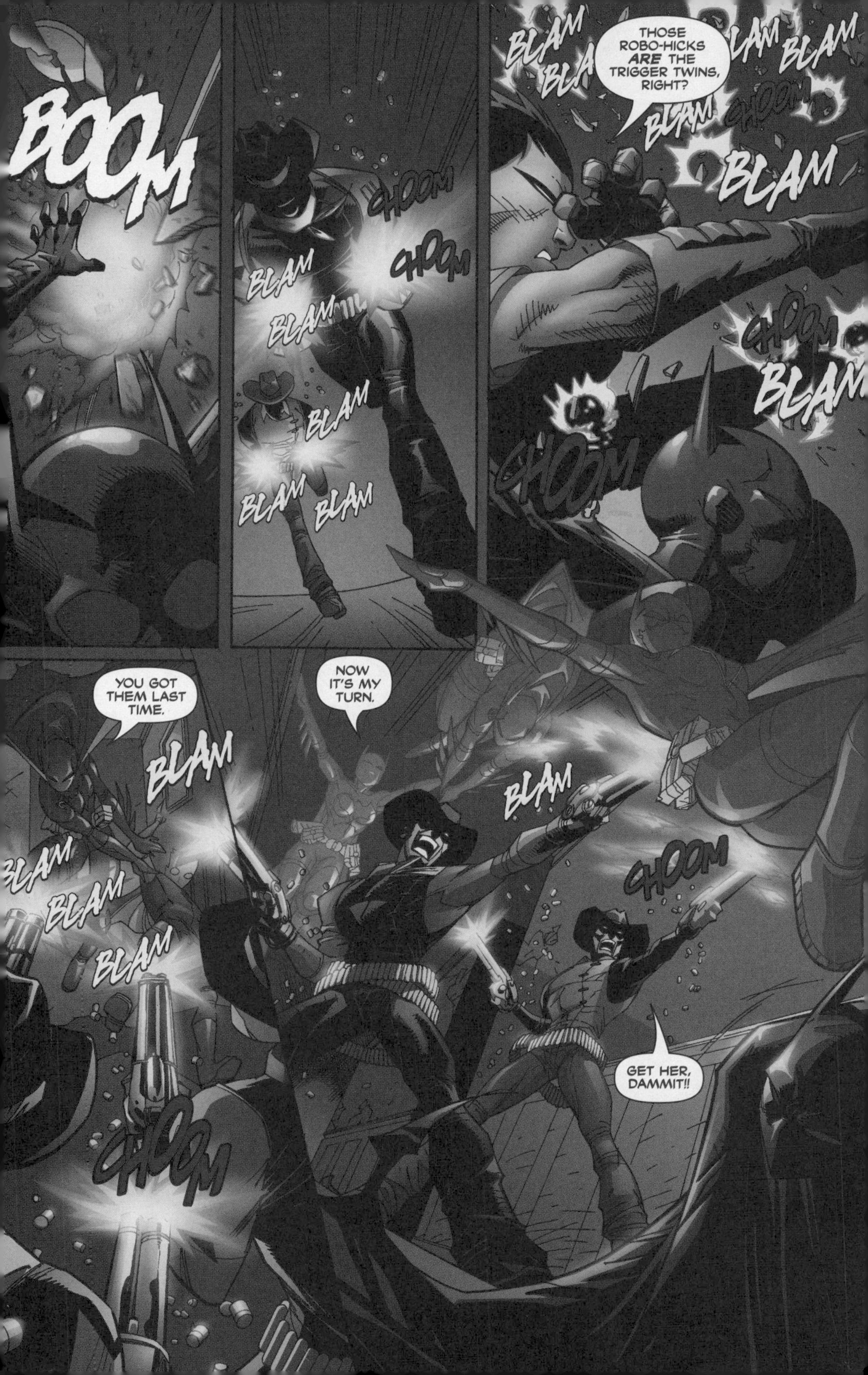
BOOM
CHOOM
CHOOM
BLAM
BLAM
BLAM
BLAM
BLAM
BLAM
BLAM
THOSE ROBO-HICKS *ARE* THE TRIGGER TWINS, RIGHT?
BLAM
CHOOM
BLAM
CHOOM
BLAM
CHOOM
YOU GOT THEM LAST TIME.
NOW IT'S MY TURN.
BLAM
BLAM
BLAM
BLAM
BLAM
CHOOM
CHOOM
GET HER, DAMMIT!!

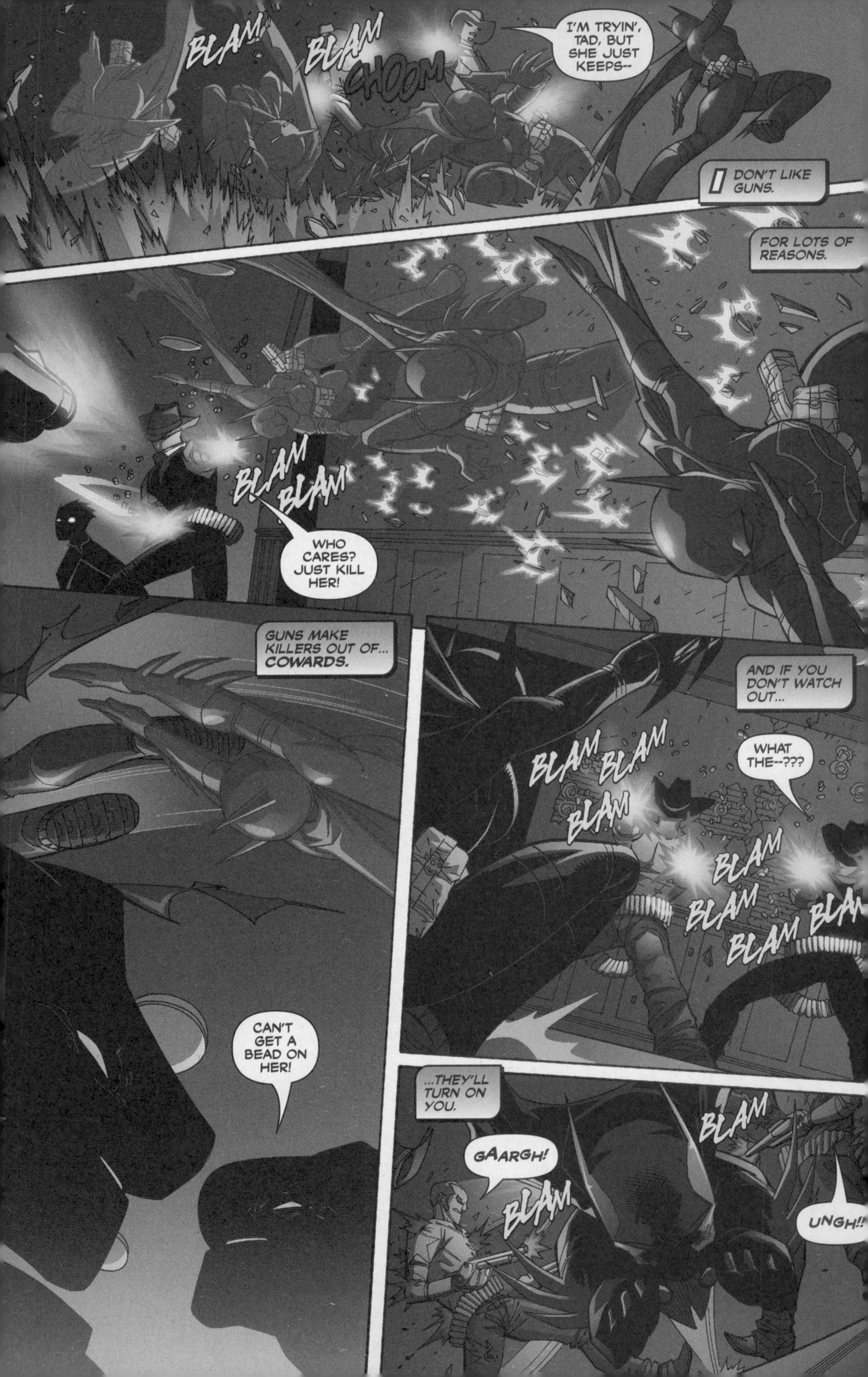

BLAM!
BLAM
CHOOM
I'M TRYIN', TAD, BUT SHE JUST KEEPS--
I DON'T LIKE GUNS.
FOR LOTS OF REASONS.
BLAM
BLAM
WHO CARES? JUST KILL HER!
GUNS MAKE KILLERS OUT OF... COWARDS.
CAN'T GET A BEAD ON HER!
AND IF YOU DON'T WATCH OUT...
BLAM BLAM BLAM
WHAT THE--???
BLAM BLAM BLAM BLAM
...THEY'LL TURN ON YOU.
BLAM
GAARGH!
BLAM
UNGH!!

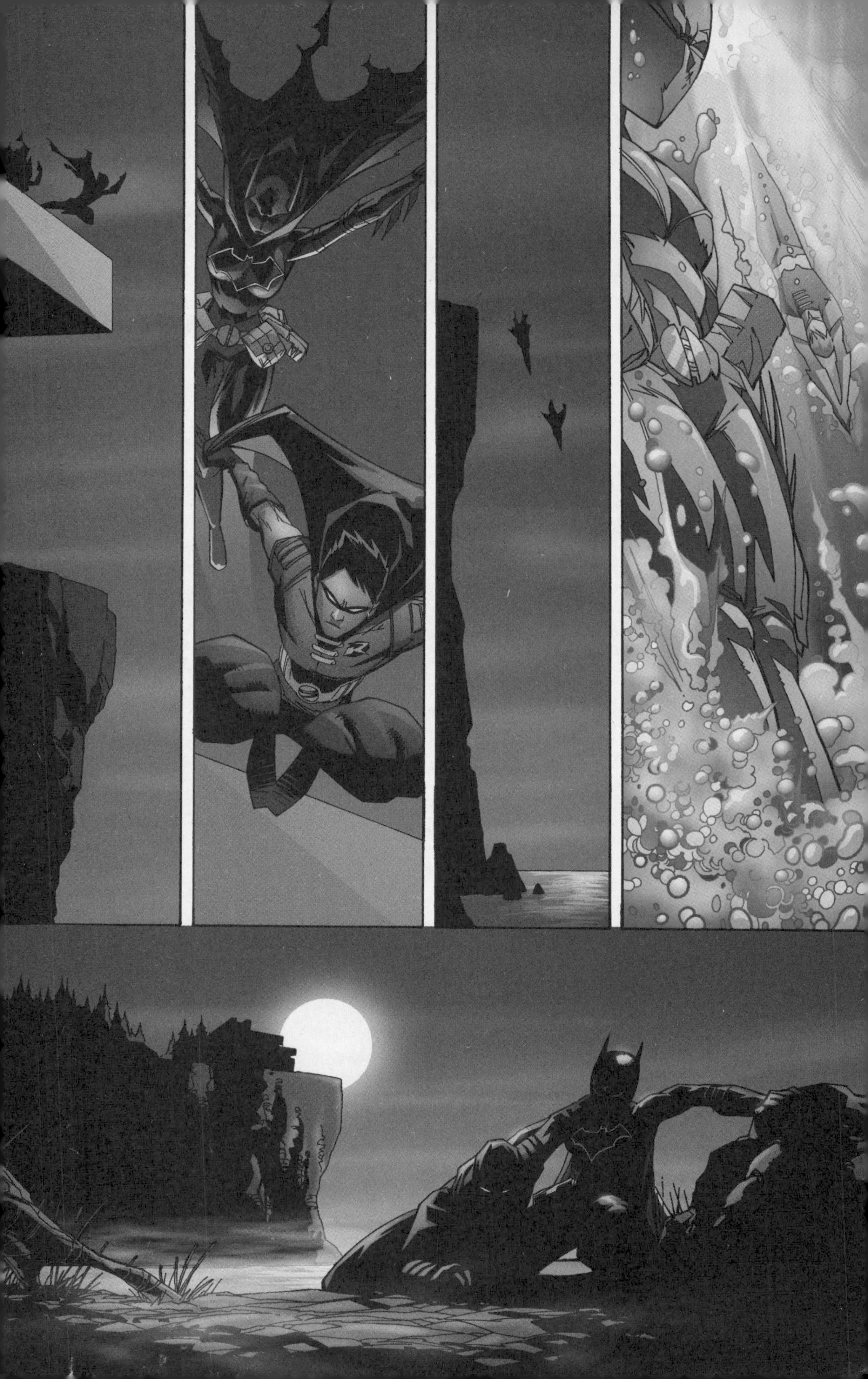

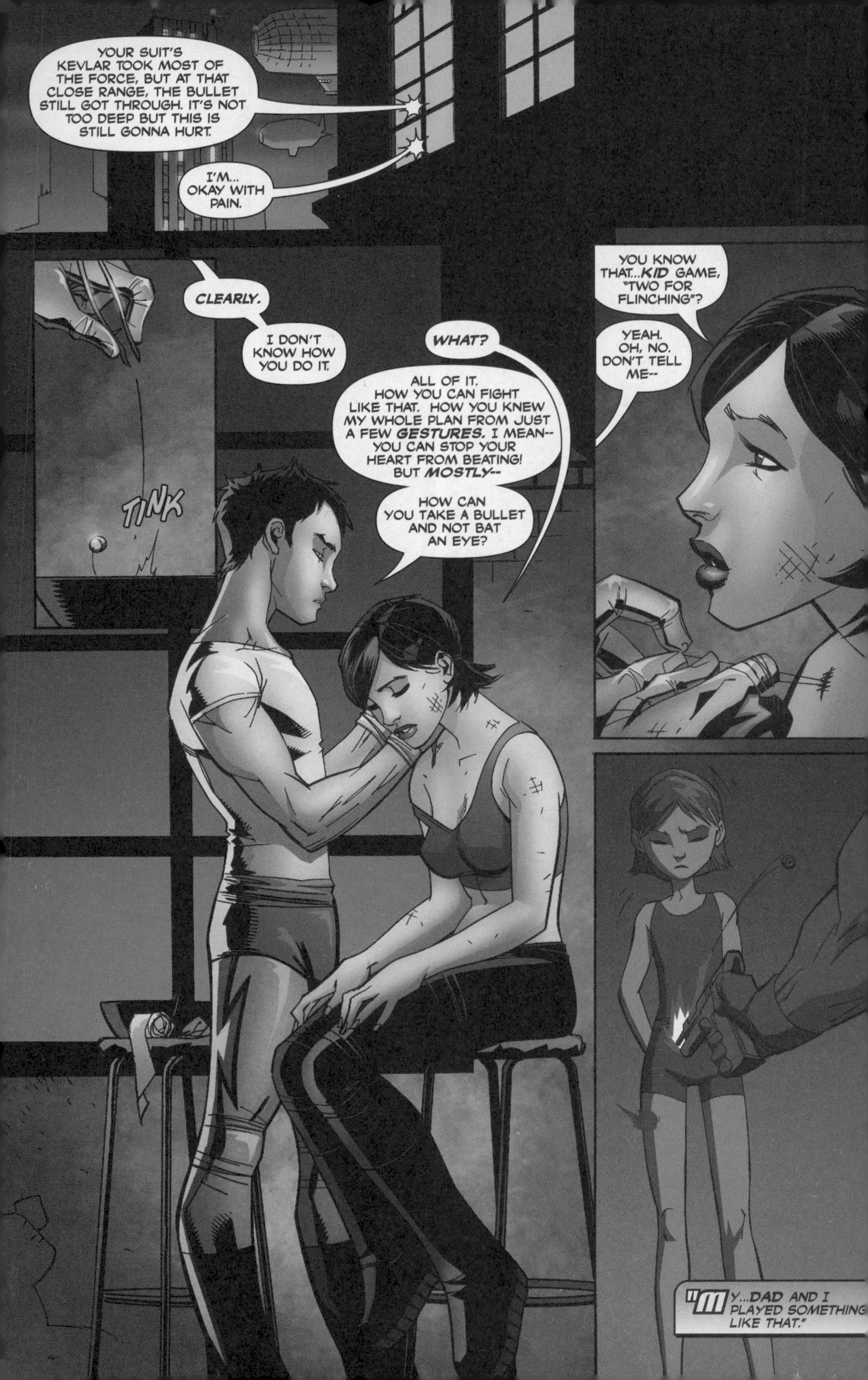
YOUR SUIT'S KEVLAR TOOK MOST OF THE FORCE, BUT AT THAT CLOSE RANGE, THE BULLET STILL GOT THROUGH. IT'S NOT TOO DEEP BUT THIS IS STILL GONNA HURT.
I'M... OKAY WITH PAIN.
CLEARLY.
I DON'T KNOW HOW YOU DO IT.
WHAT?
ALL OF IT. HOW YOU CAN FIGHT LIKE THAT. HOW YOU KNEW MY WHOLE PLAN FROM JUST A FEW GESTURES. I MEAN-- YOU CAN STOP YOUR HEART FROM BEATING! BUT MOSTLY--
HOW CAN YOU TAKE A BULLET AND NOT BAT AN EYE?
TINK
YOU KNOW THAT...KID GAME, "TWO FOR FLINCHING"?
YEAH. OH, NO. DON'T TELL ME--
"MY...DAD AND I PLAYED SOMETHING LIKE THAT."

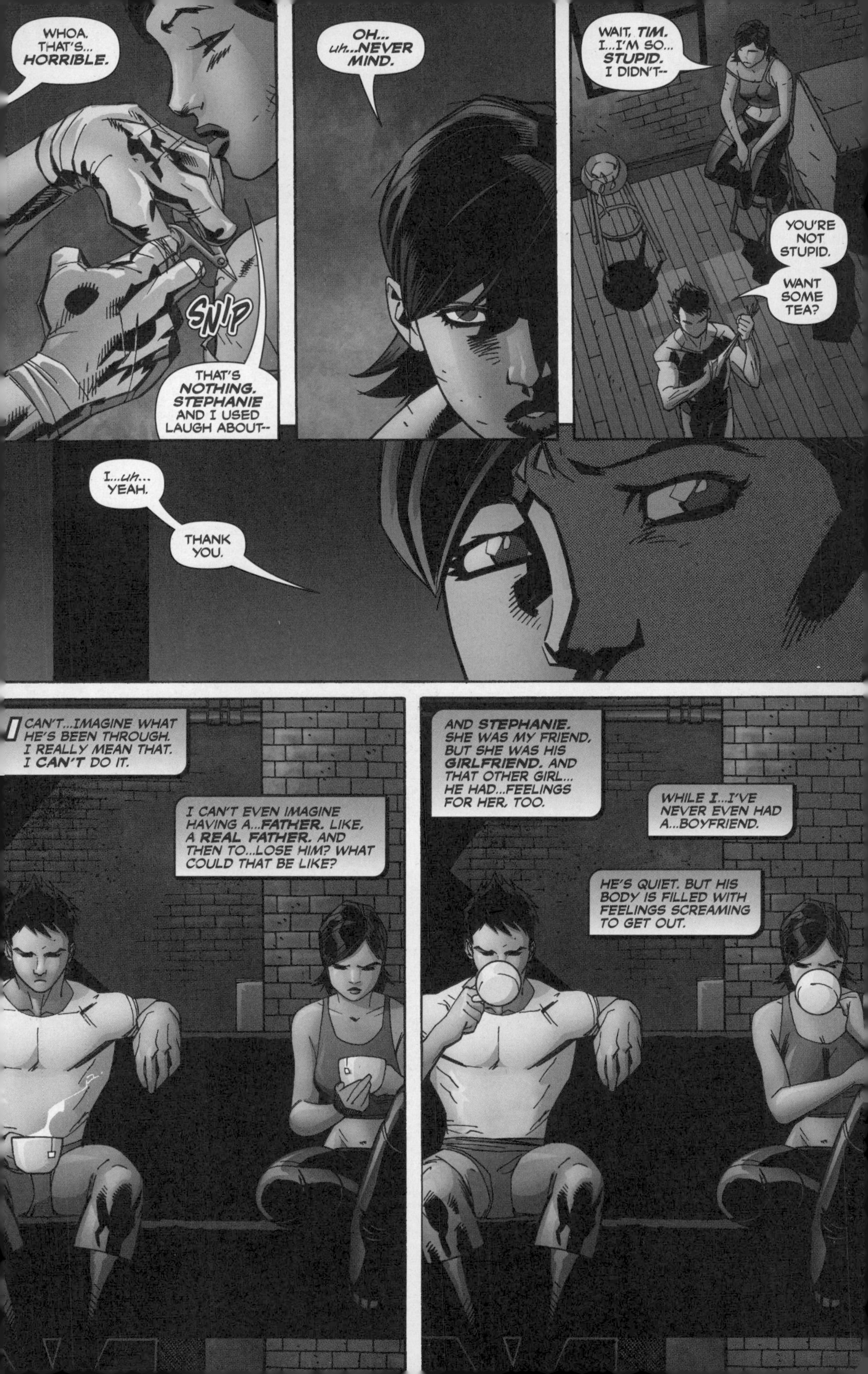

WHOA. THAT'S... HORRIBLE.
SNIP
THAT'S NOTHING. STEPHANIE AND I USED LAUGH ABOUT--
OH... uh...NEVER MIND.
WAIT, TIM. I...I'M SO... STUPID. I DIDN'T--
YOU'RE NOT STUPID.
WANT SOME TEA?
I...uh... YEAH.
THANK YOU.
I CAN'T...IMAGINE WHAT HE'S BEEN THROUGH. I REALLY MEAN THAT. I CAN'T DO IT.
I CAN'T EVEN IMAGINE HAVING A...FATHER. LIKE, A REAL FATHER. AND THEN TO...LOSE HIM? WHAT COULD THAT BE LIKE?
AND STEPHANIE. SHE WAS MY FRIEND, BUT SHE WAS HIS GIRLFRIEND. AND THAT OTHER GIRL... HE HAD...FEELINGS FOR HER, TOO.
WHILE I...I'VE NEVER EVEN HAD A...BOYFRIEND.
HE'S QUIET. BUT HIS BODY IS FILLED WITH FEELINGS SCREAMING TO GET OUT.

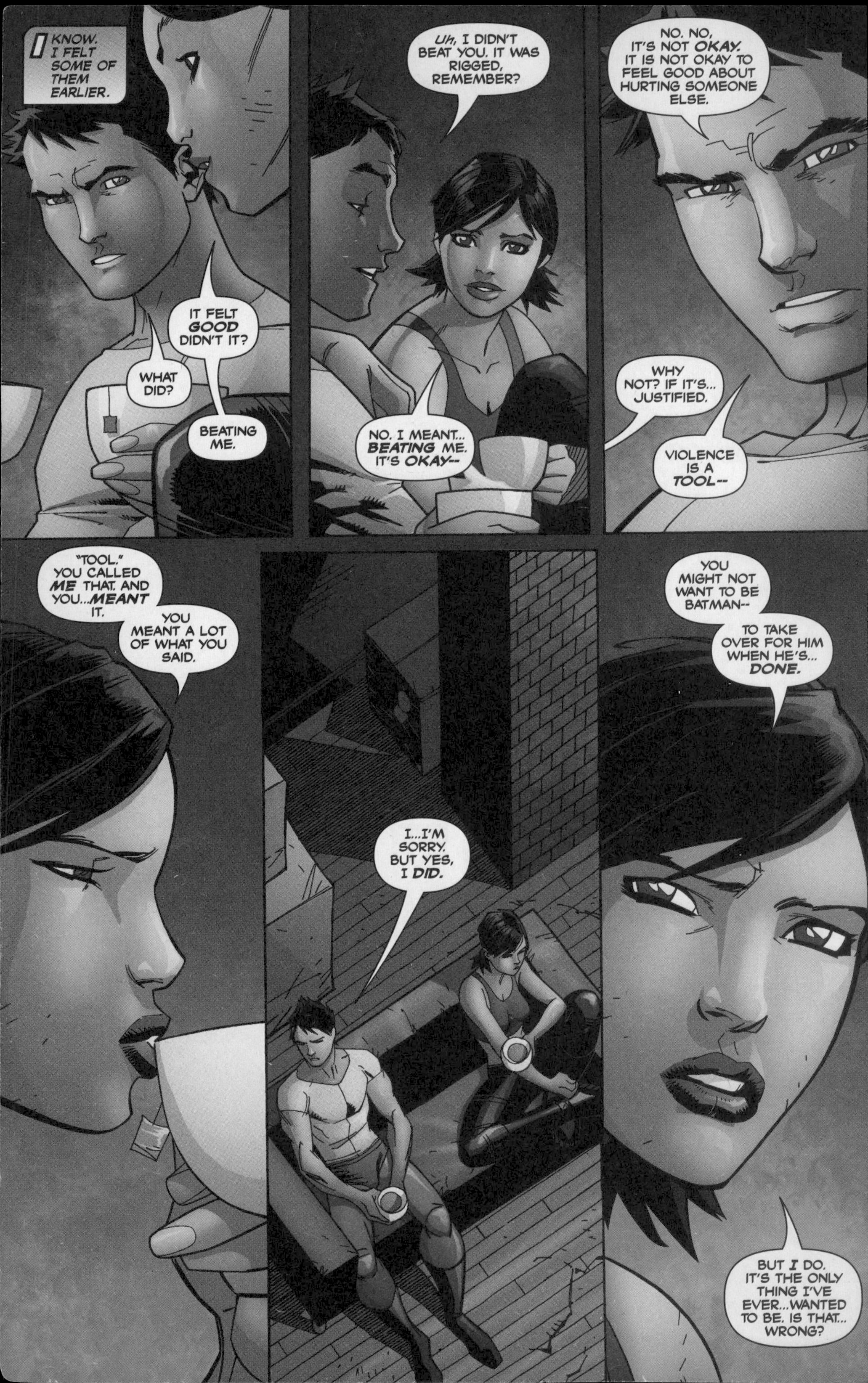
I KNOW. I FELT SOME OF THEM EARLIER.
IT FELT GOOD DIDN'T IT?
WHAT DID?
BEATING ME.
Uh, I DIDN'T BEAT YOU. IT WAS RIGGED, REMEMBER?
NO. I MEANT... BEATING ME. IT'S OKAY--
NO. NO, IT'S NOT OKAY. IT IS NOT OKAY TO FEEL GOOD ABOUT HURTING SOMEONE ELSE.
WHY NOT? IF IT'S... JUSTIFIED.
VIOLENCE IS A TOOL--
"TOOL." YOU CALLED ME THAT. AND YOU...MEANT IT.
YOU MEANT A LOT OF WHAT YOU SAID.
I...I'M SORRY. BUT YES, I DID.
YOU MIGHT NOT WANT TO BE BATMAN--
TO TAKE OVER FOR HIM WHEN HE'S... DONE.
BUT I DO. IT'S THE ONLY THING I'VE EVER...WANTED TO BE. IS THAT... WRONG?

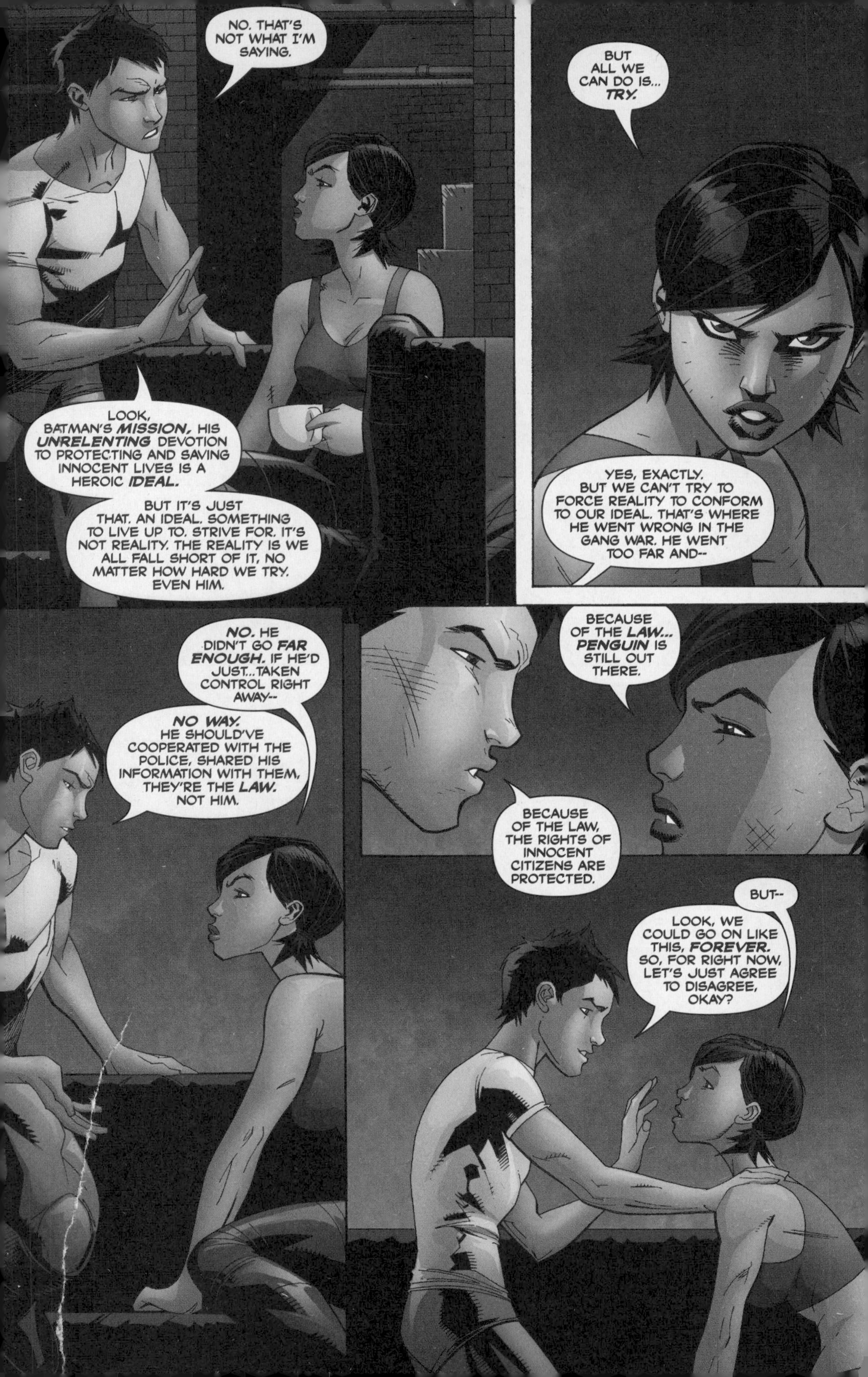

NO. THAT'S NOT WHAT I'M SAYING.
LOOK, BATMAN'S MISSION, HIS UNRELENTING DEVOTION TO PROTECTING AND SAVING INNOCENT LIVES IS A HEROIC IDEAL.
BUT IT'S JUST THAT. AN IDEAL. SOMETHING TO LIVE UP TO. STRIVE FOR. IT'S NOT REALITY. THE REALITY IS WE ALL FALL SHORT OF IT, NO MATTER HOW HARD WE TRY. EVEN HIM.
BUT ALL WE CAN DO IS... TRY.
YES, EXACTLY. BUT WE CAN'T TRY TO FORCE REALITY TO CONFORM TO OUR IDEAL. THAT'S WHERE HE WENT WRONG IN THE GANG WAR. HE WENT TOO FAR AND--
NO. HE DIDN'T GO FAR ENOUGH. IF HE'D JUST...TAKEN CONTROL RIGHT AWAY--
NO WAY. HE SHOULD'VE COOPERATED WITH THE POLICE, SHARED HIS INFORMATION WITH THEM, THEY'RE THE LAW. NOT HIM.
BECAUSE OF THE LAW... PENGUIN IS STILL OUT THERE.
BECAUSE OF THE LAW, THE RIGHTS OF INNOCENT CITIZENS ARE PROTECTED.
BUT--
LOOK, WE COULD GO ON LIKE THIS, FOREVER. SO, FOR RIGHT NOW, LET'S JUST AGREE TO DISAGREE, OKAY?

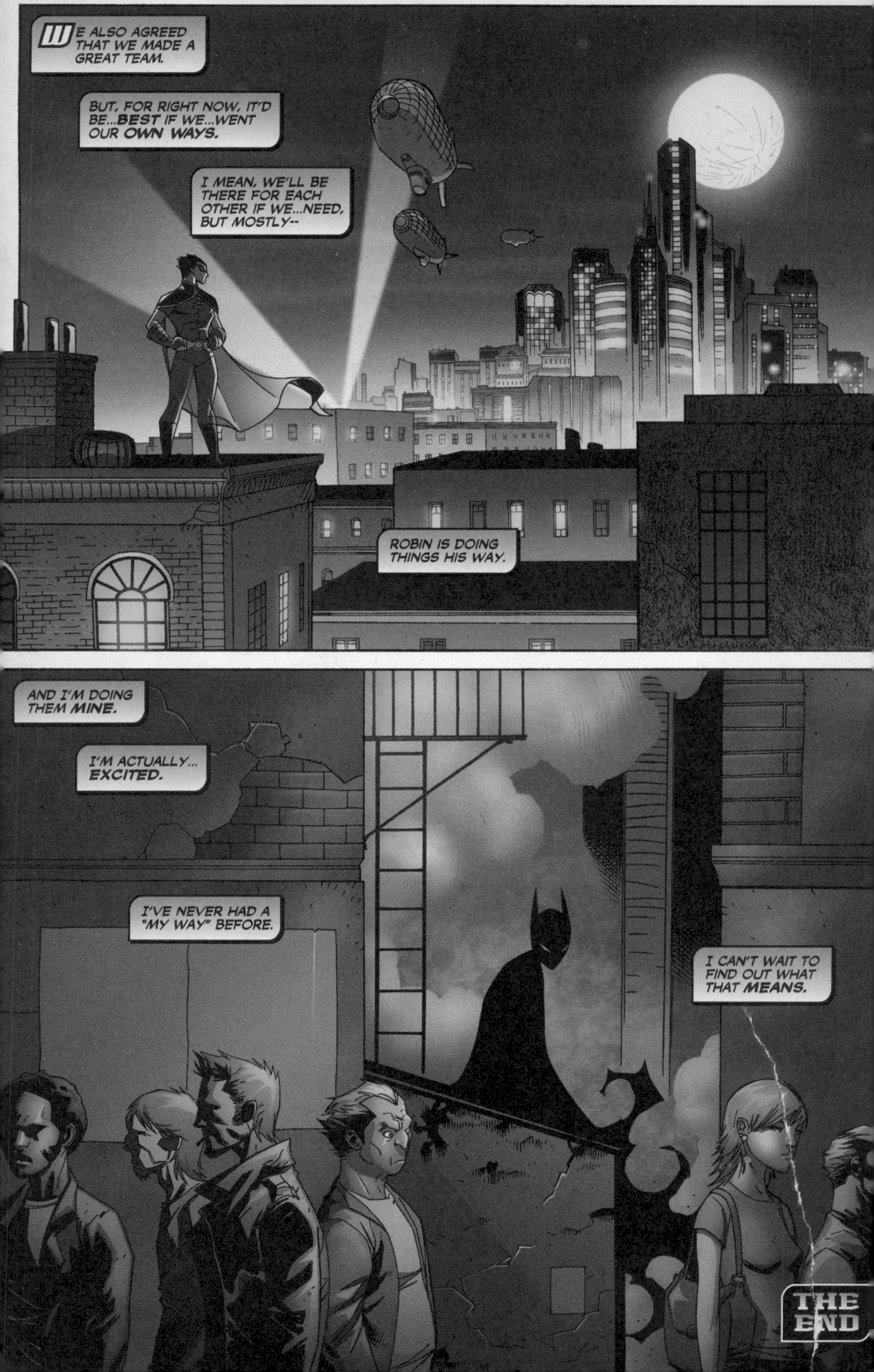
WE ALSO AGREED THAT WE MADE A GREAT TEAM.
BUT, FOR RIGHT NOW, IT'D BE...BEST IF WE...WENT OUR OWN WAYS.
I MEAN, WE'LL BE THERE FOR EACH OTHER IF WE...NEED, BUT MOSTLY--
ROBIN IS DOING THINGS HIS WAY.
AND I'M DOING THEM MINE.
I'M ACTUALLY... EXCITED.
I'VE NEVER HAD A "MY WAY" BEFORE.
I CAN'T WAIT TO FIND OUT WHAT THAT MEANS.
THE END

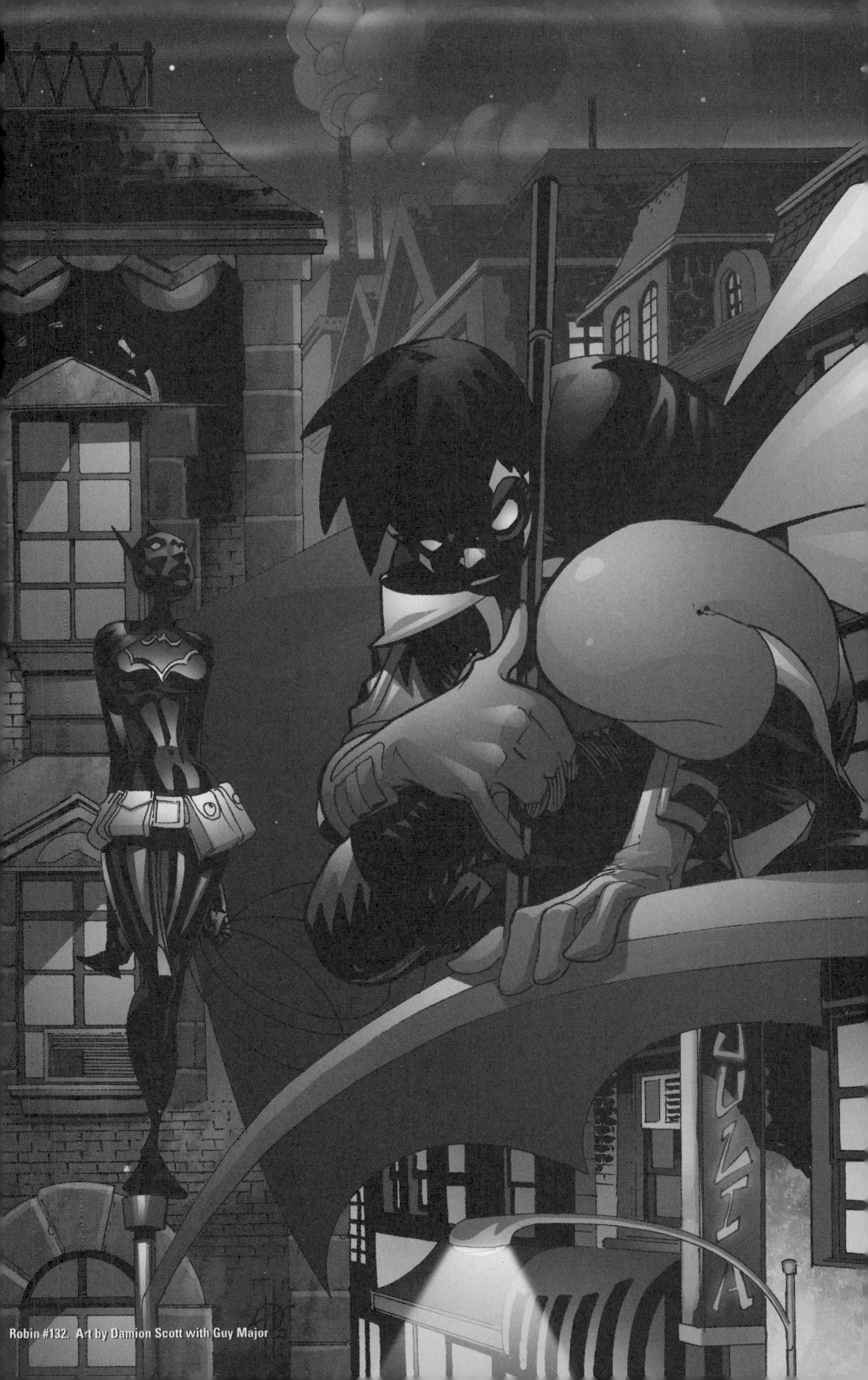

Robin #132. Art by Damion Scott with Guy Major

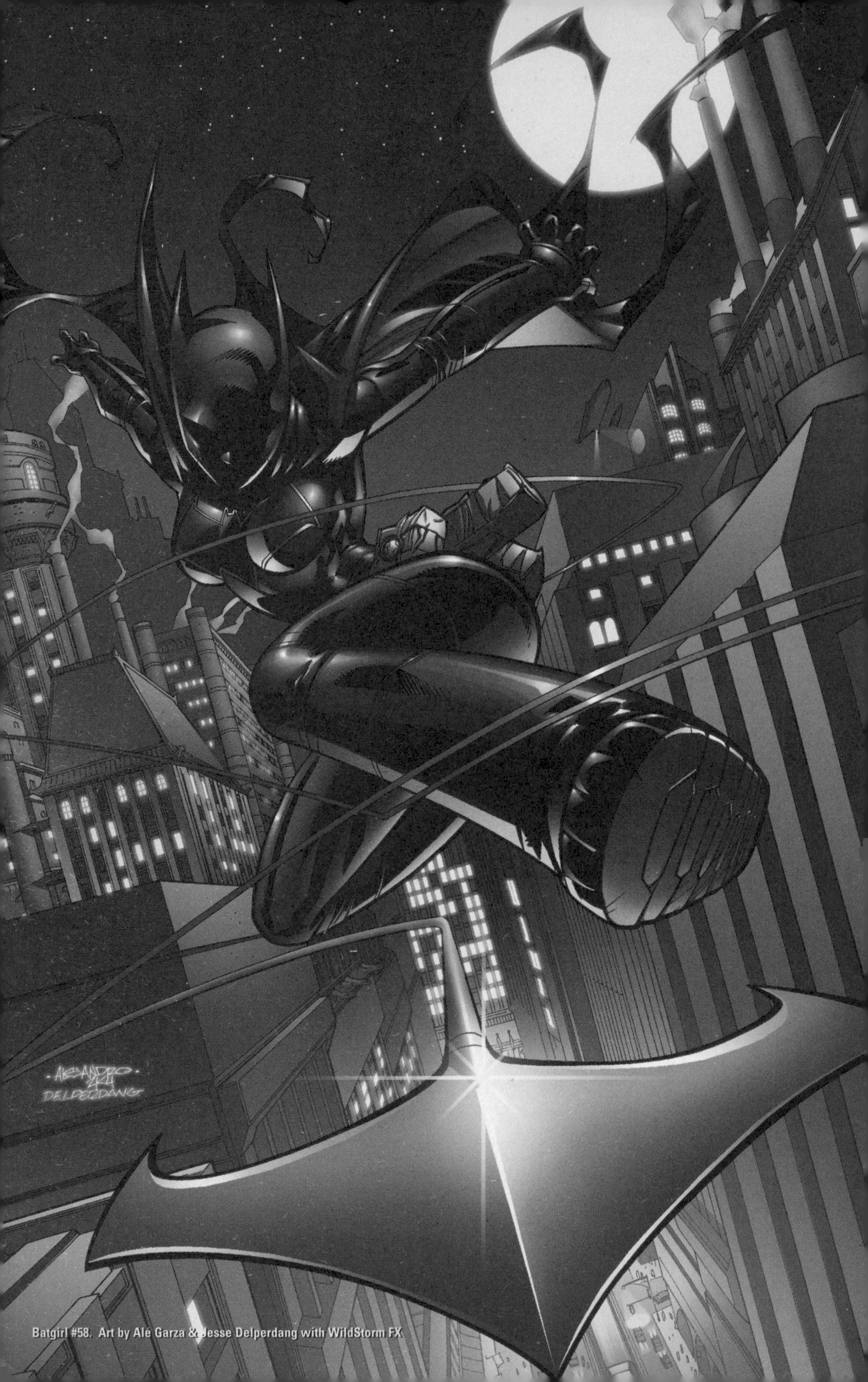
ALESANDRO
2K4
DELPERDANG
Batgirl #58. Art by Alé Garza & Jesse Delperdang with WildStorm FX

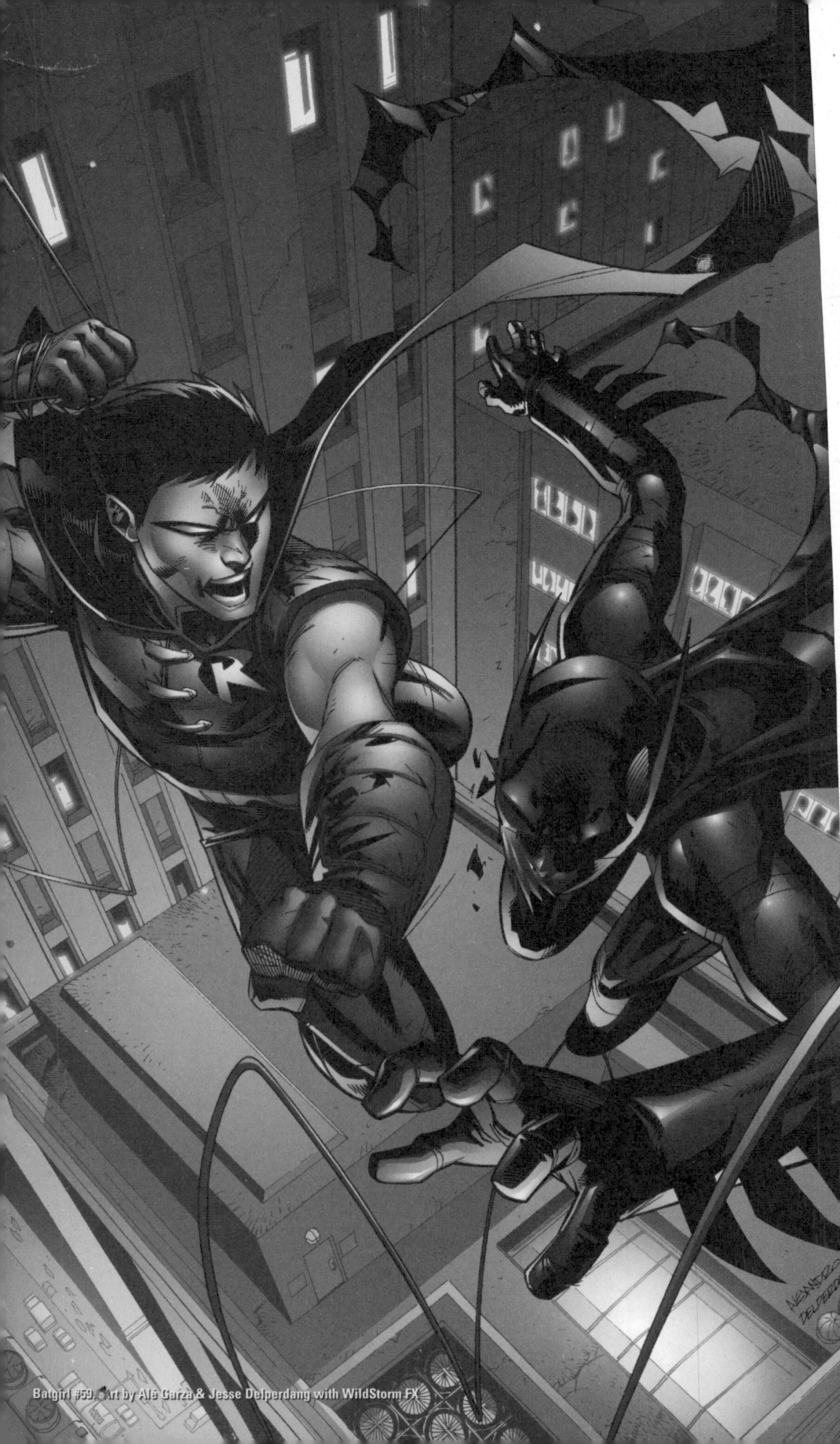

Batgirl #59. Art by Alé Garza & Jesse Delperdang with WildStorm FX

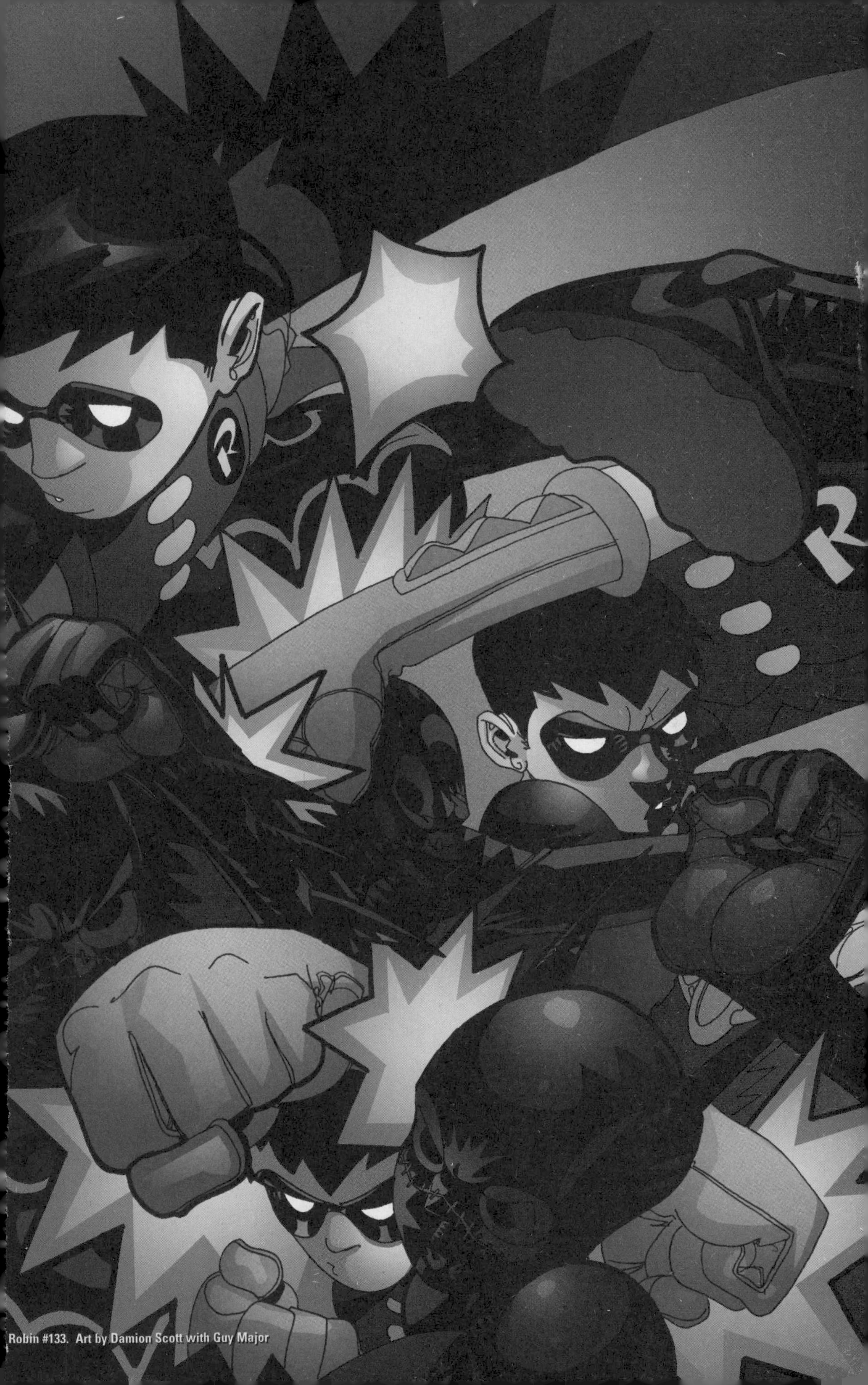
Robin #133. Art by Damion Scott with Guy Major